Antelope Hill Writing Competition 2022
Small Victories

Small Victories

SECOND ANNUAL

Antelope Hill Writing Competition

—2022—

Sponsored in part by the White Art Collective,
Will2Rise, and Media2Rise

Cover art by sswifty.
Contest judged by the Antelope Hill editorial team.
Edited by Margaret Bauer.
Interior formatting by Margaret Bauer.

Antelope Hill Publishing
Antelopehillpublishing.com

Paperback ISBN-13: 978-1-956887-62-4
EPUB ISBN-13: 978-1-956887-25-9

Contents

Publisher's Foreword ix

POETRY

Selected Poems by Author

Nullus Abnormocracy 3

Ed Altura 7

anonwriter1899 8

Bill Atheling 10

Godfrey's Bouillon 11

Christian 12

Cleon II 13

Anya Colgan 14

Corydoras 16

John David 17

Sue Denim 18

Ella Dennis 20

Dark Enlightenment 21

Servius Aurelianus Episcopus 22

Paul Fahrenheidt 23

Fraxinus 32

Bando Gora 34

Victor Holz 36

Cool Hoolan 38

E.W. Howard 39

June.....40
Mrs. Kestrel.....41
Carson Kilgrey.....42
Tucker King.....43
Nemo Knows.....44
Dogenes Kynikos.....47
Wren Lane.....48
Lachlan Lindenmayer.....49
M.....51
Bernhard D. Massey.....52
Samantha Matz.....53
Jack McKraken.....55
Grace Moore.....57
Joe Morris.....59
T.J. Murray.....61
Vladyslav Nazarchuk.....64
Ndabaningi.....70
Thomas Nyquist.....72
Greg Partansky.....79
Arthur Powell.....80
Tyler Rannus.....81
Andrew Roemer.....84
Austin Stephenson.....85
M.A. Thomas.....87
Seamus Tout-Cœur.....88
Lue-Yee Tsang.....90
Nicholas Walker.....92
J.B. Weyland.....93
Terry Williams.....94
Max Worthington.....97

Poetry Winners

Honorable Mention: "Dearly Beloved" by Firebrand Jay 104
Honorable Mention: "Erwachen" by Corvan A. Miller 108
Honorable Mention: "Small Fool" by Nathaniel Lucas 116
Second Place Winner: "Wastelanders" by Cloud Buchholz 118
First Place Winner: "For a Love of Skies" by Romanized Visigoth 126

SHORT STORIES

Selected Short Stories by Author

Aethelweard The Wake 132
A.J. Bell 141
Cloud Buchholz 148
Charlie 160
Paul Dempsey 163
Jack Irkman 167
J. Michael Kearney 174
Ludwig L 178
Nathaniel Lucas 181
Ndabaningi 183
Grant Norman 189
Carl Penda 193
Mrs. Saxon 198
Seax 203
Mark Time 207
Turn_Coat 219
Memento Vivere 231

Shorty Story Winners

Honorable Mention: "The Door" by Casey McDonough 234

Honorable Mention: "Marble Redeemer" by Rune Stenbock...........................240

Second Place Winner: "As the Spirit Moves" by Joe Morris 254

First Place Winner: "The Castle" by T.R. Hudson 264

Publisher's Foreword

Antelope Hill Publishing is proud to present our Second Annual Writing Contest. Last year, we held our first ever writing contest with the ambitious goal of making it an annual project, and we are happy to see this goal accomplished for another year. The wellspring of talent continues to overflow in our community, and we are honored to publish and preserve its fruit.

While last year we accepted a number of essays as a response to the "Why We Fight" prompt, this year, we wanted to focus only on poetry and fictional short stories. We chose to do this in order to inspire more creative writing, as essays and articles are common in our sphere. This year's theme, "Small Victories," lent itself quite well to creative writing, as the contributing authors crafted unique narratives to highlight the little ways we can find hope and exercise courage in the face of our struggle.

In addition to all the talented authors featured in this year's book, we would like to thank all those who submitted. The quality of submissions this year was markedly improved over last, and we had a more difficult time choosing which we would select for publication. It was harder still for the team to agree on the winning pieces. Ultimately, we chose poems and short stories that together showcased a variety of styles, complexity, and approaches to the prompt as well as originality and intrigue.

Certainly the evaluation process is highly subjective and we hope no authors are discouraged if their piece was not selected this year for publication. We hope to inspire more writers in our sphere to produce quality literature for our people, whether we're able to publish it or not. In many ways, the growth our publishing house has seen over the last year is our own small victory, and we intend in no way to rest on our laurels.

We extend our gratitude as well to our generous sponsors, the White Art Collective, Will2Rise, and Media2Rise, without whom this project would not be feasible. We hope you enjoy these unique works as much as we have, and we look forward to many more years of sharing your talent with the world.

Antelope Hill Publishing

Poetry

Legacy

Nullus Abnormocracy

Cobblestone memories,
Her sweet flirtatious jest,
Wrought-iron balconies,
Lovers on a grand quest.
She calms my restless blaze,
Faint smoke sweetens the air,
A sheltering embrace,
Amber perfumes her hair.

Consecrated chapel,
Blessed matrimony,
A newborn arrival,
Procreant harmony.
Melodious choirs,
A song of the nightingale,
Euphoric new parents,
Decompress and inhale.

Cherish the delicate,
Europa is alive!
Embrace the exquisite,
Your descendants will thrive!
Celebrate your language,
Indigenous credo,
Recaptured heritage,
It all belongs to you!

Rex

Nullus Abnormocracy

Ancient defender,
Noble jousts, majestic walls,
Serene pedagogue,
Meditation, pious halls,
Nebulous mornings,
Air so crisp it wakes the lungs,
The freshly baked bread,
With the eyes closed, one succumbs.

A boy’s adventure,
Carrying sticks, playing war,
Climbing, exploring,
These ramparts stand evermore,
God and man embrace,
Tiny cliff and ancient bone,
A young man’s journey,
It defines this cornerstone.

Charming nostalgia,
A distant recollection,
Triumph and defeat,
Embodies this collection,
Devotion, honor,
Formative maturity,
Wisdom and patience,
Rex, the kings of destiny.

Unconditional Union

Nullus Abnormocracy

Drifting in adoration, I curl up in her womb,
Floating in the calm of this liquid balloon,
Covered with devotion, longing for perpetuity,
The warmth of this unconditional unity.

Torn away from her heart, light becomes cold,
My eyes burn; inside I shiver a thousandfold,
Forever broken from the comfort of mummification,
The warmth of this unconditional unification.

Thrust into competition, fighting alone,
Merciless is the dilemma of the unknown,
Strength, resilience, and power govern this dominion,
Over and done is the warmth of this union.

Matters of character bear upon the mind,
Casual conquests have long been left behind,
In her eyes hoping to see that familiar perfection,
The fine art of this relentless confusion.

Rekindling a memory comes with time,
My unconditional love for her is sublime,
One thousand triumphs can't compare to the joy of giving life.
My son cries, felling this familiar strife.

An old man is often considered a sage,
Realizing too late that his life was but a cage,
A life well lived, or fits of insanity,
I could not understand its perplexity.

I slowly drift away into the abyss,
My heart soars back to find the tomb I miss,
Before I go, this the holiest communion,
The warmth of this unconditional union.

To Make Statues

Ed Altura

Frozen here amongst the ruins is untouched marble,
These strong old hands of mine set to work,
Silt and clay I reject, for a thousand years can't weather solid rock,
Carving, shaping, smoothing,
Seasons change but I press on,
A once muddied surface reveals a shining core,
My chisel sinks in for the last time,
Finally, my work is complete.

He breathes in,
An image I've made to stand forever,
His bright eyes beam with gratitude,
"But what am I supposed to do now?" he asks me,
"Go away, far away from these ruins," I say as I grant him my tools,
He begins a somber walk, looking back at me every once in a while,
He's going to the mountains, he's going back home,
Oh, how I wish I could spend my days sculpting with him, but I'm tired,
So I contently return to stone.

The Bird That Once Was Blind

anonwriter1899

As a tired and old man,
I took a look outside my window,
At a cold land, her fire,
Now like the embers of a widow.

Into the glass with my own eyes,
I saw a small bird crash, then fall to die,
Its skull was crushed, its beak was cracked,
Its vision blacked, sockets filled with blood.

Then to its aid ran a small lass,
My neighbor, the local angel of love,
For whom my heart broke, as I watched her scoop it with hope,
Into a tiny box.

A dream of keeping it alive.
A dream it could one day return to the skies.

I turned away from this cruel sight, this cold world,
Which surely could only disappoint this young girl,
Or so I thought.

For that winter when its flock,
Decided to depart,
Came back the girl with her little box.

Out of it popped the head,
Of the small bird I thought long lost,
Rising high to join its friends.

And on its wings now soars my heart,
For I have seen how the bird that once was blind,
Now flies.

We Are the Flame That Will Not Die

Bill Atheling

We are the flame that will not die,
Whose stock is strong and true,
Time honored blood of noble line,
Forged by struggle, shaped by time,
Our nations thrived and grew.

We are the flame that will not die,
Nor wane, nor know an end,
Though foemen cursed and spat their scorn,
The fire within was always borne,
By kith, and by kin, and by friend.

We are the flame that will not die,
And tides and time still flow,
Though seas of hate, churn all around,
The sacred fire cannot be drowned,
Our journey shall not slow.

We are the flame that will not die,
No more to wander alone,
If each of us should play their part,
And keep that flame within their heart,
We'll find that looked for home.

The Morning Light

Godfrey's Bouillon

Deep shades of burgundy round where I stand
Wrinkling my toes in the earlymorn sand
Gazing as Gloom draws back her curtain
For now is the hour dawn ushers in certain.

Suddenly, Apollo, the vanguard rider crests,
Upon blazing chariot that never rests
Shards of gold dazzle cross the water
Bright medallions of soldier after slaughter.

I can feel the air shift slightly now
The long Night is over, she took a bow
Now comes the time for smile and ease,
For morning enlightens, and morning frees.

My Victory

Christian

As another grain of sand falls
So too my inhibition shows
A little devil gnawing at my conscience
The root of my endless throes

While battles rage inside of me
Between who I am and who I'm supposed to be
The little devil holds on tight
My vigor turning to a blight

Perhaps once more I shall embrace
The little devil's "final" wish
Remaining far from divine grace
A vice I don't want to miss

The little devil lets me go
Confident in my demise
And leaving me with no hope
For this craving to subside

Then slowly I begin to realize
How my future is in decline
If this devil never dies
Today, for once, victory shall be mine!

One by One

Cleon II

So often I feel like a lout
Because I feel the sting of doubt.
Did my forefathers feel this way
As they stood up to face the day?

I look at what they had to face
And how they bore it all with grace.
Do I live a life they'd respect
In this world that I reject?

Evil crawls at every turn
And always wants to loot and burn.
Sin and vice are always lurking,
A certain tribe looks on smirking.

It's almost enough to break you
And I just ask, "What can I do?"
At first, I thought I'd surrender,
'Til I'm given a reminder.

I see proof that I'm not alone,
That there are others who bemoan,
They learn and build and somehow grow,
Defying that which sets them low.

The pace is oh so torturous,
Yet they are somehow boisterous.
When I see how they still do fight,
I know I too must do what's right.

Reinforce my spine with courage,
With conviction shout the message.
It is never a guarantee
That one's own people will be free.

One by one the struggle expands,
New brothers now defend our lands.
Every battle starts with one,
And isn't over 'til it's done.

Melancholia

Anya Colgan

Melancholia, a comfortable fog
A hearty duvet pressing in against your bones
Smothering your will to shower and make healthy food decisions
This spiritual ailment should be beaten about the head
Scolded like a naughty child and sent for a time out

Recrudesce

Anya Colgan

This isn't my first rodeo.
I have been kicked in the teeth before.

That dark passenger of depression has stood at my bedside
Delicate nimble fingers in phantom velvet gloves
Pressing into my chest cavity.
Hollowed, shrunken, crone-like
Shadows in my periphery.

The fear awakens
My muscles go slack and I let myself fall
My body hits the floor but I keep falling.
The tunnel comes to an end.
I have dug myself a well
A hidey-hole to calm me
Swaddle me in familiar darkness
Rest my head on conjured maternal comfort
My earthen den
My purgatory outside of space and time.

My fear of falling evaporated
I have hit bottom
Toes wiggle in damp soil
Fingers caress roots.
I look up.

Epitaph

Corydoras

No vaunted marble will bear my name
Unmartyred, my bones will find no rest in reliquaries
My hand grasps neither banner nor sword
Ink and time alike forget my deeds.
Distill my life, then, into 4 simple words
Carved in common stone, amid ranks of common stone
"Loving Wife and Mother."
Greatness does not stir my blood
I withdraw from pride, from ambition
From the chorus of worldly praise and paychecks
To serve instead, like a cool breeze
Doing the ephemeral work of love.
A diaphanous life of no renown
But one spun from unnumbered small sacrifices
The cribside sleeplessness, the dust-covered hobbies
My body made a home for outstretched hands
I am not my own.
History eschews my indulgent smiles, my homemade meals
Swept floors and scale cleaned from bathroom sinks
Ignored by the nodding arbiters of merit
And yet, here I stand
Indispensable.

Thoughts of Home

John David

Her call is like a whisper,
In the air that fills my lungs,
I hear it always listener,
You know it too in familiar tongues.

Is it a thought that decays?
A garden of flowers that now rot and wilt,
Of a travelling land that forever fades,
Whose soil always turns to silt;

Where yet, I am, held fast by its precious sun,
Whose hands are clearly felt,
Plunder of a heart not yet undone,
Like reflections in ice that is yet to melt.

Here, in this homely land,
Where fear and dread are all away,
With no dunes to know the desolation of sand,
Ne'er is contentment lost in the comely May.

Our humble dwellings amber in the sun,
Bird chorus fills the sky with verse,
Between the land for which I come,
And the gentle stream at the edge of our universe.

How my home does beckon me,
Though I may no longer walk its streets.
How my home does beckon me,
From memories I'm yet to greet.

That tug on my wandering soul,
To return to that fair isle.
To pass atop the rolling Earth,
On the axis of that mile.

Small Victories

Sue Denim

To Great Victories the glory,
Retold, remembered, survived by history,
Pored over by scholars, dissected, debated,
Common knowledge to common men, celebrated,

To small victories the shade cast by the Great,
Forgotten, at best remembered late,
Obscure, niche, neglected,
Excluded from the histories and poetry collected,

And yet the Great owes the Small,
They push the Great to prominence tall,
While they squat behind, unseen,
As the knight's steed is hidden by its rider's sheen,

The sand dune is a mound of grains,
The Great stride the sum of small gains,
The try-line crossed after many phases,
The novel penned with many phrases,
The city built in many stages,
A people, a nation, though many ages,

Remember Small Victories, however small,
Without them there is no Great at all,
The dune does not scorn the grain that props it higher,
The cold the spark that leads to fire,
The first inch along the journey of miles,
The last page to finish thick files,

Nothing is too Small to lead to Great,
No action futile or too late,
None above the lowest or beneath the highest men,
None complete, not worth doing again,

All men can win small, should and must,
Let them be bold, in themselves trust,
Be tempted not by plots of Great victory in one fell swoop,
Nor for the small wins to be too lofty to stoop,
Be the grains and let the dune form,
Be raindrops rather than the storm,

Lay the bricks upon which the next man may lay more,
Let him work so the next can do his chore,
Someday a great monument over your bricks will stand,
The credit to the last sculptor, the thanks to your hand,
It will be a Great victory while yours was Small,
Yet without it yours stands, without yours it falls,

Take pride in your Small victories, strides and gains,
They may not win you glory but let them cause you no shame,
They are wanted and needed and you must provide,
That one day Great victories are remembered with pride,
And who knows, perhaps you will be that last grain of sand,
That lets the dune taller than the others stand.

No, I Overcame

Ella Dennis

I am able to complete all that is of my mind
To finish any feat little by little at a time
Sometimes by surprise will come a substantial kind
Of clear-cut crystal vision coming from this mind of mine.

Through the gritty gravel, the splattering of rain
Through suffering the senselessness through arbitrary pain
Through dire dust where we swear we'd give up but
We adjust and then we ponder until trying again.

I try I try trying to overcome
Fail after fail slightly forward toward each one
Not to realize visions I formed had really gotten done
When can one say when one has won?

Did I simply win or lose?
No, I overcame
As of now,
Victor is my name.

To My Son, Upon Becoming a Father

Dark Enlightenment

Sit by the fire, and drink deep my son
Let me give thee wisdom our fathers have passed on
While thy wife gives birth in blood and pain
Ours but to pray and wait
Why thy mother was in thy wife's place,
Said thy grandfather unto me, and his father unto him,
Be not o'er proud, lest the fates cut thee down
Love and work thy native soil, with might and main and toil
Build a life for thy wife and child, shelter them in care so mild
Honor God, do thy duty to our city
On the widow orphan aged infirm have due pity
All thy life thy shall reap and plow
Till thou are aged as I am now
Then having loved thy wife and sons
Do as I have done, send thy sons into the world and find a wife
Risk thy precious boy in war, strife, ventures near and far,
That he might return to do his ultimate duty,
To lay a son in his mother's arms, and raise his son to do the same.

Prophetia Abbatis Ischyrionis
(The Prophecy of Abba Ischyrion)

Servius Aurelianus Episcopus

Yore have the sage and rev'rend monks bespoke
Of what would once befall the latter tide.
An abbot, asked by disciples, broke
His longsome Silence; thus he wisely cried:
"We have fulfill'd the Laws of God, our Lord,
"And those who shall hereafter come will do
"The half of what we bore and meekly warr'd."
"But, Abba, shall the last ones too?"
Someone besought, to which he thus replied:
"The men of th'End Times shall achieve no deed;
"A great Temptation, Will, and also Pride
"Shall overcome them; many will concede.
"Nevertheless, whoever keepeth faith, by Grace,
"Shall more than us beknow our Lord's sheen Face."

Heaven a Roof (Originally, Eight Spokes)

Paul Fahrenheidt

Canto I: The Shining White City

Hear me you Saxmen | you sons of far stars,
That you may recall | the song time has marred.
This dirt we stand on | foreign to our feet.
Long lost to us | is our home of wet peat.

I beg your ears | for my forefather's guide,
This song was once sung | by men more than I.
The sons of the Saxmen | they have no need,
For their father's fables | only their greed.

And yet they've gathered | round this ancient oak,
The chiefs of their clans | are yet to have spoke.
Their spear-shafts of ash | all cast to the ground,
Their ears are intent | to hear this Skald sound.

The rites of this moot | still sacred it seems;
    Not yet cast away | by haughty black kings.
Yet I see the ire | in envious eyes,
    Of those who despise | their forefather's things.

By the name | "Sigmund the Skald," which I wear,
I'll sing of the songs | the Saxmen must bear.
As few find the time | to learn of their kin;
I must remind them | why we sit in sin.

In times last recalled | by no living man;
The men of short-swords | the greatest of clans.
And yet their bright blood | goes back further still,
To ice-coated lands | yet untouched by chill.

Cities of magic | by rainbow's light lit;
Here the world's wyrd | was carefully knit.
And ancient green groves | were verdant with life;
Plague was as foreign | as hatred and strife.

Back in those times | when men had true honor,
    Their women were honest | prudent and chaste.
They gave to the gods | and thought first of God,
    And all living men | remained in their caste.

The shining white form | the wise one-eyed took,
Stood strong in the sky | where many did look.
I ask for his boon | may I drink his mead,
So tongue in my mouth | may never mislead.

Long was the reign | of the wise one-eyed lord,
'Twas not once unjust | nor took up the sword.
Yet there are some things | the wise can't impart,
And black rusting envy | poisoned men's hearts.

So too did their thoughts | turn base and perverse,
The foul fate of men | put on them a curse.
They turned on their kin | betrayed their own kind,
They murdered and maimed | and made themselves blind.

They too grew debauched | their women were whores,
    No more were the streets | where men would once build.
The ancient green groves | once landvaettir's home,
    Were cut down and burned | were lined with men killed.

The shining white form | of wise one-eyed king,
Did melt from the sky | like snow in the spring.
The rainbow's light left | the nights without stars,
In God's soul was grief | in men's souls, a scar.

Flung from that city | and into the frost,
Our foolish fathers | were naked and lost.
So too were their families | thrown out alone,
And on the cruel Earth | they hoped to atone.

The Earth was our land once | our father's home.
Its forests and fields | were ours free to roam.
The landvaettir stayed | with us for a time;
Wotan still loved us | despite all our crimes.

Forever left lonely | outside the gates,
    Of that magic land | where once men were men.
We poor cast out sons | were burned by the sun,
    Never let back | into heaven again.

Canto II: The Rise and Fall of Earth

You Saxmen may laugh | but I say it true;
Your forefather's folly | was what made you.
If you lent your ears | to tales of the skalds,
We could have stayed | within those white walls.

Outcasted to Earth | our fate filled with dread,
We made a new home | in paradise stead.
A place where the plains | met mountain and sea,
Though we were cast out | we still were called free.

When landvaettir left | we bonded with beasts;
We tied them to carts | and set for the east.
So too we west | and northward and south,
From old ice-wall's edge | to ocean's blue mouth.

We spread through the world | took tribes as our prize,
    We conquered and killed | and mixed our pure blood.
And when men's urges | tainted their honor,
    Wotan wiped world away | with a great flood.

Ten-thousands of years | passed fathers and sons,
We died and revived | one after a-one.
Off to foreign fields | we planted new roots.
In blood and in soil | so called we new moots.

Names in the hundreds | we came to be called,
Some grew their hair long | some cut to be bald.
Some sailed off to sea | to seize foreign shores,
On land most remained | to fight countless wars.

By horse and by sword | by spear and by shield,
Against mighty foes | did none of us yield.
Built we great kingdoms | which fell to our kin,
Not one place on earth | where we had not been.

And as the time passed | we learned newfound tricks,
    To harness the force | of powder and steam.
Did we so want | our white city again?
    Or was our desire | born from haughty dreams?

We cloaked the blue sky | with thick choking smoke,
We made it a point | to cut every oak,
We raped the earth's soil | clawed gems from her womb,
We never knew | we were building our tomb.

If you, brave Saxmen | laid eyes on their work,
What say you to these | the makers of murk?
Who turned rivers black | and set them aflame,
And rushed to forget | from where they had came?

They built iron mounts | and slaughtered their beasts,
Hate poisoned their minds | forgotten was peace.
They brought up from Hell | a weapon they'd made.
Invisible fire | broke bones and skin flayed.

They thought such power | was worthy of them,
    Each of the Saxmen said | "Stave off the end!"
No king ever listened | and weapons were launched;
    The green Earth was burned | which no man could mend.

Some possessed wisdom | that thing no one keeps,
When wisdom is needed | honor is cheap.
Worthless white husks like the dead | stalked the Earth,
Our folly-made hellscape | gave a new birth.

Our scattered old tribes | spread outside walls white,
Made our way back | to that beacon of light.
Great Wotan was there | the wise one-eyed king,
And waiting for us | several gifts did he bring.

Ourselves we recalled | and place we had lost,
We gazed on our folly | and realized its cost,
We built mighty ships | that sailed astral seas,
We brought back our beasts | and saved many trees.

We'd failed to protect | our Earth green and gold,
    Yet our task remained | to pay back our sins.
We boarded our ships | that sailed through the stars,
    Towards foreign shores | like our hero twins.

Canto III: The Green Thunder Dome

Atop ships we built | we too built a dome,
With rivers and soil | to copy our home.
The few sacred oaks | from Earth's dirt we saved,
Carved runes in their bark | were they so engraved.

Above this great dome | was heaven, our roof;
The sun that stood high | was not one in truth.
A bright ball of fire | that we'd artificed,
Nor did we rebuild | the great walls of ice.

When nighttime would fall | the dome would be clear,
The sea of the stars | adorned on that sphere.
Below lay our mountains | our forests and groves,
And herds of white sheep | from which came our clothes.

And we made it such | that clouds came to be,
    Beneath the great dome | which Saxmen preserved.
Yet something was missing | not all was well,
    The hole in our souls | was what we deserved.

For four hundred years | under dome did pass,
It seemed more and more | like sky than like glass.
So just as before | did we soon forget,
That we had to pay | our outstanding debt.

As many years passed | old Earth left our thoughts.
The dome was our *heimat* | elsewhere was not.
Soon the thoughts which | brought down Earth had returned,
No one remembered | the world we had burned.

Many small chiefs | would ordain themselves kings,
Every false skald | crafted glories to sing.
So born were bands | which with brothers would war,
So too did women | return as their whores.

Our new home fell | into pointless old strife,
    Thankfully wise Wotan | gave only steel,
We'd proven unfit | to wield weapons worse.
    Each petty king | sought to make Saxmen kneel.

These pointless wars | fought for generations,
Each king saw himself | head of our nation.
Then to the humble clan Bremer | was born,
The man who would mend | our tribes that were torn.

Albrecht the Storm-Born! | Donner's brave son!
And with his birth | a new people begun!
His arms were iron | which no man could best,
A lightning filled heart | thundered in his chest!

When he had grown | from a boy to a man,
He set out to mend | his greed-cursed land!
First he fought Bersi | the weakest of chiefs,
When he was brought low | Albert claimed his fief!

So too fell Wulfgar | and Godric, and Hild.
    Within five short years | the Saxmen were one!
From Albrecht the Storm-Born | came Albrecht, King!
    Against men's black hearts | brave Albrecht had won!

Wise Wotan was watching | his grandson's great feats,
And when Albrecht won | he called for a feast!
The wise one-eyed once king | crowned his own blood,
Proclaimed that his birth | brought this tribe from the mud.

And Albrecht's companions | men brave and true,
Were gifted with rings | and clans that were new.
So Saxmen who sit here | thence come your folk,
Whom Albrecht the Storm-Born | freed from their yolk.

Just as the hero's life | came to a close,
    Our ships made landing | on our newfound home.
And Albrecht remembered | and shared our tale,
    He named it Niwegeard | We broke from the dome!

Canto IV: Niwegeard

It was not long | until Albrecht had passed,
He gave one last gift | that gift which was caste.
When we left the dome | to settle this Niwegeard,
Each man had a place | no more tempers flared.

When the brave body | of Albrecht broke down,
No man could be found | worth wearing the crown.
So his companions and clans | built a bright pyre,
The crown was destroyed | with Albrecht in fire.

This left us kingless and | sin stalked our thoughts,
Was this the end | of all Albrecht had wrought?
Wotan was absent | he'd sent all he could.
Yet he stood watching | disguised in a hood.

So the first moot was | called under an oak,
    We took from our dome | to plant in new soil.
Though we had failed | Albrecht made a new start.
    The Saxmen could stand | without any man royal.

Albrecht's companions | and clans made a pact,
None would take arms | nor another attack.
While this new homeland | was fertile and green,
A great many threats | lay seen and unseen.

In the form of brute beasts | gray wolves and bears,
Such that all men | needed shields they could wear.
And swords they could swing | against more than beasts,
So too had come here | the men of the East.

Albrecht's eight companions | as many clans,
Went eight directions | claiming their own land.
But they kept between them | our ancient dome,
So that we'd never | forget our lost home.

Wotan gave a smile | and vanished from sight.
    His sons had made peace | and left their own hell.
With Albrecht's example | their eyes looked out,
    In land that he'd gifted | they'd learn to dwell.

Now let us sing | of clans given root,
By our king's bondsmen | who called the first moot.
Who come from their eight | spokes of land each year,
Back to this dome-taken | oak we put here.

First was fair Oswald | his clan just as Just.
Next came strong Cedric | arms untouched by rust.
So too came Aella | not once was he beat.
As did good Godwin | of foot very fleet.

And when Egbert came | it's said Albrecht hailed,
Next honor-filled Ulf | whose faith never failed.
Then lucky Vindur | whose eyes saw all things.
Fraywulf was last | besting all but the king.

Each of these bondsmen | swore an oath sacred,
    Their clans upheld | upon each of their deaths
So long as the Saxmen | stand on this world,
    No brother-blood shed | when we still draw breath!

A fair word of warning | you gathered chiefs,
There's gods-given reason | why I'm not brief.
For I start to see | old urges rebirthed,
And I don't desire | to make second Earth.

Hence why wise Wotan | decreed that the skalds,
Sing songs of our fathers | cast from ice-walls.
So before every moot | a skald must remind,
That envy and hate | made our fathers blind.

And with this wisdom | I ask you to hold,
Make not the mistakes | of ancestors old.
But temper your hearts | with love and respect,
For your actions here | our sons will reflect.

So ends the song | sung by Sigmund the Skald,
    Our four and five hundredth | year on this plane.
And now that our burden | has been remembered,
    This moot shall begin | I solemnly claim!

Just a Clump of Cells

Fraxinus

They want you to think that her life is of less consequence than yours. That your daughter in the womb, for whom you eagerly await would be better not being at all. "It's just a clump of cells" comes tumbling out their putrid maw.

What fell beast would have you believe, this child of mine were by chance bequeathed, subject only to man's law. Forgive them father for they know not what they say, their sins are their own and without redemption, a grave toll they will surely pay.

Small wonder that her very being breeds contempt in the hearts of these demons abound. Her light in this imperfect darkness makes for the ideal surround. It envelopes me as a shroud of blue-painted sky across the crumbling ceiling of the rotten illusion seen from below, I'm enamored with each day I have by her, and relish in those devil's woes.

Life before her was nothing but a void. Abyssal wandering without purpose, my dreams were bare, moribund, destroyed. My eyes laid upon her for the first time in life, my burning soul wept in ecstasy as it's relieved of its strife. Pale white skin as of sheets of crisp snow, the scarlet rubies that are her lips did glow.

Divine design gave us our bairn so beautiful, completed our family for which we did yearn. An accomplishment open to all who are true of moral fiber, qualities that should be easy to discern. This wonder of mine should no evil befall, woe betide the unfortunate soul that would run afoul of this pitfall.

Life itself weaves through her, as a thunderstorm through the clouds. Each spark, each smile, each quirk does beguile, and it's not enough to simply say I'm proud. It's scarcely believable that these monsters would discard such beauty, utterly inconceivable. Death will be the only eternity they deserve, neither the fruits of maternity nor paternity.

Our enemies are numerous and these times grow darker, our manifesting differences are starker still. Treading water in this mire weighs me down beyond belief and for a second feeling like forever I felt that there would be no relief. But as quickly as the trepidation set that my life was incomplete, she sprung forth and is guiding me on what is my greatest feat.

Coward Man's Chagrin

Bando Gora

You disgust me, coward man
Your beady eyes and greasy hair
Your face half stuck in your favorite scoff
Your tepid stench lingers in the air
The reptilian flakes of your scalp shed
Yet aren't a fraction as venomous as your actions
Your frigid blood undetectable as you slither
Frictionless from disappointment to deception
Nauseating all who catch a glimpse of your nature
Stay away from me, coward man.
Who couldn't go so far as to look your mirrored image in the eye
Without resigning to your fate or
Blaming someone else
Able to unearth excuses anywhere,
A man who is most confident when defeating himself
Stay away from me, coward man.
Who would sooner judge a subject than talk to that subject
Too meek to question the validity of that which you hear
Reselling it without hesitation at face value for your leisure
How dare you gossip my fall from grace
When the furthest you have ever fallen is from groveling on knees
To bowing on face
Stay away from me, coward man.
Too scared to take the leap
And suffer the epiphany that
Not only was the water deep enough to break your plummet
But the shore was close enough to grasp
And you could exit baptized
Having forgot your purpose for life
Stay away from me, coward man.
Who is too busy forming a reply to the first word
To consume the completed thought

Either so sure of yourself or so worried
That you might be categorically wrong
That you must poke a hole in the first target you sight
Measure your perspective, coward man.
Your comprehensive lease on life
Your worldview in its raw, uncut totality
Let it be tepid,
And greasy,
And disgusting,
And nauseatingly incorrect
For sunlight disinfects
And makes it much easier to repair
The consequences of one's actions
I know personally
When I stand in the sun
I feel damn courageous.

A Volte-Face

Victor Holz

A world of dust and ash
The ruins of greatness surrounding

All around, limping beasts
Stumbling into the darkness to die.
They don't look around in wonder, amazement,
    regret or disappointment
Heads down, simply shuffling ahead.

Corpulent and soft,
Hollow behind the eyes.
Dead.
Contented but not.

Some on the periphery,
Self-removed from the herd
Watch the others pass by.

Disgusted by what they see around them,
They gather in small groups.

Vomiting the vices which were force fed to them
    back into the world,
Some curled fetal from the effort.
Their shared excision a joining force.

Once rid of their darkness and shame,
A hand in the ashes, and a mark of the Light
    smeared above their eyes.

Together they stand.
Backs straightened, faces to the wind.

To walk opposite the others.
Taking any like them who will come.

Back to whence they came.
To a light unseen, beckoning from beyond the hills.

Crainn a Phlandáil

Cool Hoolan

While deer ate all the sapling
Our waterways turned to sand
Ancient cities crumbled, we
See paintings carved with crayon

Faerie phantoms drum the beat
Awakening dormant clan
Wading in the yellow peat
Transmit dreams to make me stand

Will you drown your brothers' hearth
With the waters in your hands?
Or wrap white birch 'round the earth
Sowing thistle in your lands?

Lugh's bellow slowly hurt me so
I'm a son that turned astray
But who are we, me fellow,
When we sit alone to pray?

As mystic marches inward
Lo the grail lie on a tray
Time we dig down in the soil
For Excalibur today

We plant the dear new sapling
Our fresh waters braise the land
Ancient cities rumble, we
Are greatness carved again

Clwyd

E.W. Howard

Britannia's eyelash flickers
An SOS in snare
An Elwy spire glitters
By candles lit for prayer

Here the trowels and forks still swing
And bailers jive till dusk
Quilted hills and dales sing
And cloak the rasping husk

Festering din and doner
Washes from town to grave
Dry-stone dykes we honor
As friends beyond deprave

Crenelated armistice
A searing lull to bare
Tippled choirs stir in us
Spring tonic soothes the air

We sow, chant, and drape our sores
Weaving merry braids of gauze

Matron! Quickly—Matron!
She shifts
She sighs
She stares

Don't Waste Your Days

June

Words cannot describe my fear,
That all my life be wasted here,
That work and grief shall be my chains,
To choke and bind my corpse remains,

Murdered by my lack of cheer,
Killed as though I wasn't here,
Meaningless, devoid of reason,
Alone through every passing season,

For I should spend my waking days,
Consumed by that my heart relays,
A choice to have a joyful start,
Or pain me so till life depart...

Motherhood

Mrs. Kestrel

As I lift up my burgeoning toddler
I can feel the momentum of 100 women before me
Embracing in their arms their own children,
Like an infinite zoetrope playing the images of our nurturing
If they had not raised in their arms their own children
I would not have the opportunity

At night I lay my precious children down for bed and tell them stories,
Some I make up and some that have been told to me
I pass down a tale whose mere existence is a miracle,
Its manifestation old and its persistence admirable
Sometimes I will have to sing them to sleep,
My voice sounding like my own mother's
The triumphs of the matriarchs before me echo

Providence Swing

Carson Kilgrey

I cut myself off,
I take myself out
Of the portrait.

Shock and awe or
A disgusted pause
Before words whispered,
"How could you?"

The slippery difference
Between us,
Is it only years
Or providence swing?

I bind myself thus,
I commit myself to
The renewal.

Slack and slow to
This laborious phase.
Men about me chanting
With one voice.

The holy fire lit
Amongst us,
Is it only worldly doubts
Or providence swing?

I cast my guilt out,
I raise my sword up
With my brethren.

Home and hearth found
In we, the ignited,
The titanic mass demanding
Our world back.

This martial bond swelling
Within us,
Whose hand could it be
But providence swing?

What loss could compare
To eternal defeat?
Such men I have found,
With many yet to meet.

A Forgotten Plot

Tucker King

To the west of my plot
Lay a wood long forgot

Thick the vines have grown
Constricting the cherries and the oaks
Across which refuse is thrown
Left by vagabonds and careless folks

The dying trees hang over my hearth
Ivy from foreign places grappling branch and trunk
Slowly pulling them to the earth
Threatening my home
These invasives left alone
Will rip the roots out of the dirt
To drop their wood corpses on my modern thatch roofed bunk
My dominion I must reassert

With ax and saw I labored forth
Felling, bucking, hauling
Piles built high of brush to be burnt

Though most won't see the effort it took
To clean the land that I call home
'Fore too long will sit a chicken coop
And a garden to feed my own

Temperance Hymn of the Newly Reclaimed Soul

or T. Total's Tune to be sung with Triumphant Bird Chorus

Nemo Knows

I

"I don't recognize thou, new me, sober and soul clean
"Whence went thy mud-dragged ragged dreams once propped up aloft?
"Impossible thoughts have filled thy head with contentment
"What was unimagined now lives as if infinite!"

    This begins my first spring march
    Again it starts; life as a gift of living
    Art of knowing that poison's worth avoiding!

A robin's peep-peeps mark the street's many musics
And I'm full of bird-song, amazed-glow, absorbing all
Van Winkle's crumbs tumble boulder-like from my tear ducts
And mirrors abundant guide my green glad meander.
Now near nine months passed since vine's drafts were left abandoned

"Thine eyes hunger like a she-horse fatigued from birthing
"And thy long lungs pull sloshing fine lines all about thee.
"Whose white scleras are these nested 'midst the just-stretched flesh?"
But wince of time's ice raps on many passing windows
And somewhere a young girl's long-off laugh fades into clouds

    Yet here I still stand, new-born babe-me!
    I coo too with the rock dove today
    Strength of peace abides me, throughout me
    Prayerful, proud without war-seeking

All those old red chains have bloomed into autumn-dry leaves
Swiftly crunched and strewn to pieces 'neath white leather shoes
Sloughed away and shoved off away to some n'other place
Never again to be seen nor dreamed of nor pondered.
No man blocks me, still I wrestle my lone way onward

II

Rebel, I heard thy song
"I need thou no longer!"
"And yet *it all* remains!"
Uncleanable marks, unyielding unknown parts
Everything, everything, yes I remember.
Let those burdens lie silent entombed
Let musty memories grow green flowers
Let bygone cups not shadow our now
Let's wish, but know this, something below still fevers unhidden
Out from behind that curtain, hero!
The goats have been perfumed and christened
Choruses rise unbound 'tween bleachers
And great flocks have gathered to watch thee,
To tie thee center stage to pyres.
Imagined reprisals fantastic
Will manifest with perfect timing
Ending as embers and funeral dirges.
All will be forgiven, all urges
That's when the flocking chorus will begin their dramatic murmurs:

Peep-peep!
Karoo ka-reee!
A'kreee-kitcha'kitcha—
It's a mighty spring what consumes a wrinkled witch!
To hell foul hag! Headless, boweless, wordless she went—
No bone un-bit, all matches blackened and spent;
A laugh of sulfur; a mug full of spit! All bashed and at last made molten!
Upon heaps of ashes, here we dance! Entranced by hearth stones still dewy-wet
Garbed up and gathered, at last out from under our useless rootless yellow cocoons—
A gleeful reunion!
And the first voice beckoned, said: "I feel human!"

A merry meter marks the sweeping out and sings:
Count twice, thrice, be wiser then when tomorrow rings
Below the lowest line we sank and found the sober sound there
Under which no one, no more, alone or unknown, goes drowning!

The music is fine, then fades away
There will be mourning to come, but stay.
Never mind the lost time, never mind
As sure as glaciers must find the sea, I have found thee.
Long strong roots lash us on and beyond
Down and bound the now un-winding way

One More

Dogenes Kynikos

One more wipe till all things are clean
One more effort so the room is pristine
One more page to finish the book
One more meal you prepped and cooked
One more rep when you can't do more
One more set when muscles are sore
One more swim when your arms are busted
One more lap when legs can't be trusted
One more choice that is not convenient
One more time you haven't been lenient
One more thing you chose not to partake in
One more time you are not complaining
One must imagine Sisyphus smiling
Pushing his stone every time it's falling
Keeping in mind what this is worth
Eternal struggle is eternal growth

Simple Gifts

Wren Lane

A dim lit room tucked down deep in the South
A smile breaks across a tired mother's mouth
At the sound of a babe not yet a minute old
Giving out a cry so hearty and bold.

And to witness it here, there is nothing that charms
Like the triumph of a father with a new son in his arms
And the joy of the children as they meet their new brother
They waste not a moment to ask for another.

The truth of the matter, it's no more unique
Than any great deed our folk cherish and seek
But from this vantage, after much toil and worry
This travail becomes your crowning glory.

The world will spin on and out of control
But there will be stillness in your heart and soul
The coo of your baby, the man by your side
It's the little things really, that will swell you with pride.

What I See

Lachlan Lindenmayer

I walk by strangers I could never have known
I see the screens and don't believe what I'm shown
I smell the poison on which our children are grown
I look down at my hands and have regrets of my own

Yet;

When I gaze in my mirror what do I see?
The faces of forebears staring at me
Who mastered the ice and the storms and the sea
Who gave all and more so that I could be

They tell me;

"Within your hands that once brought shame
"Lies the potential for beauty and gain

"Beyond the mindset that wants to give in
"Is the world itself for he who dares win

"And inside the hearts of our confused race
"Sit the answers of purpose and place

"Keep walking forward son, keep standing tall
"Every victory you have is one for us all"

So;

I clean up the mess that cluttered my mind
I leave behind habits uncouth and unkind
I cultivate only what makes me refined
And when I stumble I get up and retry

Though I am not yet amongst the wise men
There's one thing I learned from my life back then
I'll tell it to you now, remember my friend
It's never too late to stop
And try again

Untitled

M

Victory is not wingèd
As was that of Samothrace
Lilies from the acorn wringed
So lacking in every grace

No more the beating of the tambour
Than the singing of the lute
No more richness of an amber
Than the blooming of the fruit

What is a century?
A moment in the night
What is a victory?
The spirit of blight

Unable to rule as Gods
We suffer as simple kings
Little more than cosmic bawds
In the mere realm of things

ACAB Ballade

Bernhard D. Massey

I sit alone and pray for God, to please show himself in time. A one bedroom's become a pod, and the human soul deplete.

In the empty public quad, you can see the true defeat. A society that's been trod, another time cycle repeat. Living with this profound deceit has become the eternal crime, surrounded by all concrete, complete loss of the sublime.

I sit alone and feeling odd, amongst the muck and grime. But since I've dropped the façade, I feel like I'm complete.

To my folk I'll give a nod, lest we become obsolete. Now that I've found my squad, we know that we cannot retreat. So for now we stay discreet. All for one, yours is mine. Never again will we retreat, we're guided by the divine.

Consolation

Samantha Matz

The embers dull within the hearth burn low
And fiery sun concedes its vast domain.
Beyond the windows chilled with winter's ice,
The shadows ever longer reach and sprawl.
The barren trees sway feebly as if dead
While their plucked fruit, consumed, is all but gone.

With night sets in the terror of the dark,
Of slaving beasts that prowl ravenous
To hunt and prey upon the travelers
Who laugh in haughtiness and know no fear,
Of blinding night that makes men lose their ways
And wander aimlessly across the land
From paths beset with snares on every side,
Of wicked tyrants, gorged on murdered blood,
Whose people grow content to live in fear,
And of that silent, oft-forgotten Death.

Within that house, still weary life remained,
Their little fire burning through the night,
So gently kindled by a woman's hand,
And kept alive by rough-hewn logs of wood.

Upon her husband's breast that woman laid,
And gazing on their fire, spoke to him,

"How long must we endure this solitude,
"This barrenness and night so full of death?
"Would that the days were shortened for this strife,
"Of gnawing hunger, seldom to be filled,
"And grieving dreams of plenitude and peace.
"How long ago those days of green appeared,

"When people danced and played not knowing fear,
"When arrogance made fools of us all.
"No thoughts had we for darker days ahead,
"No dream of this dark night we would endure.
"Console me, bridegroom, cast away my dread,
"Make sweet your voice of truth upon my ears."

And from the silence, he replied to her,
"Take heart, beloved, gird yourself once more.
"Thus far you have endured and further will
"Until this pain will run its fearful course.
"Your will like iron, you have firmly set,
"But let not grief transform your heart to stone.
"Your eyes with tears now run because you see
"With watchful eyes, man's penance for his sins.
"The wrongs of all the world weigh heavily
"On you whose heart is willing to endure
"Such suffering that others might be spared.
"Close off your ears from all the lies of men,
"Do not give heed to voices urging ill,
"Nor those who offer safety in false hope.
"Long is the path and narrow which you walk,
"Without a star or lantern on your way.
"My voice now follow; let me be your guide,
"For I desire happiness for you,
"A joy so precious, bought with suffering.
"As when a lump of steel is forged in flame
"And bent so many times when soft from heat
"Until it takes the blacksmith's perfect shape,
"So are you now, and all who likewise grieve.
"For when these days have passed (and pass they will)
"Then you who sowed in tears will reap great joy.
"For love is taught to grow in solitude,
"And likewise hope, when all is desolate.
"These treasures of the soul are planted now
"And will sprout up to flourish on that day,
"When all the world to justice is restored."

The Thaw

Jack McKraken

These days it's not that difficult to fall to misery
When every day is crime and graft and it's so plain to see
But me? I laugh it off and keep my head held to the sky
Am I special? No sirree, I just count my blessings high

I couldn't tell you the amount of times I wished to leave my job
Just up and vanish without a trace and leave behind these slobs
The boss is dumb, he's barely there, he's as rude as he is crass
But it's okay, because I know, this spectacle can't last

I barely got any sleep last night, the dreams? They're naught but bad
There's vagrants walking down the streets attacking old granddads
There's perverts in the bathrooms, at work and school and church
Yet through the fog of anguish I see a glory lurks

Our politicians are bought and sold by men from foreign lands
They count their treasure eagerly and wring their bejeweled hands
But in my house, and many like it, I can't save a dime
So we share a drink and plot the course until judgment time

Because in these days of oppressive yoke that we all survive in
We're cradled softly back to slumber through every flavor of sin
And for those of us who refuse the call of meaningless escape,
We grow smarter, stronger, better off with every blow and scrape

For now the world is but a thrall of disgraceful men up high
Who prepare a moonlit sacrifice of my brothers, even I
Life is hard, it makes no sense, danger always lies in wait
But we don't let it get to us, we know their timeless fate

Our courts are all a mockery, violent criminals are deemed saints
While men like me are strung up high as they toss out all our plaints
Democracy chooses Barabbas and gives you four hundred years
But still I smile, because I know, it's us he truly fears!

And when they can't use their laws to bully and convince
They'll unleash their many rogues and killers to beat you into complacence
They'll march and burn and tear things down in a sickening ballet,
But none of it can get to me. My kid? He's due in May

And finally when we get the courage to leave our warm abodes
We cannot tire or slacken yet, our eyes are on the roads
Dark drivers with a bone to pick want to hit our children as they flee
But lo, a sound! What is that call? It beckons NJP!

Though the tally of my blessings might seem like quite a lot
Even I can't help but succumb to the gloom and moral rot
The years they go, the seasons change, and I'm still standing here
I'm older, slower, not as a sharp as I though I may appear

A cold wind blows now from the north, it's like this winter never ends
I'm weary from this slush and snow, please nature make amends
But when you let the sun climb up and warm these somber bones
Let it fill me with the strength of knights, lords, and golden thrones

I may be dead and buried before I ever get my say
But knowing that gives me the strength to fight on anyway
The winter, yeah she always comes, but it always leaves us too
And her storms always rage the hardest before the thaw's debut

A Fight Against Love is Best Lost

Grace Moore

For L, my best loss, my sweetest death

Honey coated walnuts
And deep blue pools.

Can you swim?

I never really learned, just
Jumped in, fought a war against the water,
And tried not to drown.

Just as I am trying now.

I jump in and I am trying
Not to drown, but your eyes
Are so deep and blue.

It makes me nervous.

I always hated the ocean
Because the unknown scares me and
I am terrified of not knowing just as much
As I am terrified of losing and never being loved.

How do you love?

I love sweet like honey coated walnuts,
Like orange cinnamon syrup, like
I have only ever won against the water, like,
Nothing in this world has ever hurt me.

Have you ever hurt?
Would you like to try?

I will tell you what it is to be hurt, to
Every day die a little death. It feels just
The same as loving, as being in love.

I have always been afraid of drowning, of
Losing the fight, of dying of love.
I avoid blue at all costs.
If I can.

But your eyes,
I should like to drown in them.
I should like to lose.
I should like to die sweet.

White Flesh Burns Black

Grace Moore

Do not look up. Do not
Look up. You will walk
And you will not look
Up. They can scream and
You will not look up. Hurl
Insults and you will not look up.
But what if instead you
Look up. Look them
In the eyes. You look
Them in the eyes. Eyes
Look back. They look
Back at you. At your eyes.
Eyes meet.

And see nothing.

When you were three
You fell into the pool. You were
Walking and you did not look
Up. You did not look up
Until you were looking
At the sun, broken into pieces
Through the blue
Above you.

And when your lungs
Were done fighting,
You saw nothing then, too.

How easily the world seems
To break into pieces, as easy
As a sun beam through water.

What is water to you
Now that you have undergone
Another baptism? One of
Gasoline and spit and blood. All due to
A phenotype, due to an
Irish ancestry you
Can have no pride in.

What is pride,
But a black hole?

Refuse it. Refuse to drown
Face down in black
And gasoline and spit and blood. That
Is your only hope of victory when there is
But one more baptism
Waiting for you.

And when the fires rage
And the riots with them,
And they swallow you,

Do not look down.

You are a sun beam
Sliding through water,
A knife through flesh,
A pale sign of some lost history
They cannot see.

Because they see nothing.

I, the Magician

Joe Morris

On the wild tundra plains
'Twas I who schooled the sons of Thanes
Taught how to fight and how to rule
The moon and stars revealed my school
I, the Magician.

In Druid rings I tended groves
By sacred altar lit the stoves
Linked ancestors and gods to tribe
Ensured that wisdom would survive
I, the Magician.

With quill and pen preserved the myths
From prying eyes and jealous fists
Clues for Kings I left within
So when they woke, our folk would win
I, the Magician.

At Arthur's side I served my part
With skill and wit, I used my art
Advised and listened, helped in the quest
Preserved his soul, in sacred rest
I, the Magician.

In darkest hour and blackest night
I've lit the fire, reclaimed the light
Tradition's torch I will defend
To kings reborn, I will attend
I, the Magician.

Usurper rats may run the show
And banish kings to down below
Bind and chain, folksoul to kill
Yet even here I'll work my Will
I, the Magician.

I lurk in shadows casting spells
I wake my kings and arm them well
With symbols, stories, myths I steer
Aiming true as Odin's spear
I, the Magician.

In years to come the rats will see
How kings reborn find victory
Stories told and lessons taught
Small victories, each one hard-fought
It was I, the Magician.

Whimper

T.J. Murray

I.

The time is soon coming,
For the torch to be passed,
To the young men of my
Generation.

Only the flame has been
Put out, leaving us without
Light for the coming darkness.

Darkness, in the shadow of giants,
On whose shoulders old men now
  stand,
Barking down at us to make
  something
Of ourselves.

Their broken promises all
Foul, false, and mad.
A Pandora's box opened up
And filled with sand.

We're sitting in padded cells,
To which there is no key.
Sitting in that open door,
Never to leap into the sea.

Praying for a God like Gilgamesh,
Whose heart was like a bole.
Hoping that he may renew the
Desires of a haunted, muted soul.

Walking in the streets with
Immigrant corners, with keyboard
Lights, with merciless machinations
That keep us in our beds.

Accepting the bondage blinders,
The whips, the chains, the digital
Masochism that rules over us and
Violates our heads.

Traveling every day to faraway
Places without leaving home.
Dreaming of ancient hermits,
Who at least had nature to roam.

The Indians died only for our free will
To be stolen and bought and sold.
Cameras on every street corner,
Making obsolete the myths of old.

II.

Who is responsible for
The surrogate life we live?
Baphomet, Moloch, Set, Satan
Who among you has blame to give?

This lonely suffering with
Fake dollars and pornography.
The last man writes his own
Laws with Satanic stenography.

His sacred machinery runs
Blood money into sterile streets.
His veins, his heart, his spirit,
Red, wriggling, insectoid meat.

Banks, tanks, and ruthless
Whimpering year after year.
Prisons the only things made
Better now made better ubiquitous.

His foundations pave concrete over
Love, brotherhood, national pride.
Stay back, close the doors, wonder
Why we're all inside.

Urban 3-floored somewheres,
Overwhelmed by parking lot
nowheres,
Overtaking the last few images
We have left of past Eden.

Now nuclear missiles hang over our
heads,
Life begins at thirty they so said.
Remember this, remember when, you
must
Remember, how things were then.

Give them an inch,
They'll take a mile.
Looks like we won't get
Ours for quite a while.

I feel atheistic apathy to
These week-old religions.
I feel only contempt for
These corrupt stool pigeons.

Who look for trappings in your
Heart, those with nowhere to go.
But the lot of us are now trapped,
Inside this cannibal dynamo.

III.

Life is now lived second-
Hand, not doing much.
All one may now do is
Look, but not touch.

We've all become
Tourists of the Earth.
Taking pictures, riding
Gondolas from our birth.

We serve the little plastic
Dolls we put on our shelves.
Taking the place of priests,
Friends, family, and the self.

Self-sacrifice, dumping
The sands of our lifetime,
Into the black pit of
Complacent jail time.

We each have our own cave,
With those shadows on the wall.
But now we can choose the shape
Of them, and show them to all.

In this age we can have
A life of many years.
But to never truly live is
What we've come to fear.

Hell has frozen over, as we
No longer believe in it.
Our joys are spoiled by use,
Pleasures lay at their limit.

The pearly gates, have
Been destroyed by rust.
As we who were once good,
Are now consumed by lust.

Is it over? Are we finished?
So soft have our feet become
In silk slippers, that our
Country has diminished?

Future days are yet to come, as
All days have yet to be put to text.
You grow old by deserting your
ideals,
And the appetite for what comes next.

The Epic of Sir Martin

Vladyslav Nazarchuk

I.

Great heroes rise, great heroes fall,
But all still hear the rousing call
Of truth eternal, of light profound,
Which pierces all from sky to ground,
Of darkness come and good delayed,
Of injustice which had so far prevailed,
Of evil clothed in garb unseen,
And acts that draw from soul unclean.

When right is wrong, when wrong is right,
When people are lost and blind in fright,
Then someone will undoubtedly rise
To stop humanity's demise.
His fate is sealed, and bravely in his heart
He follows it, and herefore does his part
Of a soldier loyal to his battlefields,
Who never crumbles, and thus he never yields.

Alas, such brave men often walk alone.
But they fear not, for in his throne
Our Heavenly Father watches them from high,
And angels caress them from the sky.
'Tis better to live well than just to live,
And most important, never to misgive
One's heart, and hand it over to despair;
And keep inside your soul undying flare.

II.

Our tale begins with Martin:
A soldier from the regiment
Of those who fought for Mercia
Against the men of Kent.
A brave commander he was,
Returning from the fight,
With scars to prove his prowess
And dents to prove his might.
Returning to dear Aylesford,
The town where he was born,
He rode close to his home,
And, in the pink of morn,
He saw a great, dark shadow
Sweep inside the door,
The screams of his dear maiden,
The spirit's devilish roar!
In haste, he galloped closer yet,
And what do you think he found?
The fiend had grabbed his wife,
And, turning himself around,
He sped forth through the door,
The hinges bursting forth,
And, clutching the fair Gwyneth,
Set off towards the north!

His horse exhausted, nevertheless,
Martin gave him chase,
And through the rustled ferns and
grass,
He followed the spirit's trace.
His horse collapsed, and Martin then
Dismounted and ran on foot,
Until he saw the thing no more,
And stopped before a wood.

He sat on a stump, and began to
think—
His thoughts were all ablaze:
Who was that being, who was that
fiend,
Who, in this maddening craze,
Had carried his one love away,
Who he had longed to see?
"Who can I ask that knows
How I can get her back?" thought he.

III.

After a long and restless night
That Martin spent alone,
He decided to visit
A man he had once known.
His name was Anselm, who was a
priest,
A chaplain to his lord,
Who now lived quietly alone
Of his own accord.
A learnèd man he was, of course,
A philosopher at heart,
And beside his church he lived
Practicing his art.
Martin found him at his desk
While reading some old tome,
And Anselm invited his newfound
guest
Into his modest home.
As friends, they greeted and embraced,
And happy memories were told,
And Martin then relayed to him
The woes he had now to behold.
Anselm was a pensive man,
And so in silence thought.
And when he organized his thoughts,
His wisdom he to Martin taught:

"Dear Martin, child, now listen well
"To what I have to say,
"For I now think that I do know
"Who took your love away.
"It was the enemy of men,
"Who corrupts and enslaves us all.
"It was the Devil, who for his pride
"Had suffered his tremendous fall.
"Unrepentant he is,
"And puts his pain on us,
"Trying hard to trick us,
"To rob, to blindfold thus.
"I fear he stole your maiden,
"He who troubles all that's good,
"But do not fear, and do go back
"To that forsaken wood.
"Enter, weapons ready:
"Sword and cross in hand,
"And find the darkest hollow
"In that accursèd land.
"There, you'll find your Gwyneth,
"And maybe the Devil, too.
"And there'll be many trials
"That you'll have to go through.
"But fear not, you're a soldier, yes?
"Then simply pray and fight,
"And all the doors will open
"To your celestial light."

"Oh, how grateful you make me,
"But this is all so scary!
"How can I ever defeat
"Such a great adversary?
"Aside from God, I cannot think
"Of someone with more power.
"And there are tales of such great men
"Who before him would cower!
"I'm a measly soldier—
"How can I compete?
"The Devil, with all his strength,
"My will would surely deplete!"

Anselm glumly looked
At his fearful friend,
And thought of something wise
That his fear could amend.

"Martin, where do you think the Devil lives?
"Who or what him residence gives?
"From Heaven he was ousted, defeated by the Host.
"From there, where would he prefer to go most?
"The depths of Hell! But as you know,
"He there was faced with even greater woe.
"Christ did into Hell descend,
"And Death's power did He amend.
"So, what is left between Heaven and Hell?
"Only in our world can he now dwell!
"He is the weakest that he's ever been,
"And maybe we are God's kingpin
"For driving him out of our lands for good?
"Don't fear him more than any mortal should!
"Gird up your heart, and steady your soul.
"Remember, you are in control.
"Goodbye, brave knight, here's my adieu!
"My prayers always stay with you."

IV.

Martin rode back to the wood,
And entered it with fear.
And, as he wandered further in,
It did to him appear
That he was followed by a group
Clad in armor of dark steel,
With eyes of burning embers
Eying him with zeal.
Now he looked around,
And saw that he was trapped.
"Prepare to be butchered!"
A looming figure snapped.
Martin drew his mace,
And lifted up his shield.
And then came a clashing
As if on a battlefield,
As dozen arms with weapons
Collapsed upon his head.
Martin dodged and parried
(Trying not to be dead).
Then, he saw his chance and swung
At the looming foe,
And landed squarely in his face
A devastating blow.
He fell, and with him, all the rest.
And Martin saw, that lying abreast
Were mail and breastplates of them who died,
With nothing but pure air inside.

And as he from exhaustion swayed,
He knew he must not be afraid.
He caught his breath and carried on,
Admiring the first few rays of dawn.

V.

As Martin trotted on, he saw
A small, neat cottage, with a roof of straw.
It had two windows on one wall,
The first was short, the second tall.
In between them was a door,
Which was carved with gold galore.
And out of the door came out a troll,
A woman and a beast mixed in her soul.

The troll came up to him, and said
"Oh, dear Martin, let's get wed!
"Why do you need to endure this pain,
"When there is so much here to gain?
"I will give you such great gifts, if you marry me:
"We will live together and alone, blissfully, carefree.
"Look at all this gold I have, ornaments and rings!
"I have horses, swords, and shirts, and so many other things!
"Look into my hands, and see
"What good gifts I bring to thee!"

In her hands was a pile of gold that she mustered.
Martin's eyes filled with the shining luster,
And his mind was filled with greed,
Forgetting any moral creed.
His hand reached up to touch the gold,
But then, his faith of him grabbed hold.
The film removed from his two eyes,
He saw right through the troll's disguise:
That she was lying, nothing she had held
Except for dust and almonds shelled.
Her wealth was an illusion, as all wealth becomes
When used not for good, but for selfish outcomes.

Thus Martin did not choose this bride,
But rather to her he had cried:
"Don't you touch me, heathen wench!
"I cannot even bear your stench!
"Leave me be, my love is true
"And I shall not sell it to you!"

And as he left her far behind,
He at his weakness sighed,
But nonetheless, he trudgèd on,
Following the light of dawn.

VI.

It was day, and yet under the trees,
There was no light, and only a still breeze.
Martin's boots had sagged in dirt
And the soles of his feet hurt.
But then before him, he beheld
Trees and shrubs coming into a meld
At the center of the wood
That looked darker than it should.
"Well, I seem to have arrived,
"And I seem to have survived
"Through the trials set to me.

"Maybe now my maiden I can free,"
Martin thought with hope and glee,
And prepared to the Devil his plea.
Then he stepped into the hollow,
And awaited the troubles to follow.
There was silence for a spell,
And then out of the ground arose,
A great horned being, that was half-man,
But then half-goat, with hooves for toes.
He was thrice the size of man
And of evil he was made.
With a prayer in his head,
Martin walked to him, afraid.

"Dear Devil, if you were to be so kind,
"Would you help me my maiden find?
"I have done nothing to offend,
"So maybe Gwyneth to me you can send?"

The Devil roared with unearthly rage,
"'Nothing to offend,' you measly page?!
"Every time a prayer leaves your lips,
"My hold over you unfailingly slips!
"Every time for Christ you yearn,
"In my soul I feel a burn.
"You pain me in every which way,
"Repeatedly, nigh every day,
"When you commend my foe!"
His demeanor changed, though,
As he grew calm and with trickery full.
"Listen, why do you fight me like a bull
"That is pulled by his horns in vain
"By those pretentious men of Spain?
"Maybe I exist for good?
"Maybe, walking through the wood,
"You've seen how predators and prey abound,
"And not one single group is found
"Without having enemies of its own?
"This keeps the wood from being thrown
"Out of balance by a single thing.
"The forest lives without a king!
"So why must you fight me?
"I think we can all agree
"That good cannot exist without some evil
"Or else it wouldn't be good, but more like upheaval
"Compared with the carnal stability which I provide.
"Why must you your passions hide?
"With me, you can be free,
"Wouldn't you agree?
"Speak now, peasant, for I tire
"Of your dead countenance, like that of a friar."

Martin listened to the Devil's words,
But those of his friend were still dearer.
He listened to the chirping of the birds,
And moved his hand nearer
To his heart, and spoke in full voice:

"Dear Devil, why do you rejoice,
"When you are in the wrong?
"Haven't you forgotten, how headlong
"You were thrown from such high grace
"To the most forsaken place?
"True, evil cannot live without some good primeval,
"But good can, and will live without any evil!

"Thus, your words are all but dust
"And I my plea continue must.
"You have no power over me,
"So won't you let me Gwyneth see?"

The Devil shrugged, and said, "Alright,
"I might as well pick an easier fight."
With that, he disappeared, and sunlight
surged,
As Gwyneth from the trees emerged.
And there was happiness and love,
And right above them flew a dove,
A symbol of both love and the divine,
But what's the difference, as both do
shine
Of light and beauty, and all that's true?
In the air swirled airy dew,
As eternity continued on
Towards the cheerful light of dawn.

And then Martin and his maiden
together spent the night;
And thus ends our story of Sir Martin
the knight.

Ninth of July

Ndabaningi

And now they come [again]
The shouting, gesticulating horde,
Still silenced by distance
Faces contorted, loose-limbed
Snippets of cacophony carry to our lines

The cold, early winter wind
The veld; dry, blond grey, between
Them and us
A vast world, between
Them and us
A hundred and fifty years, 350 years, 40,000 years, between
Them and us
Natal, Van Riebeeck, the Great Trek; Of course, between
Them and us
The Industrial Revolution?
The Age of Exploration?
Ages upon ages in the blood
Generations of forethought and winter larders, between
Them and us

And on they come
What is ours must now be theirs
The shifting mass; strange waves over the veld
Smoke rises in the hazy hinterland
What is ours must now be theirs
Broken, stolen, littered; shattered glass

And the flames, always the flames,
What is ours must now be theirs
Where they have been
Destruction, burning, smoke billowing

What is ours must now be theirs
On they come, our backs against the wall
Whites of their eyes now
What is ours must now be theirs
Isn't the country enough?
Isn't "freedom"? Government? "The Vote"?
What is ours must now be theirs
And what do we really have left? After centuries of toil?
Generations of sweat and sacrifice
What is ours must now be theirs

The noise hits us; a physical blow
We are here, it is now
When will we take a stand?
Now
When will we break the chains of lies?
Now
When will we cast aside our doubts?
Now
When will we take our own side?
Now
They're close, closer; coming on
Now
Now
Now

Dead to Me

Thomas Nyquist

For M.S.

We don’t talk anymore.
He just sends me money
On my birthday
And Christmas.
I convert it to crypto
And forget for 6 months
Until the next guilt offering

He bought my brother
And I guess that’s why
We don’t talk either

One last look at the shores
Of the island paradise
Where he built a petty kingdom
That protects him from the
Government’s thieves
And I sought out the hills
I had known as a child
Seeking refuge for my mother
Her body broken
Her spirit withered

They would have seen my mother
  in her grave.
He already saw her buried
In the court
Years ago
When he took up a native lover

I tried for so long
To be the son he wanted
But I could not forsake
The man I needed to become

In these hills I am far from friends
I am far from anything I had come
  to rely upon
So I learn
More than ever before
To rely upon myself and my God

My mother is alive
And my life is worth
Living to me

Paths to Valor

Thomas Nyquist

I. Shield of the Gods and of Men:
The Path of the Hero

King Leonidas awakens
To chambers that never were fated
To shelter the issue of third-born sons.
This is the last time his eyes will behold
The sacred room where his son was conceived.

He was never destined to be king.
He was always destined to be king.

He takes up his shield,
His brother of bronze,
"This or upon this,"
The words of his mother,
The words of his wife,
Forgiving no weakness,
For weakness was given
As Lacedaemon's tribute,
The price that was paid
For spirit and shield.

"Honor the gods,"
So, his army he leaves
To Apollo Karneios,
The Archer to bless.
"Honor your people,"
The guard falls in line
Three Hundred and helots
To burn before Greece,
A Holocaust to honor,
Unquenchable by Lethe.

March until bloodied;
Rest is for weepers
And Greeks who make bathhouses
Out of a fortress.
Build up the wall
That shall not forestall
Xerxes' tide of horse and spear.
But into a channel the blood
Of uncounted Persian sons
Will irrigate the fields of the glory of Sparta,
Each Greek corpse a temple
To Laconian law.

When they come he does not tremble,
Nor his men, nor their slaves.
The earth shakes with its burden,
But his purpose remains.

Warborn Leonidas,
Usurper of unworthy brothers,
Kneels not before
This woman-chosen king of kings
Whose shield of slaves seeks
No brother's protection.

Twelve mighty labors
His blood holds in mem'ry,
The thirteenth shall spill it,
Wine for the Storm Father,
Lightning returned to Olympus
The gift-spring.

Unlucky this labor to
One without vision,
Apollo Farseer's
Oracular exchange.
To Zoroaster's heathen
And deniers of the gods,
His death will be meaningless:

The Persians are not stopped.
The Greeks are not saved.

But his death is meaning itself:
It will win the wars to come.
It will build the iron will,
Stronger than bronze shields,
Stronger than ten thousand immortals,
Stronger than immortal death.

For the shield he earned with manhood
Was not of wood and bronze,
But leather bound by living flesh
Of heroes' bone and blood.
"This or upon this,"
When last his eyes close,
Leonidas obeys.

II. The Shepherd's Tools in Flesh and Blood We Are:
The Path of the Pilgrim

The eyes of William Bradford will not close.
The tumult of the ocean and the woes
Assaying all forbid God's Blessing, Sleep.
To prayer, he dedicates himself to keep
His soul from weakness and from error.
He shall not worry, nor whelm to terror.

"Thy Rod, Thy Staff, they comfort me, my Lord.
"Thy Perfect Law is bread to all aboard
"This vessel taking exodus from sin,
"Corrupted kingdoms where unholy din
"Attempts to drown the music of Thy Word,
"The clamor, the clangor, the ululant, absurd
"Resounding repetitions of the vain
"Betrayers dressed in filthy rags bestained,
"By multitudinous iniquities
"Incarnadined, their crimes a crimson sea.
"Yet, seeking freedom from the wicked's blade,

"We've wandered to the valley of death's shade.
"No evil do I fear, for You abide
"Where two or three together forgo pride,
"Abase themselves before the saving Name
"That pardons the repentant, heals the lame."

And so, he continues
Seeking strength and wisdom,
For faith like a beacon
That straight lights a path,
For the ocean is broad
And beckons destruction,
Yet just so the comfort
Of the Tempter, Approval.

The captain, Myles Standish, also braves
The thunder and the darkness and the waves.
His prayers do not like his fellow's flow,
Yet ardently his steadfast heart bestows
Whatever blessing there may be to give,
That ship and souls survive the night, and live
To see the Promised Land across the sea
Where though they lose the world, yet they be free.

The Hero John Smith's replacement
Is not without trepidation.
Like Bradford he has brought his wife,
Who even now is taken ill.
He knows that danger will await them,
A savage land with savage tribes.
Croatoan, Roanoke,
Warning to those who
Dream honey and milk
When Providence provides
Only tears to drink.

Yet, as Bradford leads them higher,
So Standish shall their ground be;
The leader make a people,
The soldier set a city.

With Staff and Rod together borne with strength
The flock shall find its holy home at length,
And as the raging storm departs with night,
Both Pilgrims raise their eyes to greet God's light.

III. Red Heaven's Sword: The Path of the Conqueror

Alexander does not weep

The blinding light of
Irradiated ley lines
Burn the surface of the Earth
His Retinas registering
Their gruesome glory

Millions dead
Millions to die
His enemies
His people

They will regain the strength
They knew under His Namesake
The ages of decadence
Immolated in the Inferno of His Will

The might of Mars behind Him
He is Judgment
He is Glory
He is Redemption
He is the Two-Edged Sword
That will cleave to the very heart of the wicked
That will cleave the hearts of the pure to His Own

Earth is the first
To bear His Fury
For she was first
To bear the race
And though her children
Have spread to the stars

There will be no far-flung outpost
No refuge
From her Greatest Son's
Cleansing Love

His chariots descend
Purifying pollution
Preparing the soil
For the feet of its Master

He breathes in the air
His great-grandfather knew
And thinks of the lands
His forbears knew not
Awaiting the caress
Of His Law
Old yet new
The hundreds of suns
That shall shine on His Face

Alexander does not weep
For there are countless worlds to conquer
And this is but the first

My Princess, Europa

Greg Partansky

They left you alone, they left you abandoned.
They crushed your spirit and beautiful heart.
They said you weren't worth it, that you'd be alone, and no one could possibly want you.
They've lied to Europa. They lied to you, darling.
The wounds they have dealt you, the unforgivable pain.
The thing no one has told you when you cried those hot bitter tears.
That a Knight was out searching, for his Sweetheart, his Princess, his Queen.
O Europa, you're perfect. You're worth it. You're everything a man could possibly dream.
Not a drop over spilling, not an inch left to be filled. You have always been more than enough. Since the beginning of time, you've filled the cup to the brim.
I'm sorry my darling, that it took me so long. There was more than one dragon that I had to take down alone.
Wipe your eyes now my darling. It's over. You have been found.
You have been loved by a love that's forever, that knows no beginning nor climax nor end.
EUROPA! My darling! Our love is forever! Your heart has been mine from the start.
My Love, I'll protect you. Before any devil can get you, they will meet the wrath of my sword.
O Europa! They lied to you, darling! They've lied to you, angel!
That there wasn't one that could love you. Your body, Your heart, and Your soul.
They've battered and bruised you. Your precious, beautiful heart.
But O did they know though, that you were a Princess?
One that was worth it, desired, and loved.
EUROPA! My Princess, I've found you! Let me fall in front of you on my knees!
O how glorious is your beauty! How divine is your heart!
O how lovely you are my dear Princess, and how in love I am with you and your scars...

Of the Thulean Vedas

Arthur Powell

When the winter wonder comes
I stand outside in silent joy

Imagining days of yore
When man saw first snow

His heart would rise upon
Sight of white, for

All the work is now done.
Boreas unleashes his cold winds

But we are bundled up and warm
Hay dry and ready

In
Cold short days we work and play
Later
Retreating into Candles glow

Long nights stand vanquished
As tales are woven amidst the stars

Playground Escape

Arthur Powell

The stick in hand,
A sword in mind
Exploring a foreign land
Many a treasure to find

What key unlocks the past?
Blood memory pulses
As playtime ends too fast...

He sighs and groans
Marched back to class
His face drawn
What lies beyond the glass?

The bell rings loud
He dashes back outside
Armed once more
No further classroom lies.

Far from Most

Tyler Rannus

One evening my nose started to run,
Then I began to sneeze,
It moved to my lungs, but what could be done,
To put myself at ease?

I was sick with a cold and sick of the city,
I needed to get away.
Away from the nitty, away from the gritty,
Gone by the end of the day.

There exists a place free of smog,
No towers of steel and glass.
Where the only mist is a morning fog,
And the valued green is grass.

The place I went was far from most,
Void of city streets.
I set off right then, away from the coast,
'Til dirt replaced concrete.

The clamor dissolved, the sky expanded
To deep, refreshing blues.
Nature restored what the soul demanded,
Not neons and sirens and fumes.

The sun started setting and tinting the sky
An amber-golden hue,
On the horizon I caught with my eye
A farmhouse pop into view.

It was battered and beaten from ten renovations,
The siding a hundred years old.
But it stood and it shielded for ten generations
From rain and from heat and from cold.

I went to their farmstore in the backyard,
And spotted their milk in jugs.
No bulletproof glass or security guards,
No robbers or thieves or thugs.

They had apples, bananas, cherries, and peaches
Each with their own jar of jelly.
There were eggs and butter and various cheeses,
Screaming to get in my belly!

I grabbed what I wanted and carried it all,
And took out a wad of money.
Just then I saw what hangs on the wall,
Above the sweet jars of honey.

Not a screen or stranger who's glaring at you,
With a face that elicits disgust.
No device to keep watch and record what you do,
Just good, old-fashioned trust.

A ledger, a pencil, a basket of change,
Were all that we here need.
To everyone else, that's stupid and strange;
They're stupid and strange to me.

I wrote down my take and what I had paid,
And dropped it in the bowl.
I thought I'd not waste such a beautiful day,
And have myself a stroll.

It was a quaint, quiet family farm,
Nestled in hills of green.
The meadow and trees surrounding the barn,
I swear I saw in a dream.

The coop gave shade to calves and cows,
As chickens waddled along.
The shepherd, I saw, was a vigilant hound,
Guarding them all day long.

I watched them in silence, before I walked off,
Goodbye to the grass and the trees.
And I thought to myself, as I let out a cough,
This is how our life should be.

Darkness crept in as the sun set,
That day forever gone,
If we remember, we'll never forget,
What follows a dusk is dawn.

I ask you, dear reader, what did I do?
And yes, my sickness has healed.
Let us just say, my new morning view
Is cattle grazing a field!

Kinder

Andrew Roemer

Dreams smashed in an instant
Give way to the light of day

Things that went unspoken
Now I have much to say

Holding onto my little child
Branches stretching from the tree

Will that little precious boy
Ever know that he saved me?

The Drowned Man

Austin Stephenson

A quieted rage within me creeps
Above the surface, in trickling might.
The old man within, though drowned, still sleeps
Till waters disperse and he comes to light.

Lunging against the wood-covered well,
While anger from the stones' mortar seeps,
The elder's irascibility swells
And geysers forth from his simmering steep.

The unrestrained fury entices a fight
Within the torrents released from his cell,
Deluging the earth in rancorous spite:
The flood not enough for quenching my hell.

Though artesian forces came from the deep,
Unleashing pressures long where they dwelled,
The pain from the rock's crevice still weeps,
Alluding to troubled waters not quelled.

Unable to drown him from whom springs my plight,
The old man is caught in currents that sweep
Him away over rapids of great height:
Cascading wrath is the reward that he reaps.

The passion now channeled, the flowing foretells
Of justified anger to defend what is right,
Rather than capsize the ship tolling a knell,
It will be drawn up to nourish a future that's bright.

Heavenly Beads

Austin Stephenson

Across a sharp precipice I limply hang,
Forswearing a call I desire to heed,
Reenacting a fall that elicits pangs;
My descent is halted by heavenly beads.

With humble affection I whisper the words
I've intoned in times of sorrow and need,
Grappling firmly as strength in me is stirred
To conquer the cliff by aid of the beads.

A Year and the Seasons

M.A. Thomas

These days stretch on and still I toil,
See as leaves fall it's not spoiled,
Steel myself, prepare the soil.

Frost buries world and all,
Fire keeps me standing tall,
Heart remains, with grace spring shall call.

The land rises ready to be plowed,
That from above spills to the trodden ground, Flickers
Become beams, gray becomes green—it's found!

Radiance ascendant, rays of gold produce
Bounties, Sweetest of fruits, no longer do I doubt
Thee the dead are no more, life rises proudly.

Small Victory

Seamus Tout-Cœur

Under a green-robed monument to an ancient god
I fell in love with a wisp.
Its shape changed as soon as I came to know it,
A time and again.

It held—or was as in a cup. For itself might lift and pour—
Or if disturbed, billow out when taken up.
I sought to imbible, have off'ring flow

Over lips, past teeth, till I be in indiscreet fashion.
Drink of drinks would compose my heart
And its taste mine each passion.

A riddle brought gibe and suff'ring lo!
Touched to face frightly.
Touched my face and I could not place
Horse nor cart. I hung there, a cliff—
But by a few joints
Pressed in brace tightly.

I dared not call out for an aid
In my fear and in my shame.
I brought hand close to disguise nigh pang.
A sound? My savior? Nay, high plague—
To wit not yet known.

"Fly to me my child, my own!
"Your flesh is yet crisp
"And your skin without sallow.
"You must be kept close and cool,
"Shorn and shallow."

I distinguished not call's tenor and tone
But wisp knew well—and stirred quickly.
In that instant it lifted and flew,
Twisted anew, and was at once
In wondrous withdraw.
I was again then as before—alone.

There and to that god I spoke a vow—
Troth which I cannot repeat,
For it is yet under lock's law.
I knew not the power of a lock and of a vow,
Or that these might be put beyond one's own allow.

In my youth I spoke foolishly.
I have hope that youth be forgiven—
By wisp I know not nor by god—

But by earth envoke hymnody:
Creature within and upon ground that under us thaw!
As we be soil again—
Together I pray we amend.

I stood and it was vast before me.
I blinked and it was vast within me.
As I walked it diminished, but as I blinked it grew.

And now, when I step seeing puff, see vapor,
See vision—in hall or history
I take each and claim for self its concision
As small victory.

Studiorum Victor

Lue-Yee Tsang

Why Latin? Why this extra class to fail,
Tacked on to all the others? So they said,
As if the language were a pinned-on tail.
    Are we Melchizedek, old Salem's head,
No father, mother, start of life, or end
Of days, that into sunset we should tread?
    This nation here, this life the fathers lend,
Is no Athena, sprung full-formed a child
From nought, to give a bow you deftly bend.
    But if you are Odysseus, beguiled
You are by your own mind if you forget
You had a home, in Ithaca, defiled.
    While suitors ply your wife with gift and threat,
When will you string your bow to punish them
And cleanse your household? Take the sword and whet.
    To hear it from a mouth of Chinese stem
Perhaps unnerves you. Am I a Trojan horse,
A crafty Sinon come to kiss your hem?
    Come off it! You're the cunning Greek, of course:
No need to play at being hoodwinked here,
But face your dangers at their very source.
    Your house is spoilt, and will you take a spear
To tilt at windmills? Answers lie within.
The matter's in your heart: let it be clear.
    Wise fool you'd be to judge this by its skin
Rather than who you are from yesterday,
And who your fathers make you in your grin;
    Or think what happens when you've left the bay,
Vix e conspectu, and the deep seas surge,
Disclosing both their floor and how you pray.
    Three things and four too wonderful, the urge
To ask, to love, to fight, to repossess

A goodly heritage from death and dirge.
    Lo, quivers full of arrows fathers bless,
Old paths renewed, through axes singing true;
Or see Troy's ashes bear a new impress.
    Rome fell, but crumbled Rome is made anew
And tumbled into starry vaulted height,
Its windows luminous with jeweled dew:
So *tolle*, *lege*, gird your loins and fight.

Alexander

Nicholas Walker, Australia

Hopelessness.

It is lost.
We have lost.
Why bother?
I should sink into the bottle of pills again.
A self-destructive escapism.
There is no future.
I open the cheap bottle of whisky,
The third time this week.

Then she shows it to me:
Two pink lines on a white stick.

Responsibility.

It is not lost.
We cannot have lost.
A grey smudge on a dark screen.
My reason to deny escape.
There WILL be a future.
I pick up the barbell,
The third time this week.

She cries in agony,
Our two lines are becoming one.

Zeal.

We are winning!
The tides have turned!
Her contractions come closer!
Anticipation! Why would I want to escape?
This is our future!
I take her hand,
The third time this minute.

She pushes a final time,
And I hear his beautiful cry.

Love.

We have won.
We witness perfection.
I am a father. I am a father!
My reason, my charge, my future!
I weep for love and disbelief.
I stroke his perfect face,
The third time this minute.

Our small victory.
Why we fight.

Why we WILL win.

No Small Victory

J.B. Weyland

Swelling dawn o'er-takes the darkness
So too does day the night
Seasons spin the eternal dance
Coldest winter gives way to verdant might

Kith and kin keep fast hold
Onto the gifts of hearth and home
Binding all within by luck and frith
Ancestral blood to familial stone

Fret not upon the worldly wheel
As it turns time and tides
For heroes have hewn our stories strong
Wielding eternal hope against the lies

Willing sons of Wotan were they
Men against time apiece
Driving spear and sword through heart and word
That connive to corrupt our peace

Though each they faced eventual defeat
No small victory they had secured
Our sons and daughters may battle on
Proving heroic blood hath endured

Sword hand aloft in honorable salute
Eyes ablaze and vision clear
Kith and kin, we shall soldier on
Bold wyrd hath forged a sharpened spear

Inspiration is not born of intellect alone
As the din of darkened armies roil
Lest they forget our Gods are we
Hail victory, for blood and soil!

If Today Was My Last Day

Terry Williams

I can't imagine today being my last day
Making your lunch before the day begins.
Waking you up and telling you good morning with a smile.
Getting you dressed.
Brushing your hair and teeth.

I can't imagine today being my last day
Running your forgotten lunch bag to you as you leave for work.
Texting you to drive safe and have a good day.
Throwing the tennis ball with my favorite dog.
Getting myself ready for the day.

I can't imagine today being my last day
Slamming the door to the house as we all make our way to the car for school.
Wishing you a wonderful day while on the way to school.
Giving countless kisses, hugs, and goodbye waives before finally walking away.
Laughing with my sister about anything and everything like every morning.

I can't imagine today being my last day
Trying to decide what to eat for lunch.
Going to get you from school.
Asking you how your day was.
Pumping you up for your first day of t-ball practice.

I can't imagine today being my last day
Sharing a meal together and actually talking you into trying something new.
Changing your diaper or walking you to the potty.
Wiping your snotty nose.
Breastfeeding you almost every 2 hours.

I can't imagine today being my last day
Texting you to find out how your day was.
Asking what would you like for supper.
Arguing about something stupid and pointless.
Telling you I'll see you soon.

I can't imagine today being my last day
Sending pictures of our girls to you.
Watching my sister take pictures and spend time with her nieces.
Accidentally dump sand from your shoes onto our living room floor.
Cooking you supper.

I can't imagine today being my last day
Visiting with you and telling you about my day.
Giving my oldest permission to hang out with her Ammaw while I go home to prepare supper.
Hearing my mom knock on the door.
Getting texts of what the cat drug in.

I can't imagine today being my last day
Giving you a bath.
Decorating our holiday tree for the next upcoming holiday.
Playing with you in the floor.
Reading you a story or two.

I can't imagine today being my last day
Praying for you to have good dreams and wake up refreshed.
Rubbing your ever-growing back, arms, hands, legs, and feet.
Kissing you goodnight.
Telling you I love you.

I can't imagine today being my last day
Discussing the day we had.
Worrying about our messy house because it's not like we actually live here.
Realizing each little mess is a little memory left behind.
Mindlessly scrolling through my phone before getting ready for bed.

I can't imagine today being my last day
Realizing I don't remember the last time I hugged some of the people I love.
Being disappointed in myself for not telling others that I love them more often.
Taking pain relievers because I'm getting old and out of shape.
Feeding the dog scraps.

I can't imagine today being my last day
Rocking you to sleep.
Making sure the house is locked for the night.
Setting out your clothes for the next day.
Closing my eyes while lying in bed.

I can't imagine today being my last day
Being a daughter.
Being a sister.
Being a friend.
Being an aunt.
Being a wife.
Being a mom.

I can't imagine today being my last day
I take my last breath.
Smiling for the last time.
Leaving you with memories.

Today I'm thankful because every day, every moment, every milestone, every memory is a gift.
Cherish it.

A Brutal Pageantry: Prologue

Max Worthington

The seed of love you sow, will only come
When you've let go, to know the bloom of Us.
Crushed by your grip we drowned by storge,
Pray our cause I beg Saint George.
Slates lay anew, a coup! Of reverent heart.
Flowers of the Saints arise, banners, flags
They fill the skies as dogmas weigh the
Shield, their caged hearts revealed.
Slovenly soldiers all! Slavers plough your
Freedom, severed roots lay waste our Eden.
Hark the bulges play the chorus,
Organizer of chaos, trapped! His shelves are
Sunk by our decorous. Pride in reason,
Half men! Share their fate with treason.
Return to me departed Angels, to the
Divine nation of Us. Rendered serfs
Of stolen soil, unsettled dust from foreign feet,
Fate sends our yields to spoil. Sheep
To the loom! Sedition slips the tongue,
Drowned by unholy spirits, men
Are made conscripts of the bottle.
Future proof the barricade! Awaits us
Lies the next crusade. May the kiln of
Battle forge your heart, their backs are
Known to all. Make friends their knees with
Sand! Supple hands of feeble grip,
Let banners fall and rifles slip. Hollow chests
Adorned in dusty medals swell the heads of
Wealthy beggars. Their helmets lose their fit.

Ablation brought by time the vandal
Sets eyes upon mystic mortar and leaves
The pile to crumble! Our enemies made
Humble. Beckon ancient hilt, Summer
Nigh, your dress lay gilt, as Heaven split above
By columns raised to honor God, by columns
Mustered to the sword. The tide of
War may take a turn, momentum lost and
Cities burn. Cast into marble what we've
Done, the heroes made and battles won.
Take repose, the Sun retreats, tomorrow
Calls the rested. Preserve your rags
And looted garb, give rented nobles a taste.
We'll turn their Black books red.
Fear? Disgust? It matters not! We'll draw
The quarters of the lot! The time of doubt is
At an end. God has told us who to send, execute
Traitors he condemns. We'll fight until the bitter end.

St George's Athos

A Totem

Max Worthington

Stelae talks,
Of drowned cities and walks,
Through narrow paths and fallen trees,
The once proud man falls to his knees.
"What price have you for honor?"
He shouts as though to mock her,
A woman mixing ash with snow,
Stucco formed beneath him.

Searching his heart for blued bronze,
He stands upon the stela,
With piercing pilum flying past,
His eyes alone could feel her.
Stood by his side are coppiced men,
Who vow to take the fight again.

His spear takes its shine.

With Eyes to Spy Out, and Scare Evil Spirits

On Beauty's Edge

Max Worthington

The pleas of those who tow the line,
Drowning out of which sublime,
Consign their eyes the sight of soil,
To straddle toil, silence fell overboard.

The crown of Artemis shows its peaks,
It grows as does the callus wreaks,
Men's labored hands and galling hold,
My commission rested well,
If only for the moment's sake,
The realization fell.

True beauty lies beyond our realm,
We dearth a comprehension,
To only those who've seen the Edge,
To those who near ablation.
Bestriding struggle and its grace,
I have seen the Edge.
An aesthete blinded by his pride,
I have seen the Edge.

In reservation of the hale.

HONORABLE MENTION IN POETRY

Dearly Beloved

Firebrand Jay

This poem is dedicated to my wife, and so am I.

Remember, dear, the steps we took
That brought us to this place?
How far we've run together now
Along life's sacred race!
Do you recall that blessed fall,
The leaves upon the ground?
I met you there in chilly air
At a bus stop two blocks down.

I asked your name but had misheard,
The wind had been my foe
I smiled and thought to ask again
But then you had to go.
I agonized for days at that,
How could I lose your name?
What then to call a lovely girl?
"My lady?" "Miss?" Or "Dame?"

By God's sweet grace we met again,
In classes teaching dance.
I took your hand. We took the floor.
Your hair had me entranced.
The lovely braid had swung about,
A cord of beauty fine.
It swung about and hit my face.
I caught your name that time.

That couldn't be the end, of course.
I had to know you more.
We gave our numbers after class
As we went out the door.
I walked you home and talked about
All kinds of pleasant things.
I saw you safely there then left,
And then I heard you ring.

You watched me from the windowsill
And called to say goodbye.
You said you had a lovely time,
And I said, "So did I."
We couldn't bear to say goodbye
A second time that night,
And I'm not one to let you down;
We talked 'til morning light.

We couldn't stay so long apart
As dance class once a week.
To be together more and more
Was our new aim to seek.
Remember that old restaurant?
The silly trick I taught?
And all the laughter and the jokes
And merriment we wrought?

Before too long, I saw you in
A way I never knew.
I looked at you and saw myself
And all our future, too.
I told you underneath the stars
The love I felt for you.
You told me that you felt the same,
Our lonely days were through.

Again, again, again we'd meet!
We couldn't stay away!
The iron hot, the time had come
For which all lovers pray.
I asked if you would be my wife.
I knew what you would say.
"Duh," you said with confidence,
Your charming little way.

We set the date—a day in spring—
A year ahead or so.
A blazing summer, crisp fall air, then
Blanket winter snow.
We felt our in-bloom wedding was
Too far beyond our reach.
We dreamed our dreams of honeymoon,
Of romance, and the beach.

But time has funny ways of things,
As tick by tick it went.
It never seems to pass at all
Until it's all been spent.
That year was lightning, blazing fast,
But slow as glaciers, too.
It felt as though it wouldn't end,
And then we said, "I do."

"Dearly beloved, we gather here…"
I'll spare you all the rest.
You recall our vows in full,
And I recall your dress.
Your tired eyes still shine like stars,
I see it in your smile.
But why not let them close for now
And rest a little while?

Your toughest day was yesterday,
Forever changed we'll be.
To see you sitting in your chair,
It all came back to me.
The triumph that would top them all
Now sits across your knee.
Our greatest little victory
Weighed in at six pounds three.

Honorable Mention in Poetry

Erwachen

Corvan A. Miller

How is it some do not succumb,
When faced with death, or stricken dumb, to
Hopelessly wallow in grief,
Or selfish thoughts, however brief;
Where do they get this fortitude,
Who never sigh or sulk or brood?

For me, my friend, I must be clear,
That I could never hope or fear,
To take my ranks among the caste,
That does not shy from Agon's task;
In fact, I was in such despair,
That I no longer valued air,
Nor food, nor drink, nor Bacchanal,
Nor even anything at all;
I swear to you, although it's queer, the
Following is crystal clear:

Not long ago, the first of May,
I had the most disturbing day.
As usual, I walked along,
That sandy shore where I belong, and
Here, good sir, is my recount, of
The events and all my doubts, for
As my thoughts began to smother,
One omen followed another.

Number one arrived by sea,
Though I know not how this could be,
For from the shore I saw a man,
With sword and shield in each hand;
I know it's strange, but it's no joke—
I don't intend here to provoke—
No sails or oars kept him afloat;
A swan, somehow, had towed this boat.

Approaching him was not by choice, but
Enthralled was I by his voice,
And I admit I felt a tremor,
When he called out in a tenor:

"I come to you from fair Brabant,
"Writ by the hand of the savant;
"His pattern sends me to a place,
"That dwelleth not in time or space;
"In transformation and through pain,
"You'll find treasure hard to attain, and
"Once you go beyond the pale,
"Begins your quest to find the Grail."

Before I had the chance to act,
Or question this confounding pact,
His bird had turned and then withdrew, and
Left me there without a clue;
What treasure is hard to attain,
That comes from suffering and pain?
What's more, can I believe my eyes,
When such absurdities they spy?

I shrugged, and then returned once more,
To my patrol along the shore,
But this time kept myself aware,
For anymore Walpurgis flair.

Not long had I resumed my walk,
When over me it seemed a flock,
Fled hastily from some great thing,
That blocked the sun with massive wings.
With dread I turned my eyes to hail—
What happened next, description fails—
A giant eagle soared above,
And clasped a branch, much like a dove.

A branch? Not on my second take,
That creature's carrying a *snake*!
Again, I had no time to wonder,
Before a new voice could thunder,
Down the hills, without a face:

"I speak not from Hel, nor any place.
"Retract your claws, I mean you no harm, but
"Keep them sharp, and coated in charm;
"Look at my friends, my eagle and snake, and
"See how they both can make their escape.
"Bite one head off, another will grow, and
"You'll never know how deep the roots go.
"Now one more thing, and remember it well,
"No matter in Heaven or Earth or in Hel, it's
"Within your body you set yourself free,
"For it has more wisdom than philosophy.
"Farewell, good man, we hardly knew ya!"
And thus, I guess, spoke Zarathustra.

I knew by now my mind had gone, and
Thought I'd better saunter on, for
Nothing more here could surprise me,
And by now the moon shone brightly.

That was when the fog rolled in,
And chills ran down my spine again;
I thought I could make out a shape—
A tail and a prickled nape?

Ah, it's nothing but relief,
It's just a canine, oh, how sweet!
"Hello my friend, I'll scratch you there."
He met me with a dev'lish glare;
"Egads! This demon is no dog."

"Indeed, I've come for dialogue."

His speech rattled me to the bone,
And suddenly I longed for home.

"I challenge you to a debate;
"Infuse me with all of your hate,
"And fears and doubts and secrets, too,
"For after all, I'm part of you.
"If you confess all of your crimes,
"Return, I will, water from whine."

"I find you familiar,
"Like a shadow in the mirror;
"Always slightly out of view,
"But what am I to say to you?"

"Nothing more, that will suffice,
"Now watch as I display your vice!"
Barkéd he an incantation,
And produced an aberration—

Foul witch in tattered clothes,
With crooked teeth and crooked nose, and
Crackéd lips on sordid mouth,
That opened as a worm crawled out:

Siegfried's horn and Donner's hammer,
Tragedy and Göttedämmer,
Bring the sorry lot together,
And cast them into the weather!
Now that folly's been removed,
Think how much time I'll have with you;
Never will such things adore ye, once
We rewrite your history!

My stomach turned and brow was creased;
Revolted, I turned to the beast,
"What can you mean, to show me this?
I'll not be scared by parlor tricks!"

"Don't fret, my friend, you're unaware,
"That this one's just part of the pair!
"Now watch as I prepare for you,
"What once was one turns into two!"

How, indeed, I've no idea,
Next appeared my dear Sophia!
Gracefully, just standing there,
She gave the most discerning stare. No
Words were needed here this time;
Her meaning was clear in my mind,
That striving towards the feminine,
Brings out the very best in men, and
When we falter, fall off course,
They're always there as our recourse.

Then to the dog I turned and said,
The first thing that came to my head:

"This sorcery grows tiresome,
"And now that I am accustomed;
"There's nothing more for you to show me,"
And I moved to back up slowly—
Before I could, his jaw unhinged;
It opened wide and quickly binged,
On both figures, fair and grim, and
Gave me the most wolfish grin.

I stood transfixed and horrified,
Unable to believe my eyes,
"Vicious creature of desire,
"Clap my hands and light a fire,
"Leave me here in peace and quiet,
"Or I'll cause you such a riot!"

Though my words had no effect,
His eyes were no longer grotesque, and
After all that hellish ranting,
Smiling, the dog sat there panting;
If that's not the strangest thing,
I bid him to come home with me!

I hope, my friend, you'll think me sane, but
I think I can speak again,
And hear and see and move and shout;
There's more to life, I have no doubt,
And if there's one thing that I've learned,
It's that you need not be concerned—

Invoke the folk, and if you're true,
One day the folk might invoke you.

Honorable Mention in Poetry

Small Fool

Nathaniel Lucas

I'm explaining
Thunder and lightning
But she's not buying.

Thunder is what you see
Lightning is what you hear.

But sometimes I see
And don't hear or hear
And don't see, she jeers.

Yes cause we're inside
Or too far away...
(I slip into prose,
Which is a sure sign
Of losing the argument)

They must be different.
She takes the world as it appears
Like Tacitus' sailors
Watching steam rise
Where the sun rents
And boils the ocean,
Or Homer's wine-dark sea
That proves either their grapes
Blue or their Med burgundy.

She sings the psalms at night
In bed in her own way,
Waiting for me to join her
And I think of Chaucer:
And smalle foole maken melodye

You know, she says later,
I think lightning and thunder
Is God showing he's master.

Second Place Winner in Poetry

Wastelanders

Cloud Buchholz

I.

The sky is a blue screen of death waiting
To be rebooted. The clouds are a brush
Of white noise against the jagged steel teeth
Of the city's jowls. Its metal maw of progress
Bellows out of the earth like an electric yawn.

He is a downtown window watching
The red pollution bleed the horizon
Into a violent lesion. The day will die
By the time he reaches his apartment.

He gathers his essence into a wallet
And wears his phone like a mask
As he ambles through the cubicle maze.
His spirit is a rib-thin rat gnawing
The mechanical fumes of progress
As he trudges the hammer-strikes of thought.

He chisels his memory from a slab of yesterday
Hoping to carve an ideal of himself:
    a marble titan; muscles smooth, features
    fixed on eternity, a man of renown,
But the miracles of his forefathers are
Discarded fat in his diet of screens
And scrolling news feeds.
His pantheon of emojis demand tribute.

The black screen is smudged with streaked fingertips
Like souls worming out of fresh graves.
Its proximity is a comfort, like the grandmother
Flicking her thumb across a rosary. He crosses himself
In headlines and memes as he enters the elevator.

II.

She is a caravan of mauve fingernails
Tapping the day's wage; a wastelander wandering
    through a desert of polyester polos, wading up
    rayon ridges, peering from poplin precipices,
                tumbling down
                        drifts of twill.

Fashion is a prophylactic for her soul.
Its empty seduction sells well in the city.
She is a mirror warping wrinkled lust into
Juvenile chic. She measures her success
With blistered heels and empty coffee cups.

She peers at the vermilion lips of sunset
    as the afternoon kisses the evening.
The chase of celestial lovers will end
    with an eruption of flickering aether
        before she reaches her apartment.

She closes out the cash register and slips her
Essence into a cluttered purse to jostle between
        pink lipstick, lavender lotion,
            discarded earrings, forgotten
                gum, and stale crackers.

Freedom is a glass of wine and
A cleavage photo for the boys
Lurking in her likes, simping
For another bite of her apple.

She walks the concrete veins of the city
    toward the train station.
The crowd is a tide of shoes ebbing and flowing,
    giving life to the steel carcasses of skyscrapers.
There is no distinction between acquisition and surrender
As the tycoons are devoured by revolving doors.

She enters the train.
Her long white legs are shimmering armor
Dancing across the mouth of a dragon's cave.
He is a rousted serpent relinquishing
His bed of gold. She wields her headphones
Like a knight's visor slapping shut.
He sucks in a breath as if to spit fire.
Her jilted gaze is a lance jousting
With his winged desire.
                    He falters.
She turns from him, shielding herself
In a silent conversation with the window.

His mind is a debunked myth.
His tongue is a furled flag.
His heart is a sword sinking
    to the sandy bottom of a lake.
His confidence is a eulogy.

The train stammers to a stop.
Its metal mouth belches free
The undigested passengers.

She is the threshold, the
    platform, the stairs, the
        pavement, the crowd, the
            blur of city streets, and then
                she's gone...

The train jostles onward. Each station is a meal
    of perfumed suits and platform pumps.
His loneliness is clad in a listless crowd
        of receding hairlines and loose ties.
Their eyes are wet matches coaxing
            the sticky heat of indecision.

He thinks about the girl
the way an uprooted tree ponders
a passing storm.

Her ivory legs were marble statues
smuggled out of a museum.
Her emerald eyes were jewels
poached from a sunken temple.
Her blonde hair was golden thread
tugged from the tapestry of fate.

His affections are a papyrus scroll
dissolving in the desert heat. He retreats
Into his phone and consults his pantheon of
emojis for wisdom:

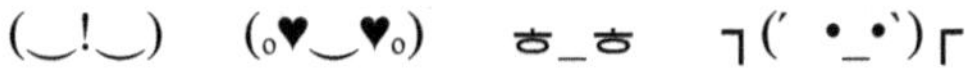

The gods have spoken.

He rubs his bristled cheeks.
The scruff is a rock garden his
Fingertips rake into rippling patterns.
The sandy stubble is not yet gray.

There is time, he thinks,
to meet the mirror of his soul.
There is time to mend his mild grin.
Time to compose a contagious chuckle.
Time to caress the supple curves
of a quiet Sunday.
There is time, he thinks,
to kiss the pregnant belly
of the future.

III.

She is a pair of sweatpants sinking
In the sofa. Her ambition is a bowl
Of soggy ice cream lounging in her lap.
Her weeknights are a spine of sticky dishes
Decaying in the sink. A brigade of suds
Will be conscripted before an army of ants
Assault her small kitchen.

She nestles her thoughts against the rigid armrest
And wriggles her toes into an unkempt comforter.
The television is a crude companion, goading her
With gaudy promises. She flirts with the fleeting
Commercials like a wine-sussed soccer mom
Stalling a suitor on a speed date.

Think different. Have it your way.
Just do it. You're in good hands.
Because you're worth it.
Obey your thirst. It keeps going,
And going, and going...

Her heavy eyelids are lulled by the soothing
Slogans of progress. She spies the padded paws
Of night prowling across her windowsill.
                    Has it gotten so late? she wonders.

She walks to the bathroom sink
And washes the beauty from her face.
The mirror is a stabled chariot
Churning minutes into days.
The depth of years are flattened into
A roadside effigy glimpsed in passing.

She eases her elbows onto the cold counter
And examines her glassy reflection.
The lines along her cheeks are not so deep.
The circles under her eyes are not so dark.
Her pouty lips are not so pale.
Her blonde hair is not yet gray.

There is time, she thinks,
            to meet the mirror of her soul.
There is time to sort her cluttered resolve.
Time to pour her honeyed heart
            into a man's syrupy passion.
Time to stitch a husband's sweltering sun
            into her turquoise sky.
There is time, she thinks,
            to tickle the toes
                        of an infant future.

She meanders to the bed, tugging loose
A trail of discarded cotton corpses;
Socks and sweatpants flung into an open grave
Of garments, a genocide of vogue pursuits.
She curls into the cold sheets not yet willing
To undress her thoughts of motherhood.

She rolls onto her side and gazes at the gown
Of starlight draped across the cityscape.
The ivory hues are punctuated by the red-blue
Wail of sirens and the mournful howls
Of concrete hounds. She snuggles the frigid
Talons of midnight as the lumpy pillow
Nibbles her nascent dreams.

She thinks about the boy on the train.
His thick arms were steel railroad tracks
        cutting through a mountain.
His blue eyes were cave walls
        painted by primitive hands.
His scruffy jawline was a turbulent horizon
        swallowing lost ships.

She dreams about his baited phrases
Grappling her pebbled riverbed—
His smoky fingers soothing the bees
Vibrating her sticky honeycomb—
His homespun lullabies cooing
A future yet to be born.

There will be time, she dreams,
            there will be time...

IV.

The sun tugs the silky gown of starlight
To caress the steel canyons with naked warmth
As the rock-a-bye highways awake, dreamlike,
To the rumbling combustion kisses of gridlock.

And the misty miled turnpikes stir softly,
Wary to wake the slumbering billboards
While the centipede sedans scurry, breathless,
To claim the lined recesses of cement hollows.

In the rustling city,
The caffeinated sidewalks find footing,
And the skyscrapers synchronize
                    with the sinking moon.

First Place Winner in Poerty

For a Love of Skies

Romanized Visigoth

A breaking dawn lends light upon a gathering of beasts.
Assembled thus, a theme discussed of greatest and of least.
With pomp and zeal, and much appeal, they set off arguing.
The question sought: What aspects ought adjudicate a king?

"At this congress," the lion stressed, "let's try to get along.
"Although, in jungle law, it states the weak should fear the strong."
With gestures of assent the elephant concurred, "That's right!
"The quality we'll all agree to heed is rule of might."

A whistled jeer and twisted ear cut short the giant's speech.
And at his back, from whence attacked, a monkey thus beseeched:
"Between the two, I'd argue that intelligence beats brawn,
"For great and many are the things that kings must think upon."

"As we make mastery of our environment through tools,
"To just dismiss our cleverness would lead to rule by fools!"
The rodent said, "Then use your head, and count us as you please.
"Our population figures as the flowers and the trees."

Another voice cut in that seemed to spring forth from the ground,
A tiny body, confident, despite its tiny sound.
Addressing all the gathered beasts, a bug issued this boast:
"If numbers count, by sheer amount, we insects have the most!"

"Ridiculous!" the rodent cried. "Methinks I have misheard.
"The bottom of the food chain, king? It's patently absurd.
"We ought to stick to vertebrates, I will not bow to ants.
"Or why not favor further still and argue this with plants?"

"Now truly, rat," the lion spat, "you needn't be so rude.
"All of you here, to me, appear as nothing more than food.
"And though the place that sits my race atop this chain is firm,
"Yet, at the end, our corpses tend the beetle and the worm."

Conspicuous in absence, overhead an eagle flies,
And beats a steady course to meet the sun upon its rise.
Above the tan savannah, with his form horizon bound,
His shadow sweeps across the congregation at the ground.

The lion, looking up, beheld him passing through a cloud,
Then, looking down again, he posed a question to the crowd.
"This meeting's invitation traveled all across the plain,
"What then might be the reason for the eagle to abstain?"

"He sees himself as special." The giraffe supplied this view.
"Of looking down on those below, I know a thing or two."
An antelope imparted, "I have ranged most distantly.
"And due to this, the news I miss is little, you'll agree."

"I've heard from other birds that on the highest cliffs they breed.
"It's there they nest, and take their rest. They only land to feed.
"As far as predators would go, I'd say they hunt with Grace,
"But hasten to regain their berth in boundless, open space."

To supplement, the elephant proposed a reason why.
"The eagle loses touch with truth from only touching sky.
"For grounding in reality, one needs to touch the ground."
"I second this," the serpent hissed, his lengthy body wound.

"To dust return our bones in death, and from this dust our birth.
"My trust is least for any beast that shuns the solid earth."
"Then you will like this story," said the monkey conferee.
"Unoccupied, one day I spied this scene atop a tree."

"An eagle in the air another flight had just begun,
"Unusually high, he seemed intent to touch the sun.
"When almost out of sight, disaster forced him to descend.
"With feathered wings alight, his burning flight came to an end."

A laughter took the gathering. In roars of merriment
The group expressed their pleasure at the tragical event.
But cutting short this schadenfreude, in mild reprimand,
The lion made request they recommence the point at hand.

So traipsed and slurred to closing words the pawed, the clawed, the hooved,
And while said, above their heads, the eagle's form yet moved,
When all at once, the monkey seemed to dispossess his cool.
He took a stand, and from his hand, he flung a bit of stool.

"I'll tell you why the eagle flies," they gathered close to hear.
"It needn't be a mystery, he does it out of fear!
"His pinions climb a longer time than any other bird."
"A coward, yes, a coward," all the animals concurred.

That cachinnation from below, the eagle did not reach,
And whipped away by wind, as well, the congregation's speech.
Dissatisfied to only glide, he climbs yet bolder heights,
Renouncing ties terrestrial through more and greater flights.

He soars towards the rising sun, he sets it as his mark.
Perhaps beyond his reach, the sheer attempt offends the dark.
Yet, at the precipice above abyss he bravely stares,
That veil his vision penetrates his grasping talon tears.

Where finds his eye infinity, there beats his potent wing,
Possessed by force of will to wrest the point of vanishing.
With spirit kissed by eddied mist in rendezvous above,
His ardor issued at the sun, to skies he makes his love.

Amongst the clouds he gazeth down, surveying worldly things,
Then soars so high Apollo's eye may even singe his wings.
I tell you now the reason why the Faustian eagle flies.
It is not for the fear of ground, but for a love of skies.

Short Stories

Small Victories

Aethelweard The Wake

His hand shook as he held the needle.

George paused and took a breath. He set the needle down and tried to steady himself. Thoughts raged within his head. Feelings swelled at his breast and threatened to explode out of him. A nervous energy ran into his legs, and he had to fight the urge to tap his foot or stand up and walk around.

He took another breath and looked around his modest office. His wife had chosen the house. She had decorated most of the rooms. But the office was his. The one small space in the world that was his and his alone.

Half of the room was dominated by bookshelves. He had put up the shelves himself. Cutting and sanding and shaping the oak had taken days. Finally he had covered two of the walls with shelves that ran from floor to ceiling. Thick leather spines stared back at him from across the room.

The titles were lost in the shadows, but that didn't matter. He had read every book more than once and knew that he would read them again in the years to come. He knew his collection, and he was proud of it. Some of the books weren't even sold anymore—but that only made them cling to them more proudly. He could find any title he wanted just from the color of the spine.

The other bookcases ran along the side wall. There were more books there too. They were dotted among the keepsakes and the ornaments and the souvenirs collected through his life. Some of the things he had made himself. Others were gifts or mementos from his family and his friends.

Everything had its place.

Everything in the room was important to him. When they had first bought the house, George had struggled to show the interest he knew that he should. His wife was the homemaker, and she was wonderful at it. His business was out in the world. He provided for and protected his family, and every day he came home to see Harriet and Millie waiting for him, it was worth it. The house was a refuge from a world that he increasingly neither understood nor liked.

But it hadn't felt like his house. It wasn't until Harriet had taken him by the hand and led him to the small door that he understood why she had insisted they buy that house. "For you," she had said. "Everyone needs a space. Somewhere to rest. Somewhere to call their own."

He remembered that day, and he smiled. She had never questioned anything he had put in the study either. He remembered the day that he had bought a painting she had said was ugly. Now it hung just a few feet away. She had helped him hang it and never said a word against it.

He remembered when she had first started putting flowers in a bowl near the door. Freshly cut from their garden and the brightest yellow. She was one of the few people who knew that was his favorite color.

There was nothing of his wife in the room, and yet she seemed to breathe through all of it. Everything reminded George of her. He felt another surge inside himself. He felt as if there was a storm within him and it was fighting to escape.

He had been through so many things in his life and nothing had affected him so much. Nothing but her, and then his daughter. And to think that she was…

He closed his eyes and took another breath. He pushed the worries away as best he could. The clock ticked behind him. Classical music sang sweetly from the speaker in the corner. He listened for a moment, and a small smile twitched at his lips despite everything else he felt. Vaughan Williams. One of his favorites.

He let the breath out slowly and opened his eyes again. Turning to the desk, he tried to focus on what he was doing. The green shade of the lamp glowed slowly. The light glinted off the brass base and pooled on the desk.

He had spread a sheet of thick paper over the green leather top of the desk. It made it easier to see the model, in case he broke off a piece or dropped something. It was almost done now, but he was still worried that he might drop or damage it.

The tools were neatly set out in a line to the right. Only the needle was out of place, sitting where he had set it down. He picked it up again and raised it. Light glinted off the shaft near his finger as he picked up the wire.

His hand wasn't shaking, but it still took several attempts to thread. With that done, he reached out and picked up the model. He squinted slightly and turned it, searching for the tiny spot he had marked out earlier when there was a sound out of place.

George's head snapped up. The door opened slowly. The person on the other side hesitated, as if they were holding themself back. Then, a small face poked around the corner. The floppy ears hung down. One trailed down towards the floor and the other half obscured the rabbit's face.

"Millie? Stop playing and come in."

A girl's face appeared from behind the door. She stared at him with wide, wet eyes. Only the lamp on his desk was on and the darkness threatened to swallow her, but her skin was so white that she almost shone in the darkness. Shadows hung across her cheeks. Her eyes, wide and wet and imploring, caught his own.

"I'm not playing Daddy…" she said. "I wasn't sure if I could come in."

"You're supposed to be in bed," said George. His daughter didn't move, and he studied her face from across the room. Then, he softened his tone. “What’s wrong, Millie?”

“I can’t sleep,” she said.

“Come here.” He gestured to her, and she stepped into the room. She closed the door, and trotted over towards his desk. Her stuffed rabbit swung limply from one hand as she moved.

George waited until she was close enough and then reached out. He grabbed her by the waist and swung her up, into his lap. Usually she would squeal with excitement—but not tonight. “Are you worried about mummy?” he asked.

She nodded. “Is she coming back?”

“Yes. Of course she is.”

“How do you know?” asked Millie. George smiled, in spite of the doubts and fears that plagued him.

“I just know, sweetie. You don’t need to worry,” he said. The idea that Harriet might not be coming back haunted him too, but he knew he must be wrong for his daughter.

“Okay…” She pressed the rabbit to her face, sucking the tip of one of the ears. He gently reached up and stroked her face. She hadn’t been crying. That was something.

George hugged her against his chest and kissed the top of her head. “Everything will be alright,” he said. He wasn’t sure if he was trying to convince her or himself. She squirmed on his lap and leaned forward to get a better look at the model on his desk.

“What are you doing, Daddy?” she asked.

“I am making a ship in a bottle,” he said. He picked up the model and held it up. The hull was already painted in bands of black and yellow, and the whole thing teemed with intricate details. “When I’m done, this will fit inside that bottle.”

Millie followed the line of his finger. She took one look at the glass bottle and shook her head. “No. It’s too big to go inside.”

“It’ll fit. There’s a trick to it,” he told her.

“Are you sure?” she asked. She turned to look at him, and her hair whipped slightly, tickling his hand.

“I’m sure. I’ve made them before. But never this one,” said George. His daughter turned and looked at him.

“Why?” asked Millie. “Is this one special, Daddy?”

“Yes,” said George. “It’s the Victory.”

“The Victory?” She frowned.

He nodded. “That’s right. It’s the name of a ship. A very old ship. A great one. Very important.” He paused. “It’s still around too. It’s down south. Maybe I will take you to see it one day. Would you like that?"

"Yes." She nodded, and the rabbit's ear still in her mouth made the doll's head nod as well. He almost laughed at the image. The two little figures, the girl and rabbit, nodding together to answer him. "Can we go tomorrow?"

"No. Not tomorrow. It's too far away. But we will go some time. All of us. Mummy too," George told his daughter. She nodded again, but he could see something in her eyes. A glimmer of something. Something dark. The same thing he had been wrestling with all day. He cleared his throat and pushed it aside. "Do you know what victory means, Millie?"

"No," she said and shook her head.

"Well, it can mean win. When you beat someone in a game. That's a victory. But it can mean something else too. When you do something you didn't think you could do. Overcome something. When you do a good job. We call that a victory too."

"So, when I get good marks at school?"

"Yes. That's a victory. Or when you learned to tie your shoelaces. Do you remember that?" Millie nodded again, and George laughed at the memory. The first time he had tried to teach her she had tangled the laces around themselves until nothing could untangle them, and then she had cried. "That was a victory. Eventually."

"And when you got the cherry tree out of the garden?" A smile crept over Millie's face, and George nodded.

"Yes. That was a victory," he said.

"You said a lot of bad words." Millie giggled, and after a moment George chuckled too.

The previous owners of the house had let the garden get far too overgrown. Harriet had asked him last summer to take out a cherry tree in the corner of the garden. He had assumed it would be easy. Millie and Harriet had sat on the lawn and played while he worked.

The tree's roots were so deep and so tangled that it had taken George most of a day to uproot and remove it. In the process he had destroyed half a flowerbed and taught his daughter some words she could never repeat.

"Yes I did say a lot of bad words," he said. "But I got the tree out. In the end. So that was a victory."

Millie reached out and picked up the small hull of the ship. George watched her, making sure that she was careful and didn't break the fine detailing around the edges. She held it up. "What did the ship do?"

"It won a very important battle. And the captain of this ship was a very important man. I'll tell you more about it another time," he said. Then he pointedly added, "When it isn't past your bedtime. Hmm?"

His daughter pulled a face, but she didn't say anything. She went to set the model down, and George reached out. He cupped his hand under it and held it out. His eyes scanned over it again, and his mind drifted away.

He thought of Nelson and the men who fought on the Victory. He couldn't help but feel that parts of life were easier then. A man knew who the enemy was, and he knew what was expected of him.

It wasn't until Millie nudged him that he came back to the moment. He looked at her, and she looked back at him expectantly. "How does it work?" she asked.

"What do you mean?"

"How does it go inside the bottle?" She pointed. "It's too big, Daddy."

"Ah." George nodded. He brought the ship back up again. His other arm curled around Millie so he could touch the masts with his free hand. "These parts here. They fold down. Like this." He gently pushed the masts of the model and watched them bend down towards the hull. "When it is flat like that it can go inside the bottle. And then I use a piece of wire to pull the masts up again." He pulled the masts gently back up into place.

"Wow." Millie stared at the ship for a few seconds. She reached out, and George let her—carefully and gently—push the sails down again. "It's so pretty."

"Yes it is. Do you want to help me?" he asked. Millie nodded. He made her hold out both hands and then carefully placed the model on her palms. She held it still as he picked up the needle.

Then he reached out and put one hand over his daughter's. His large hand covered hers and helped to steady the ship. He took a breath and pushed the needle through the spot on the mast.

"Done," he said. "Easy. And now I can use this wire to pull the masts up. So I can fold them down and put the ship in the bottle. And then I can fold it up again."

Millie looked at the model and reached up to touch the wire he had just threaded into the wood. Then, she looked at him. "Can I play with it when it's done?"

"No. This sort of thing isn't a toy," said George. "We don't play with it."

"Then what is it for?" she asked.

"It's a decoration. I will put it on the shelf," George told her. Millie pulled a face again.

"But why?"

George had to think before he answered. He knew why he wanted it and yet it was hard to explain it in a way that Millie might understand. "It's so that I remember something. Something important," he said eventually.

"Remember what, Daddy?" Millie asked. Again, he had to think.

"It's to remind me not to give up," he said. He looked down at his daughter, and he could already see the question forming on her lips. Why? He sighed and shifted her again. He turned her around so that she was facing him. "The ship is called the Victory. You remember what that means?"

"It's like winning. Or…" Millie thought hard. "Learning a thing."

"Very good," George nodded. It was close enough for her to understand, he thought. "And in life, there are lots of victories. Big ones. Small ones. And there are bad things that happen too. Like the captain of this ship. He died on this ship."

"He died?"

"Yes. But he still won the battle. And the name of the ship. Victory. This is just a model. It's small. But there is a big Victory as well." George paused. His daughter nodded, and he decided to continue. "So, this model reminds me that there are big victories in life. And there are small victories too. And it reminds me not to worry. Sometimes the big victories feel so far away that you think you might never see them. But if you only think about the big victories then you might get sad. Some days it feels like you never see the big things."

"Are you sad, Daddy?" said Millie. He shook his head.

"No. Because I think about the small things. I think about how you're growing up. How you can tie your shoelaces now. And I think about how I got rid of that tree. And I think about all of the little things I can do every day," he said. "Even the little victories are important. And they make me feel happy even when the big victories are far away. Does that make sense?"

Millie nodded. He wasn't sure if she truly got it, but it still felt nice to say it aloud. He also knew that he couldn't tell her too much. The world was not a nice place. She would learn that one day. But not now. He wanted to protect her for as long as he could.

Then, his daughter put her head against his chest. He could feel his heart thudding just against the hard curve of her skull. "Is Mummy okay?"

George opened his mouth to answer. He wasn't sure what he was going to say—but before he had to speak he heard his phone buzzing in his desk drawer. He reached out and opened the drawer, taking care not to disturb his daughter. The phone screen shone out at him with just one word. Harriet.

His thumb pressed the button, and he lifted the phone to his ear. "Darling? How did it go?"

"Everything is fine," she said. She sounded tired and yet better at the same time. They had last spoken earlier that day when George had dropped her off at the hospital. There had been a tension in his wife's voice then—the same tension that had held his heart in a vice ever since she had fallen.

"It is?" he asked.

"Yes," Harriet said. "They did the scan. I'll be fine."

"And the baby?" he asked.

"He's fine too. Healthy. We're both fine, George," said Harriet. "You don't usually worry like this."

"No. But you are important to me. You know that," he said. He heard her laugh.

"Well. You're sweet. But stop worrying now. I'm fine," she told him again.

He felt a surge of relief in his chest. He wasn't the kind of man who let his emotions rule him, but he knew that the only thing stopping him from standing up and punching the air was the fact he had his daughter resting on his lap.

"That's wonderful," he said. "Do you need me to come and get you?"

"No. They want me to stay overnight for the blood tests. But they said it's just a formality. They'll discharge me in the morning." There was a pause, and then Harriet asked, "How are things?"

"Good. I'm working on my model," he said. He heard his wife laugh again, and he smiled as well. "I was trying to distract myself."

"Did it work?" she asked.

"Mostly," he said. "And it helped with Millie."

"Millie is awake? She should have gone to bed hours ago!" Harriet said. George could hear the reproachful tone in her voice, and he cut her off before she could start.

"I put her in bed. But she couldn't sleep. She was worried about you. Do you want to talk to her?" George looked down and noticed his daughter had her eyes closed. One hand was raised in front of her, her thumb in her mouth where the rabbit's ear had been earlier. "Actually, she might be asleep again."

"It's fine. I'll see her in the morning," Harriet said. "Put her back to bed, please?"

"I will," he said. Then, after a moment, George cleared his throat. "I love you."

He could almost hear the smile on her face and the surprise on her face. "You must have been worried," she said. He didn't say those words to her often enough. He knew that. And she stayed with him anyway. "I love you too."

"I'm really glad you're okay."

"I am too. I didn't know I married such a worrier," she said. "Now come on. Put Millie to bed. I'll see you tomorrow. And George?"

"Yes, darling?" he asked.

"I miss you too," said Harriet. "Goodnight. And see you tomorrow."

"I miss you too," he said. Then, the phone went silent. He set it on the desk and reached out. He curled his arms around Millie and gently rocked her. "Are you awake?"

"Mmmm…" she said, muttering to herself. He rocked her again, and she opened her eyes. "Was that Mummy?"

"Yes it was," he said. "She said she misses you. And she'll see you tomorrow."

"Is she okay?" Millie asked. George smiled, and he nodded.

"She is. And your brother is too," he said. "But she said that you have to go to bed. Okay?"

"Will you tuck me in, Daddy?" Millie shifted in his lap and stared at him. He nodded.

"Yes, I will. But only if you go now," he told her. She pouted, but she turned and slid off his leg. He heard her feet pad on the floor as she landed.

"And I get a story too, right Daddy?" she asked.

"Another one? I already read you one." George saw her face and sighed. "Alright. One more story. But only because I miss Mummy too." He reached out to tickle her. She giggled, and then he nodded toward the door. "Go and get in bed. I'll come and read you a story. Go. Now."

He watched her walk across the room and open the door. Just before she left, she turned and looked at him. "Can I help you with your little ship? When you put it in the bottle. Can I help?"

"Yes you can," said George. "Now go. I'll be a moment."

She disappeared, leaving the door ajar. George looked down at the model spread across his desk. He only had a couple more wires to thread and he would be just about ready to put it inside the bottle. Another small victory. Literally, he thought.

Then he thought of his wife. No matter how much he had tried to hide it, he had been worried. No matter how bad things seemed to be, he always had his family. The idea of losing them…

He pushed the thought aside. There was no point worrying about something that wouldn't happen. She was fine, and so was the baby. He smiled and stood. He stretched his arms out and backward until his back cracked. Then he went to the door, ready to read his daughter a second story.

Just like Millie, he turned and took one last look into the room. The boat was still lying on his desk. The pool of light from the lamp shone on it, and the rigging cast shadows like spider webs across the paper.

He looked at the ship and thought of what he had told his daughter. The little victories helped to get through the days while you waited for the bigger one. There were days when it was only thinking of some small goal that gave him hope for the greater things to come.

George took a final look around the room—his room. Everything in the room was his, but it all reminded him of his family.

Harriet would be okay. His son would be okay. Everything was going to be okay. He smiled again. “Today was a good day,” he said—and then turned and made his way to the stairs.

Is It Bright Where You Are? Have the People Changed?

A.J. Bell

Anytime I look up at the stars at night, it makes me want to go on a journey. I've always been that way, ever since I was a kid. Not anywhere in particular, you see.

Just a journey. Just somewhere far away.

The wars stopped a lot of people from daydreaming about things like that, or even thinking about normal stuff like the future.

When the wars ended in 2080, most people's dreams never came back. Just like society, and the grass.

They didn't look up at the stars.

I guess you could say I'm an outlier in this way. But I know how they feel. The sky I look at now is not the same one I saw as a kid. It's faded, like a memory you struggle to recall. The memory of a friend who's gone.

The stars seem further away than ever. But they're still there.

My buddy and I used to talk about finding a spaceship (this was when we were kids). Something small, a little fighter that had been shot down in some forgotten battle, before the world forgot us completely.

We would dig it out of the ground like dinosaur bones, clean it up, try to repair it. Use it as a clubhouse, and never tell anyone what we were doing.

And eventually get it to fly.

We never found a spaceship. Anything valuable like that was stripped away to nothing a long time ago.

We didn't really mind. We used to joke about the fact that we'd probably be old men, still keeping a lookout for our spaceship that we were going to fix up.

More things that never happened.

My buddy started drinking, and we lost touch. Eventually the bottle got him. Now he's joined the ashes of the world.

We were never space pilots. We were never old men together.

Most days the only thing I daydream about is food.

* * *

I wear a gas mask along with my leather jacket and boots, when I ride into the cities. My bike roars like a lion as I cut through the empty streets, the houses a blur, the blown out windows empty eye sockets of skeletons.

There's still a lot of fumes, toxic gas.

You can't be too careful.

It's good to cover your face too, in case you encounter someone. You can hide, deny who you are. Be a disposable person by choice for once.

I needed to find something to eat. It had been two days.

I still felt mostly okay, but I knew that feeling was going to run out fast. And it did.

I had to stop. Generally, as a rule, you shouldn't take a break while you're in the city limits. If you're a traveler. Especially a city like this one; narrow streets, buildings close together. You have no way of knowing how many eyes are on you.

But I was dizzy from hunger. It had been hot all day. So I stopped. The bike felt heavy and sluggish beneath me. But I knew it wasn't the bike. It was me.

It happened within seconds. I only have myself to blame.

I stood there, hunched over, trying to get it together. Taking deep breaths. Not paying attention.

Just for a second.

I felt the barrel of a gun pressed to the back of my head.

"Get off the bike," a voice said. "And do it nice and slow, or I'll blow your head off."

I did what I was told, and turned around.

The guy holding the shotgun was short, stocky, wearing overalls. He didn't have a mask on. I did a quick assessment.

Then smacked the gun out of his hands. It hit the dirt a few feet away.

The man crumpled like a leaf, fell to the ground with his hands on his head, already asking for forgiveness.

"Look man, I'm sorry, I didn't mean anything by it. I was never going to shoot you," he said, staring down at the ground.

I ignored him. Picked up the shotgun. Emptied it, pocketed the shells.

I stood over him, holding it by the barrel.

I said, "Do you have anything to eat?"

He hesitated, but he looked up at me.

"Excuse me?"

"Food. Do you have any food?"

"Um, no."

"Where do you live? Do you live here?"

"No. I live just outside of town."

"Do you have food there?"

"Yes. A little."

"Take me there."

"No."

I held up the shotgun with both hands, like a baseball bat.

"I'm going to beat the crap out of you. I'm going to kill you, if you don't."

He got back on his feet, brushed the dirt off his pants. He didn't seem too impressed by my threats.

His face was serious now.

"No. I'm not taking you to where my family is. You can kill me if you want, you scumbag."

I looked at him carefully. He meant what he said.

I handed him the shotgun back.

"I'll hang on to the shells for now," I said. "Do you know where I can get some food?"

The man put out his hand for me to shake.

"Nice to meet you, my name is Oliver," he said.

I didn't shake his hand. He gave me an annoyed look.

"Look," I said. "I don't mean to be rude, Oliver. But I haven't eaten for a couple days. I need food. If there's no food around here, I need to be on my way."

"Well, you're in luck, Mr. Gas Mask Man. There's a truck that comes through here once a week, should be here just after sundown. We could take it, you and I."

"And this truck has food?"

"Food. Tools. Clothing. All kinds of stuff. It's going to an army base a couple towns over. I've been watching it for a few weeks now. And here's the best part."

Oliver took a few steps closer to me.

"There's only one guy. The driver."

I tilted my head at him.

"Why haven't you done it already?"

"I've been getting up the nerve to do it. Remember, I'm just one guy myself. I was going to go for it tonight, believe it or not. But then you showed up." He stared at his feet like he was embarrassed. "I don't usually do this kind of thing."

"Yeah no kidding."

"What's that supposed to mean?"

"You're not the type. Nothing personal. First of all, why aren't you wearing a mask?"

He stuck a finger in my face.

"You don't need that stupid mask," he said. "You're not going to get sick from walking around breathing the air. Granted, you try to grow your own food here, you're probably going to be messed up. Water, same thing. Like I said, I live outside of town."

"There's other reasons to wear a mask. People remember faces."

Oliver scratched his chin.

"This face is too pretty to cover up," he said. "Look around. This is a ghost town. Everybody hauled out of here a long time ago."

This was true. I hadn't seen any sign of anyone besides him as I was riding through.

"The driver of this truck. Are we going to kill him?"

"No. That won't be necessary."

"The guy's going to be armed, for sure. Especially since he's by himself."

"No."

"We might have to."

"We're not killing him."

"Okay fine. How do you plan to do this?"

"Come with me."

I followed him down an alleyway, after parking the bike somewhere out of sight. I kept my eyes peeled, and my right hand close to the pistol in my jacket pocket. This could be a trick.

We stopped at a dusty garage door. Oliver bent down and yanked it up.

Inside were four ancient-looking vehicles. Two smaller pickups, two sedans.

"Do any of these run?" I said.

"Nope."

"Then why are you showing me this?"

"We'll roll them out into the street, where we were just now. Form a barricade. The buildings are tall around here. He won't be able to see it until he comes around the corner. It'll be too late. He'll have to stop."

"Then we'll nab him."

"Right. As soon as he stops I'll run up and fire the shotgun into the air, right up close to his door. Scare the bejeezus out of him. You pull him out from the other side. You got a firearm?"

I hesitated before answering.

"Yes I do. What if I can't open the door on the other side? What if it's locked?"

"Use the gun to break the window. Yell, tell him to get out. Bang on the door. Remember, it's going to be dark. He doesn't know how many of us there are."

"What if he tries to shoot me?"

Oliver held up the shotgun.

"I'll be yelling and making a racket too. Sticking this thing in his face. He'll be distracted. You'll have your gun on him before he even knows you're there. If he has anything on him, we tell him to drop it. Two against one. Simple."

I thought about all this.

"What about the truck? What about the authorities? He has to check in at all his stops. People are going to notice when he doesn't show up on time."

"He'll be running late. Happens all the time. We'll be long gone by the time anyone comes looking."

"What happens to the driver?"

"We'll send him off in the direction of the army base. It's his next scheduled stop anyway. It'll take him about a day on foot."

"And we'll be long gone by then."

"Yep."

"What if he doesn't go to the base? What if he runs off somewhere else?"

"It doesn't change anything. The base is the closest thing to civilization out here, by a lot. He has to go there. He doesn't have a choice."

"So he's like us."

Oliver smiled.

"Yes, I guess he is. I'll need my ammunition back."

I tilted my head again.

"I don't even know you," I said. "I have no reason to trust you."

"You're quite right, Mr. Gas Mask Man. It's a bit of a risk you're taking. I guess hunger has clouded your judgment."

I handed over the shells.

* * *

I started traveling after my friend died. I guess you could say I replaced him with the bike.

I never worked on cars or anything growing up, so I didn't really know what to do with it at first. I made a lot of mistakes. He was always the one who was more mechanically inclined.

But I learned.

Learned to ride it, fix it, replace the parts. Improvise. I like to think he'd be impressed.

If anything ever happened to the bike, I'd be pretty pissed off. But honestly, in the grand scheme of things, it wouldn't be too bad.

Because I could rebuild it, I could bring it back from nothing. All the time and effort, all the miles. I had it all in my mind.

And if I kept it there, I would always have it.

* * *

It all went down just the way Oliver said it would.

For the most part.

I had the driver, hands tied behind his back, in the alleyway where my bike was stashed. I had him sitting down against a wall across from me. I had my pistol on him.

The moon shone bright above our heads.

Oliver was moving the truck.

I had to get my mask off. I'd meant to take it off after we got done getting the cars in place. I'd started sweating. I was going to take it off and thoroughly mop my head before the truck arrived. Then put it back on.

But things moved fast. I never got around to it.

It was bothering me. I'm sure being hungry and tired had something to do with it, but I was agitated.

I told the driver not to move.

I went just a little ways down the alley, where he couldn't see me. I tried pulling it off with one hand, but it wouldn't budge. I tried my other hand. Same thing.

I got impatient. I had to get this thing off.

I put away my pistol, just for a second, so I could use both hands.

It came off with some effort.

I exhaled. Told myself to calm down, I'd be fed and out of here before I knew it. That's when I got checked into the wall. Hit my head pretty hard, but I have a hard head. The blow knocked all the air out of me though. A voice inside kept telling me to reach for my pistol, but I felt like I was tumbling down a well. I eventually managed to roll over onto my back.

The driver was standing over me. He had my pistol in his hand. (Never did figure out how he got loose. He probably had a knife on him somewhere.)

Neither of us said anything. We just stared at each other.

I heard the sound of footsteps. We both looked.

"What the hell?"

"You put that thing down right now or I'll—"

Oliver let him have it with the shotgun. It was like blowing out a candle. I had blood mixed with sweat on my face.

I'll always remember Oliver at that moment. The look in his eye. That was the real man right there. The man who would rather die than take me to where his family was.

He had no interest in hearing what the driver had to say.

He didn't hesitate.

Oliver set the shotgun down on the ground, then walked over to check the driver. He picked something up that I couldn't see, walked over to me with this fatherly expression, like, *you alright kid?*

He held out the thing he had picked up. I thought it would be my pistol.

It was my mask.

* * *

I shake Oliver's hand one last time, as I start up the bike.

We feasted on cans of beans and cold soup. It was delicious. There was even a case of orange juice in the truck.

After that, we talked for a long time. He told me about his wife, his son and daughter. I told him about my buddy and his drinking. But not just that.

I told him about the spaceship too.

Then it was time for us both to go.

"Well I hope you find it one day," he said. "Can't be any worse out there than it is down here."

He pointed up at the sky. I thanked him.

"Tell your family I said hello."

"Oh they're going to love this. That time Dad met a Gas Mask Man. I'm going to have drawings of you on my refrigerator within twenty-four hours."

Oliver hopped in the truck and drove off into the night. I watched until I couldn't see him anymore.

The night air feels cool on my face. The mask is put away.

I race toward the stars.

Stray Dogs

Cloud Buchholz

1

Mosquito bites. Summer sweat. And freckles. That's how I remember her. Red haze hanging at the horizon, the branch holding the weight of us both as we inch further out. Her sticky fingers touching mine, yanking me closer.

Her lips warm and dry, but still perfect—the kiss I'll use to judge all future kisses.

…and a moment later I fall, breaking my arm.

A long angry ride to the hospital, Ma cursing God and me and the cars in front of us. My arm crooked and wrapped in towels that are red with blood, but all I think about is the kiss and her sticky fingers and what could have happened next.

Years later I see her at a potluck, pretty as ever, a kid resting on her hip and a ring on her finger. She smiles. I think to speak, remind her of the tree, the kiss, but instead I spoon another clump of potato salad on my plate.

The pain is sharp in my leg. The bone broken I'm sure, but I don't trust myself to look. I pile snow on my pleated, puffy pants, red and melting.

I lay my head against the tree, my eye slow to move, already swollen. My voice is soft and tastes metallic. The path isn't far off. They'll find me soon.

I paw her nipple, rough and quick, too eager for my own good, kissing at her neck like it was on fire. We twist around in the back of Pa's pickup, the stars speckling overhead, touching as much of her as I can.

Her eyes are soft in their yearning, and she nods to make sure I know she's ready. We move slow together, awkward at first, and then less so.

The crickets play our ballad as we lay there, her head resting heavy on my chest. I drive her home, kissing her before she runs up the porch steps.

I park on the dirt road, the June heat thick and sticky. I sleep outside, under a crooked oak, fearing Ma will smell her perfume on me.

And she does the next day just as easily. She shakes her head ready to lay into me, but Pa kisses her cheek and laughs, and she says nothing.

My leg throbs, the snow doing little for the pain. I pile on another fistful anyway.

I hate skis and snowy mountaintops. I told her as much before she bought the tickets. My parents will be there, she says. You need to meet them. We're getting serious, she says, you need to meet them.

...I need to meet them.

My city girl, Ma calls her, all heels and lingerie. I tell her that's how people dress in the city.

She rolls her eyes. City folk, she shakes her head. City folk.

I'm city folk now, my apartment on the cheap side of downtown with a clear view of a dirty alley.

She calls it horribly trendy. The night I sleep with her, I gawk at the number of soaps she has in her bathroom. I count them three times just to be sure. She calls me silly from the shower.

I watch her lather, the suds easing down her bronze skin, and I think maybe she's the one. I stick my head in the shower, kissing her before I go.

I holler again, as loud as I can manage, my voice echoing off the trees. My toes numb and out of reach. I tell myself it's the snow.

...and the cold. It's just the cold. They'll find me soon.

I take her to the pond, a mile down the back road past the old house. I'm still wearing the suit and tie from Pa's funeral. I show her the wooden dock he and I built.

We sit on the edge, placing our bare feet in the cold water. She tells me she's pregnant, her voice wavering. I kiss her and pull her close.

My lips are dry, my voice gone. The white snow soaks up the blood seeping from my padded pants. The sun edges past the trees, a red haze hanging like a halo around the leaves.

I flex my fingers, blowing hot air into my cupped palms. The snowflakes are powdery and soft, stinging my cheeks like spider bites. My head droops against my shoulder, my eyelids heavy.

The wet snow layers itself with more snow, soft and powdery, the red blotches of blood slowly diminishing.

2

The doctor calls me lucky. I tell him he needs to buy a dictionary. He laughs and nods. I'm not dead. That makes me luckier than most.

She hates hearing it. She scrunches her eyes, squeezing my hand. You're alive, she repeats, kissing my cheek. You're alive.

...you're alive.

I mean to tell her it'll be alright, but the drugs take hold and I drift lazily.

One eye opens slow, and I see Ma sitting in the corner, the newspaper crossword folded over her knee. She sighs and shakes her head, less patient now that Pa's gone.

I twist awkwardly, my leg propped in a sling and difficult to move.

Pa lasted longer than we thought, those last few months confined to a bed, speaking incoherently with a string of blind curses.

His only comfort being Ma touching a cold rag to his forehead, droplets sliding down his sullen cheeks.

She stands over me, staring at my busted leg. You won't die, she says, you got angels. She slides the Bible under my hand. You got angels, she says. The nurse leads her out.

The worn leather cover is a comfort. I rub my fingers across the embossed letters. The gold shine is faded and smooth.

The spine has been re-glued twice, the cover stitched in three places. The New Testament stained with an uncle's blood, my great granddad praying over an arm caught in the gearing of a tractor. He lived, a few fingers shy of ten, but the angels had to take something for their trouble.

The doctor says I'll walk, just not yet…and not all at once.

Misty tells me to be thankful. You've got a daughter, she says. Think about her.

…and I do.

I think about my baby girl, her little hand barely the width of my palm. Her mind tied to dreams still floating in the ether.

She was born on a Thursday, 2:00 a.m. and three weeks eager. I paced the hospital halls, my legs trembling too much to sit. And then I heard her crying, a melody sweeter than any I had heard…or might ever hear.

My Melody.

I reach for the cup of water on the end table, the straw a placid torture for my lips. Melody sits in bed with me, her crayons catching between the sheets.

She draws Caribbean Green trees with Tumbleweed trunks, a Denim sky with Piggy Pink snow, and an Unmellow Yellow sun. My stick figure, Outer Space Black, sprawls under a tree, the Razzle Dazzle Rose blood dripping down the page.

She presents it to me, proud and fervent. I have the nurse tape it to the wall beside my bed.

She doesn't draw the angels, but she tells me that they're watching from behind the sky. I imagine a peephole cut in the bright blue, angels crowding together on the other side, one further back, a lookout for when Jesus strolls by.

I kiss her before she goes, her mother easing her off the bed. And I'm alone, except for a persistent cough across the hall. I stare at the ceiling, wishing like hell to scratch my leg.

Pa points at the fox, its red fur brilliant. It flitters between the brush quick and elegant. One shot, he says. Anything more and you're being cruel.

I aim the rifle just below the neck, my finger light on the trigger. Put it down quick, Pa says. If you hesitate you'll miss and wound it. Days'll pass before it dies buried in a hole. You got to put it down quick.

I look down the sight, steady and calm. The rifle is loud. The bullet pierces the shoulder and heart. The creature goes stiff like a stone.

I check the kill.

The brilliant red fur is matted with blood, sticky to the touch. I heft it in the air for Pa to see. Good, he says. The chickens are yours to tend now.

I stare at the window. The hospital air is pungent with bleach, an accident in the hall, the bathroom a few steps too far.

The moon casts a stark glow against the trees and I can't tell if it's snow or light that's weighing them down.

We walk the park near downtown. The sky is bleak but warm. I take her hand, kissing the knuckle. She thinks it's silly when I mean for it to be sweet, but still she smiles, which is all I want.

I don't recall the words that lead to the kiss, only her smile and that half second of hesitation as we inch closer.

She offers me coffee. I tell her it's late and the night is already perfect. Tomorrow, I say, or the next day.

She grabs my collar with both hands, kissing me slow, standing on her tiptoes to reach my lips. Now it's perfect, she says.

The bruises on my face are tender. I ease my head into the pillow, too soft for what I prefer.

It's late, I think. I should be tired.

A lonesome owl hoots outside, seeking its companion. It's a cold night, and I don't envy it. We sit on the porch, a jug of lemonade between us. Ma eases back in the old rocking chair, mending Pa's torn jeans while Pa's naked legs rest on the porch railing, his hat covering his dusty face.

I stare at the distant green, not a neighbor for miles. Ma hums an old gospel tune, the needle and thread moving to her rhythm.

The dogs lay beside Pa, panting a grin, content with the cool autumn air.

I pull the old Bible from the end table, laying it against my chest, the weight reassuring.

I smell the worn leather and tattered pages, trying to remember the words to Ma's old gospel tune.

3

I swing instead of walk, the crutches my pivot point, my good foot taking the brunt of my weight. My ribs are still bruised, but I manage. The stairs are trouble. I climb backwards, a tense hand clutching the rail.

I sit back slow, more cautious then I need to be, the old couch sinking with my weight. I prop my busted leg on the coffee table and stare at the television. She tells me to lie in bed. She tells me to rest but I'm not tired.

Pa hammers another board into the side of the barn, the metallic thump echoing for miles. A storm cut through the day before, not proud enough to be a tornado, and busted all but the heavy frame.

Ah sh-ite, Pa hollers, his thumbnail clipped in a bloody crescent matching the hammer's head.

He sucks the tip of his thumb, staring down at me while I hold the next board.

He grimaces, his fingernail nearly amputated. Sometimes it's alright for a man to curse, he says, but you ain't a man yet, you understand? He wipes the blood on his jeans and takes the next board.

I ease my leg off the coffee table and wobble to the kitchen, leaning heavy on the crutch. I put the dishes in the sink meaning to wash them later, though I won't.

My trembling fingers grip the stucco walls, my body twisting around the hall toward the bathroom.

Pa rubs the handkerchief across his sweaty forehead. How long you gonna keep us out here?

We got work that needs doing.

Oh, Uncle laughs from under the hood. This here's a diamond in the rough. A diamond. The fool sold it for pennies on the dollar.

Is that why it don't run?

You just wait and see, Uncle smirks. Alright boy, give it some gas. Easy now, he says peering over the hood.

I twist the key and tap the pedal lightly. The engine clicks twice. I try again. Still nothing. Ah, hell, Uncle groans, and flings his handkerchief at the engine, his greasy face scowling. Pa pats my shoulder. If we set off now, we'll make it home before dark.

I inch my way toward the bedroom, my limbs shaking, my lungs ready to quit. I sit on the bed, cradling my ribs, breathing deep and slow.

She told me not to push myself. I should have listened. I pull my leg up and onto the mattress.

I'm sweating by the time it's in place. I lean back, the pillow firm beneath my head.

I take Pa's old Bible from the nightstand, thumbing through it for no particular reason. I told Ma to keep it. I told her I had no use for it, but she insisted and there was no point in arguing with her.

A third of the verses are underlined, illegible notes scrawled in the margins belonging to relatives before my time. I see Pa's name written in the front, bold and clear. Above it, his Pa's name, and another two above that.

I take a pen from the nightstand drawer, the tip black and modern. I place it below Pa's name, the ink almost touching the page.

I know the book is mine, but putting my name to it doesn't seem right. I'm not a country boy.

I'm not a God-fearing man.

I slide the old tome on the nightstand, the pen firmly between its pages.

Ma slams down her glass, the juice splattering across the table. This ain't no place for him, her voice sharp. You tell him he ain't welcome.

Pa frowns. He's family.

Fine. Ma shakes her head. You tell him what you want, but he ain't staying here. You know he ain't got nowhere else to go.

That's his own fault.

Where should I send him if he ain't welcome here?

How's he gonna learn if you keep indulgin' him? Ma scowls.

There's plenty work to be done here, Pa says. I could use another set of hands. Ain't that what your son's for? She glares at me like I started the argument.

Pa smiles, calm and confident. He's my brother. I ain't turning him away.

Ma huffs, staring at her plate. Why do I bother saying anything when you're gonna do whatever you damn well please.

Pa smiles and kisses her cheek. You sure are pretty when you're cross.

I groan, sore from not rolling onto my side. Misty walks around the bed, her shirt draped over the chair.

I glance at the clock, realizing dinner's passed. Where's Melody, I ask. I told her to let you sleep. You looked tired.

She undresses in front of me, casual and carefree. Her arms are thin and golden brown, reaching for a t-shirt in the closet. Her leg inches up, a finger slipping loose her high heel shoe.

Come here, I say, my hand reaching vainly.

She smiles and walks beside me, bending down to kiss my cheek. I touch the inside of her thigh, my fingers ascending.

She shakes her head. Not for another week, she insists, doctor's orders.

I sit in the tree, the broke branch just out of reach. I lean into the curve of the trunk, sap clumping the hairs on my arm. I watch the sun dip below the trees, red haze scattered like a shotgun blast.

I carve my initials in the bark, my hand slow and still mending. I think maybe she'll see it. I'm too young to know what I want from her, but I know whatever it is, I want it bad.

I sit at the table, my leg jutting awkwardly to the side. She gives me a plate of food, freshly microwaved. I eat it fast, not knowing how hungry I am.

She sits across from me, watching me eat, her head heavy in her hand.

Melody is scared, she says. You need to tell her everything is alright. The way she looks at you…you need to tell her everything is alright.

It is alright, I say.

She thought you were going to die.

Pa throws his hat into the dirt, shouting something I can't hear. Uncle waves him off. The tractor sits idle between them, the field barely plowed.

I stand, inching closer to the window.

Ah, Ma chides. Back to your school work. She points at the textbook by my side. What if they need my help?

Your help is the last thing they need. Let 'em be.

Pa kicks a heap of dirt toward Uncle. Uncle falls on his butt, swatting the dust with his hat. Ma taps the table with her long ruler. I won't say it again.

What do you suppose they're fighting about?

Your Uncle's been messing with things he ain't supposed to. He's got a bad habit of tinkerin' when he's drunk.

I can help, I say. I know how to fix an engine.

Ma laughs and shakes her head. That fight they're having is older than you are. Let 'em spill a little blood then they'll settle.

I stop in front of Melody's room, her nightlight casting pink lines across the hall.

She looks delicate and small, the blanket barely covering her shoulder. I stand, my leg sore and throbbing, wanting to watch her sleep a little longer.

4

I shamble up the stairs and down the hall, tired when I reach the door. The keys quiver in my hand as I enter the apartment.

Melody leans over the coffee table, crayons scattered in a semi-circle around her coloring book.

Daddy! she exclaims.

I lift her to my chest. Her tiny arms wrap around my neck.

Don't hurt yourself, Misty chides from the kitchen table, textbooks forming a defensive wall around her.

I set my cane by the door and limp to the couch, Melody already reaching for her coloring book. Kneeling is too much of a risk so I sit on the couch behind her. I grab the coloring book by the corner and put my weary leg in its place.

Melody flips through the pages, showing me the progress she's made, the colors she's chosen, the methodical process she's taken to keep the lines intact.

Daddy, she says, glancing up. Are you listening? I kiss the top of her head. Of course, sweetheart.

Pa puts my suitcase in the truck bed. I unhinge the rifle from the back of the cabin and take the shells from behind the seat. Pa accepts them with a grateful nod.

Ma stews on the porch, arms crossed, jaw locked in a frown. She shakes her head, pacing. The dogs lay sideways by her feet, nervous not to get stepped on.

Pa squeezes my shoulder and looks me in the eyes, our height even now.

I did all this for you, he says, so you could make more of your life then I did of mine. He glances over his shoulder. Don't worry about your Ma. She'll simmer.

His eyes linger on the rippling waves of alfalfa, and he steadies his resolve. Go on, he says, tapping the side of the truck. You're a university man now.

Melody tugs my shirt. See, she says holding up the crayoned page. I nod. It's very beautiful. What do you call it?

Call it? She furrows her brow. It's coloring, Dad.

Yes, I smile. I mean, now that it's finished, what do you call it? She tilts her head, examining the page. Does it have to be finished? No, I say. It's finished whenever you want it to be finished.

Then it's not finished yet. She sits in front of the coffee table, crayons scattered in piles. She adds an extra layer of Jazzberry Jam to the flowers and Blizzard Blue to the sky.

That's good, Sweetie. I comb back her hair with my finger, her neck and shoulders delicate. Pa hands me a shovel and points to the far side of the stables. He means for me to clean.

Your uncle will be stayin' with us, he says, his voice softer than normal. He ain't been on the farm for a long time. It may take him awhile to remember what it's like.

Where's he been Pa? Everywhere but here.

And that made him forget?

No, Pa says, brushing the horse slower. He had plenty of reasons to forget. You need to be patient with him the way I'm patient with you sometimes, understand?

I nod. Okay Pa. I glance over. Pa's hands are at his side. He stares at the bale of hay, vacant and sad.

I slide the coloring book out of Melody's hand, her eyes closed and restful.

Misty touches my leg, her fingers soft and warm, squeezing lightly. Does it hurt? she asks.

No, I lay back, my head resting on the arm of the couch. It feels strange, like I forgot how to be touched.

She eases her fingertips up my thigh, pushing and kneading peacefully. She lays her head on my chest, her eyes tearing up.

Are you getting misty? I ask.

What? she says defensively. These movies always make me cry. I touch her cheek, catching a tear with my fingertip.

She leans up, her supple breasts pressing into me. There's nothing wrong with crying once in a while. She smiles, kissing me on the lips, her fingers messing up my hair.

What about the movie, I ask.

Her legs straddle my waist. I've seen it before, she says, and this was never about the movie.

She kisses me again, slow, like the air was being pumped out of the room.

Before she leaves, she touches my hand. I'm not just another one of your misty girls, am I? Her fingers slip free of my leg as she walks to the kitchen.

I peer at her with my good eye. Why'd you stop?

You should eat. She pushes aside her textbooks and takes a plate from the refrigerator. I slip my leg out from under Melody and limp toward the table.

Ma slips the knife into the duck's gullet, blood seeping onto the wooden counter as she cuts across its belly. She cups the organs with her hand, placing them in a bowl to be sorted later.

Don't look away, she commands. There ain't no reason to be squeamish. I keep staring, my head barely taller than the counter.

She holds the knife upright, blood dripping down the blade. God gave us dominion over the beasts. We kill 'em and eat 'em because that's the way it's meant to be. We ain't got nothing but love for 'em, you understand? They keep us alive and strong. You cherish 'em for that.

I watch the blood pool below the knife, the smell of iron thick in the air. Misty pushes in her chair. Your daughter needs a bath.

I can manage it, I say, setting down the fork.

She kisses my neck and walks to the bathroom. Water fills the tub before I get to my feet. Uncle stumbles inside, his nose bloody, his shirt ripped. He kisses the bottle to his lips, swigging the last drop of whiskey. He knocks over a lamp as he staggers to the kitchen.

What in the, Ma glares at him more angry than surprised. Uncle lifts a fist to cover a hearty belch.

You damn, drunk fool, Ma yells.

Uncle picks at his ear, sauntering toward the couch.

Ma blocks his path. No drunkard is sleepin' in my house. Uncle waves her off.

She stands firm, giving him her practiced glare. That drinkin' is gonna kill you. One hand is on her hip, the other points at him like a spear. That ain't no way for a God-fearin' man to behave.

What do you know about God?

I know He ain't at the bottom of that bottle.

Uncle laughs. I could have told you that an hour ago.

Ma huffs, her hand squeezing into a fist. You sleep in the barn until you're sober. You're lucky your brother ain't here to see you like this. You'd break his heart.

Uncle looks away ashamed. He shambles outside, stumbling toward the barn. His Chevy is parked in Ma's flower garden, the small fence busted and bent into the front bumper.

I ease onto the couch, crayons rolling between thigh and cushion. Melody hugs the coloring book in one hand, a Mango Tango Orange crayon clutched in her other.

I brush her thin hair with my fingers, watching her chest rise and fall in the slow, steady thralls of slumber.

5

I sit up a few minutes before the alarm, the air cold and heavy. I switch off the buzzer before it wakes Misty. I limp to the bathroom, slow and quiet.

I lean into the counter, studying my haggard face. The circles under my eyes are dark, the wrinkles deeper than I expect.

I splash cold water against my cheeks and eyes, rubbing the sleep loose. I hobble in front of the toilet, adjusting my aim.

I wash my hands, her soaps cluttering the counter, some unopened, others laid out like traps for unsuspecting fingers. The light is sparse, bleeding through the gap in the curtains.

Pa bows his head, his fingers interlocking.

Heavenly Father, the preacher grips the wooden pulpit, Hallowed be Thy name. Thy Kingdom come. Thy will be done on Earth as it is in heaven.

I glance at Pa, his eyes closed. Pa, I whisper. When's His kingdom comin'? Pa opens one eye. It's already here.

Where?

It's a choice, son. You choose to be in His kingdom and you're there. Does that mean we're movin'?

Pa laughs.

Ma glares at us, pinching Pa's wrist hard.

I mix the sourdough batter, adding a handful of blueberries as I stir. I pour the batter into the sizzling pan. The air is sweet with flour and cinnamon.

My leg is stiff, the muscle tense but not yet throbbing. I feel a tug on my pant leg. Melody looks up at me, more curious then tired. Can I help? I pull a chair from the table and hoist her onto it.

The phone is silent. I hear Ma breathing. Pregnant, she finally says. A girl, I say.

But you ain't married.

I love her.

You don't know nothing about love unless you been married, Ma says. If you love her, she'd be your wife.

People aren't like that anymore, Ma. Times have changed. I ain't that old.

Can't you be happy for me?

It ain't my job to be happy for you. I'm your Ma. I set you straight. I keep you on the narrow.

I slide the finished pancake on the plate and pour more batter in the pan. The pancake bubbles light brown. Melody's tiny hands grip the spatula, my hands wrap around hers, then we flip the pancake together. She giggles with amusement.

Uncle sets the bottle in the dirt, digging a little hole so it stands upright. Come on boy, he says.

You ain't afraid, are ya? No, I say. I ain't.

Then come over here and sit in the dirt with me. I'll tell ya a story about your Pa.

I sit beside Uncle and stare at the river. The water rushes in little rivulets of white and blue like a girl's hair being braided.

Good, he slaps my shoulder and tilts the bottle toward me. I keep looking at the water.

When me and your Pa was boys, stray dogs roamed these woods. They'd scavenge farms and fields, steal warm bread from open windows, rustle dumpsters. They weren't no trouble, he says.

They never hurt nobody. They was just living. Except city folk don't like seeing strays mucking about, so they paid a man to catch 'em and put 'em down.

Me and your Pa was walking home from school, across that bridge, and we see cages stacked around this old pickup. Mangy dogs was sticking their snouts between the metal bars whimpering and yowling. Looking at 'em, I knew they was the kind of dogs that get put down. I suppose your Pa knew it too because he took a stone and laid into those locked cages. A man come running out from the tree line red-faced and hollering for your Pa to stop, but your Pa wouldn't listen. He kept busting the locks and turning loose them dogs. The man wrestled your Pa to the ground and wailed on him something fierce. Your Pa was bleeding from his nose and lip. They was both covered in mud, struggling for breath. Your Pa didn't have the strength to overpower him, but the man couldn't risk letting your Pa go neither.

They was at a standstill, then your Pa looks up at me. His eyes turn to them cages. I hear the mutts whimpering, gnawing at the metal bars. The stone wasn't but a few inches from my feet. The man didn't have the reach to stop us both. I stared at them mangy dogs. Their fur was matted and muddy, and their eyes were wild. I started thinking maybe they belonged in them cages.

I stare at the side of Uncle's face.

I don't know what your Pa was thinking. Uncle takes a long swig from the bottle. Them dogs was going to die no matter what we did. He throws the empty bottle in the river.

Pancakes? Misty smiles from the hallway. I helped! Melody exclaims.

I can tell, Misty glances at the batter smudged across the stove and wall. She gives me a wry grin. You must be feeling better.

I am. I kiss her cheek.

Withhold Not Your Hand

Charlie

There is a lot to be said about the power of a single phrase, a single word, a single thought. This is what makes modern entertainment propaganda so powerful; it easily incubates a thought across the masses in an instant. But sometimes these lies can be uprooted as quickly as they're planted. When the roots are shallow, or not planted in the truth, all it takes is the faintest glimmer of strength to erase any memory of how they could possibly be believed.

I was heading home after a long vacation, picking the flight just on the border of being a red-eye to stretch out those last few hours of enjoyment away from work, and of course save a few extra bucks. Naturally, poor weather pushed the flight back once, then again, and eventually forced us to reroute. While vacation time is worth at least double what working time is, wasting time in an airport is something I'd pay triple my wages to avoid. My co-passengers seemed to feel the same. After much fanfare and moaning, we were able to board our flight. We idled in the runway for an eerie amount of time until the crew unceremoniously announced, "Plane broke," and shuffled us off to find more suitable transport.

More time passed, more helpless tempers shortened, and at last a suitable chariot was found. I wander in to find my seat, and something catches my eye a few rows forward. A man on the younger side of elderly was berating a slightly portly young girl. His skin was the same color and texture of an old leather wallet that's been carried around for more than a decade. Unfortunately the content of his character did not have the same rugged quality.

You see, this inner city gentleman decided that he deserved to sit in the aisle seat, regardless of the actual seating arrangement. As you might expect this perturbed the girl, and there hadn't been an issue in the broken plane, so why the trouble now? Regardless, she quickly folded after only mild resistance. And who could blame her? She'd never been prepared for this situation. Unfortunately, giving in is not the correct course of action, and, sensing weakness, the colored fellow continued to berate her.

"Who tha f*** you think you are? Muthaf***ing b**** a** nigga. You sum kinda White supremaciss b****??"

"Please, I just wanted my seat…" she replied.

"I tell you watchu are, you the kinda b**** who gets her a** jumped as soon she leave tha airport! B**** a**.

Of course, I could not stand for this. There were a great many things I wanted to say and do to the old codger, but to find a course to take while also retaining my employment? That would be a bit more difficult, even for a negro whisperer like me. The other passengers were still loading, blocking my way to the mini race war, but letting me bide my time. At last, my plan materialized, and at the same moment my path cleared.

I approached the girl and noticed now that she was on the verge of tears. This would have been so much better if she was cuter, I thought to myself.

"Excuse me, you're in my seat," I said to the girl.

"What?" She looked up, not quite understanding what was going on.

"You're in my seat. Yours is back there," I said, pointing back to my now vacant assigned row.

"AH, YES, thank you," she replied, gathering up her things as quickly as she could.

I take my seat beside the enemy. He instantly tries complaining to me about that poor girl. "Can you believe dis s***? Deez peop—"

"I'm not interested," I cut him off, putting in my headphones. "I'm just going to listen to my music."

"Aight, aight, fine den."

And that's it really, the story of my outstanding courage and heroism against overwhelming odds: an unruly black. For the rest of the flight I listened to my favorite racist parenting podcast and enjoyed the extra leg room paid for by the young girl. Standing up really doesn't take much. As soon as the plane landed the antagonist scurried off, taking the hostile cues from the other passengers to heart. The girl thanked me profusely, and one man came up to me to thank me for what I did, saying he wished he had done it himself.

"Well," I replied, "If White people don't stand up for each other, *no one's* going to stand up for us."

He looked at me for a moment, eyes almost blank, then looked up and off to the right. An ancient gear in his head slowly shifted into place with a dull *clank, clank, clank.*

"You know what? You're absolutely right," he announced, more to himself than to me.

And just like that the seed was planted.

* * *

Will it sprout? Will it grow? Will it bear fruit? Or will it be choked out by the thorns and weeds surrounding its fragile life? Only God knows. But that's for Him, and fate, to decide. All that we can do is plant those seeds. It doesn't have to be a grandiose soliloquy on the finer points of esoteric political philosophies when the simple word "us" can realize a people where the enemy tries so hard to pretend there isn't one.

So sow bountifully! You'll never know which kernel of truth is the one that, when planted in the right soil, will set our people free. There's a footnote in American history named Edward Kimball. History remembers him for nothing, except sharing the gospel with a young man named D.L. Moody. Moody would later become the greatest evangelist of the nineteenth century, bringing Christ to millions. Maybe you're called to fight for our people against overwhelming odds. Maybe you'll plant those seeds of truth in the hundreds, thousands, or even millions. But maybe every seed you plant will be consumed, every sprout will dry up and die, and every leaf will wither, except one. And maybe, that one tiny seed will be the one we need.

Matthew 13:1-9 Ecclesiastes 11:6

Dangerous Summer

Paul Dempsey

It was an unusually hot summer in Saint Petersburg. Everybody told him so. Peter came there for a two-week preparatory course of the directing faculty at the National Film School. It was hard to get into NFS, especially if you wanted to become a director. Every year, they accepted no more than five students. One year, they accepted no one at all.

On a sunny and hot morning, Peter went to the first lecture. There were seventy students in a big sloped auditorium. The professor was a middle-aged man, slightly bald.

"All right," the professor said, smiling, "so all of you want to become film directors. First of all, young men, you should be able to do at least fifteen pull-ups to become film directors. I'll check it myself on the day of the entrance examination. Ladies, you don't, don't worry."

No one said anything. Peter thought that he could only do twelve.

Then there was an introduction to the course. The professor asked them to show their own films, if anyone had brought them. Peter showed a film of his own and watched the films of others. There were some decent works among them. Then the professor recommended some books to read and films to watch.

"You have to read the Russian classics. You can't become a Russian director without reading *War and Peace*," the professor said.

"What about the *Cinema* books by Gilles Deleuze?" someone asked.

"Those are the books that everyone claims he's read, but actually no one reads. Forget about it, for now. Read the classics."

The first week of the course was boring. The professor told them basic things about the history of cinema and directing that Peter already knew. Every day, someone missed the lectures. By the beginning of the second week, there were some fifty students left. Those seemed to be more determined.

After the lecture was over on Monday, Peter went to the city center to shoot something he could use in his future works. As he was going up the Nevsky Prospekt, he saw her—the girl he knew from Königsberg. Out of all places—here, in Saint Petersburg. She was smiling and looked very pretty in her light-blue dress.

"Hello, Peter!" she said. "Isn't it strange to meet like this?"

"Hello, Mary," he said. "I think it is. Why have you come here?"

"Oh, it's just for this week to see my friends here. And my father. What about you?"

"I came last week for the preparatory course at the National Film School."

"Oh, so you want to become an actor?"

"No, a director."

"That's so interesting! But what are you doing here?"

"Oh, just filming the city."

"Will you film me?" she grimaced, showing her acting qualities.

"Sure," he laughed. "All right. Where?"

"Anywhere," she smiled.

They spent the rest of the day together, talking and walking around the city. Peter was filming Mary on Vasilyevsky Island, by Saint Isaac's Cathedral, and on the Admiralty Embankment, all in the sun, and the cool wind was coming from the river. In the evening, they had dinner at a restaurant that only had five tables. They ordered wine, and no one asked for their IDs. When they came out, it was dusk, which would not become any darker because of the white nights. They walked for some more time in the night, warm and beautiful. Then there was a quiet garden with many sculptures and few people.

"How do you like this day?" Peter asked.

"Oh, marvelous."

Then Mary stood on a stone to be as tall as he was. "You see, and who is tall now?" she asked, laughing.

"Me," Peter said and kissed her.

She smelled of wine, cigarettes, and perfume. He loved the smell.

"Mister Director, do you promise me that I'll play in your next film?"

"Sure. You'll have the main role."

She giggled and kissed him.

Peter walked with her to the place where she lived at her father's and went home.

* * *

Next day, they met again after his lecture and walked by the side of the river. They bought some wine in the evening and crossed the bridge to the Petrogradskaya side and walked there, sometimes stopping to drink wine and to kiss. Then someone called Mary, and she talked for some time, while Peter enjoyed the cool wind from the river and did not want it to be over, ever. She stopped talking.

"Peter, oh sorry, Mister Director. My friends invited me to go with them to a villa somewhere near Sortavala for three days. Why don't we go together? I'm sure they'll agree to have another person, especially such a sweet person."

"Well, I'd like to go, but I have my course."

"But you said you learn nothing new. Come on, let's go there. They say that the nights are even more beautiful there."

"I'll think about it."

They walked and talked and drank some more wine, and later they were sitting on a bench in a park, embracing each other and kissing in the warmth of the night.

"Will you go with me tomorrow, Mister Director?" Mary asked, winefully.

"I will, miss young-and-promising actress."

"Will you, really?"

"Oh yes."

"I'm so happy, if only you knew!"

Then they had to part.

In the night, lying in bed at his aunt's flat, Peter thought about the next day's trip. There were three more days of the course. But he learned almost nothing new there. And then there was Sortavala, the villa, Mary, spending the nights with her, maybe it could be his first time. But then there was this course. Many people stopped attending it, though. And the nights in Sortavala, warm and white and Mary and how he would film her, probably even naked, and then, and then. He fell asleep.

The morning was very bright. It was already hot in the flat when Peter woke. He sat on the bed and looked around the room. There was his camera. He would film… What would he film, he thought. Films. He would make films. He took his phone from the night stand and called Mary.

"I'm sorry. I won't go."

* * *

On the last day of the course, the professor came up to him. "You are Peter, from Königsberg, right?"

"Yes."

"It's great that you survived until the last day. Shows you care. I liked your work and your level of knowledge. I want to see you in my group this year."

"That will depend on whether I pass the entrance exam."

"Oh, don't worry about that."

"What about the pull-ups, though? I can't do fifteen."

"You're all right. Some young men need it, though. Now more than ever. Many are too soft."

"How do you know I'm different?"

"You're all right. See you on the entrance exam."

The professor left. Peter gathered his things and went out of the building. The sun was shining. It was hot.

My Brother's Blood

Jack Irkman

I was standing with two empty glasses and a head full of worry, the sour-sweet smell of stale beer, cigarettes, and bodies hard worked corrupting my nostrils. The wood paneled walls were dark oak—so was the bar—and under the dim light the brass fittings shone like dirty gold as the punter's chatter rumbled like thunder over the nineties Brit-pop. These public houses used to be ten a penny. Every street boasted its own to keep whistles wet and the community heart beating. Not anymore.

Today, it's all too common to find public houses like The Grey Nag's Head with their doors closed to the public, the once English staple becoming so rare as to be novel. Youngins prefer clubs and themed bars these days, if they leave their homes at all. That's not to say I'm so old myself, mind you. I'm still months away from thirty. I guess I'm just an anachronistic soul.

Taking a deep breath I grimace at the tight discomfort in my chest. Born of stress it would once have remedied with a hand-rolled cigarette stuffed with tax-free tobacco. That was before I swore to God that I'd never touch another.

"What can I get you, darl'?" the barmaid asks finally, our regional accent riding her words smooth as silk and pleasing as bird song to the ear.

She's a petite woman, delicate as fine china and aged beyond her years (although I suspect she's around forty). Her eyes are a dull green, glazed like frosted glass and carrying the accumulated sorrow of a hard life without purpose. Her mousy hair has begun to gray and her skin is thin and discolored like old wallpaper stained with cigarette smoke, as though she just stepped from an old sepia photograph. Probably, I think to myself, she was quite beautiful once. Likely she never thought it would fade.

"Two pints of Stone's please, pet," I say, and the barmaid nods dutifully.

Leaning against the bar top, which is sticky and scarred, running in a horseshoe shape and filling the center of the room, I spectate the crowd of familiar strangers. They're mostly men, mostly older, and each of them probably born within a stone's throw of this place. They all remind me of my father in some way. That's one of the comforts, the familiarity. But tonight there's something different.

It's January and dark out. The air beyond the stone walls is frigid, the icy nip promising snow. But it isn't the weather that has things unsettled; it's the war. At first it seemed just another far off drama, one of those things that the state media uses to keep you hooked to their teat and that everyone talks about at work for weeks on end, picking the right side so as to masturbate their ego. Thing is, it never died down like the rest; it grew. Now the conscription has started and young men in England are being called up like the French were a week back and like the Scots will soon enough as the neutrality of their newfound republic wanes.

Already there've been funerals. One of those neighbors whose name you never bothered to learn finding out their son had been killed. There's been violence in the streets from those refusing the draft too. London is back under control but the fires of Birmingham have been glowing red as hell for days now. I'd have gotten in on the defiance myself perhaps, except the demographics weren't really what I'd hoped for. While the young, working-class, English lads march off to get massacred, the rest stay behind and fight in the streets.

The whole thing has changed the mood of the country. Suddenly there's this persistent foreboding like we've seen dark clouds on the horizon. All of that childish irony and foolishness that had characterized us has gone, replaced with threatening reality as though the English had been a child playing with a match and now the curtains have gone up in flames and we don't know what to do. It all promises to end in tears—that much is certain.

The barmaid returns with my drinks. "12.40 please, darl'," she says. I sigh, it seeming as though the inflation is racing the taxes towards driving every pleasure out of life. I hand over fifteen and tell her to keep the change. She seems shocked to see cash and sets down the electronic reader, but the tip breaks a faint smile of appreciation over her thin lips all the same.

Walking back to the table I can feel the sympathetic eyes following me as though I were ascending the gallows steps. In their minds I'm a hero, and already dead. They, the older folk, feel for me and every other young man of conscription age. The eldest among them can recall the few words their own fathers and grandfathers uttered on the subject. "Such a terrible waste," they say to one another over their pints as I pass. Yet there's no doubt in their minds that I must go. It's my civic duty to protect England's freedom, whatever that might mean.

And if I told them I wasn't going? Hate, pure as it comes. They'd call me a traitor and spit red-faced scorn all over me because it's easier than facing the truth. England's fatal blow was dealt long ago, and on their watch. Now she's got about as much substance as a shopping center and the charm of Broadmoor, but behind the thin veil of drugged up shoppers wearing dipshit smiles rests horror like you wouldn't believe, glimpsed by a few who can't close their eyes to it, like myself. The truth is I am a traitor to this, whatever this is. It's my obligation. If I stayed loyal to England now, if I fought when I was asked, I'd be excusing all of the evil that has been done to us.

George is in denial, excusing the evil, although I doubt he sees it that way. He's at our table in the nook, sitting beneath the stained glass window through which the unholy yellow light of the solar street lamp twinkles. He's a big chap with wide shoulders, solid looking and with cheekbones that each look to be made of stone axe heads. He's brooding, huffed because of our argument, twirling a flightless dart between the thumb and index finger of his large right hand. We'd both like to leave the dispute behind, but it can't be done.

I set the drinks down and take a seat across the table from him. He doesn't look up, doesn't say a thing; he just sits there twirling the dart and making pinprick holes in the varnish.

"You still riding that Royal Enfield?" he asks finally.

"I am," I say and sip at the cool pint.

"I was thinking of getting one myself for a while, price of fuel being what it is. I don't think Becky would go for it though." Becky is the harlot who's inexplicably had her claws in him for several years now, and I choose to ignore the mention of her name.

"You won't need one, not if you're going to war," I remind him.

"English bikes, aren't they?" he asks, ignoring my point and looking up from below the ridge of his brow.

"Indian, mate. Have been for some time," I reply. George tuts and rolls his eyes until they're back on the dart.

I'd thought he had more sense. For years he and I have seen eye to eye. Of my few friends he was the one I thought I'd never have to worry about. Then that bastard letter came, straight from hell, his call up papers. I can still see them sticking from his breast pocket now, and he turns up here this evening and tells me he's going, off to kill and die for nothing at all as though I'd be proud of him, eager to join even.

George raises his eyes again and looks over my shoulder. I turn. The gents on the dartboard should be finishing up soon. The fatter of the two, the one with a pink face and missing finger on his throwing hand, chucks his second arrow, which lands better than the first, nailing the treble nineteen, which pleases him. But it isn't the game that has George's attention; it's the TV screen above, the media showing scenes from Lublin, or at least what remains of her.

"Why are you going?" I ask George flatly. He shrugs.

"I've been called up. What else can I do?"

"Refuse."

"What, like those pink-haired fucks and ungrateful immigrants? Not a chance. It's cowardly," he scoffs, leveling a cold stare at me so that there can be no mistaking what he thinks of my decision.

“I disagree,” I reply. George sits back slowly, the chair groaning beneath his weight. Placing the spike of the dart in his mouth, he studies me.

“Go on,” he says, the judging eyes still as those of some taxidermied lion.

I breathe long and slow as I feel that tightness in my chest again. I have to be careful; George’s life may depend on it. Our friendship does, without a doubt.

“I’m done trying to convince you, George,” I say finally, stopping to take a drink before carrying on. “I’ll just give you my reasoning because it’s important to me that you understand. It’s all I can do.”

George nods slowly, and so I go on. “How long have we known one another?”

He takes a moment to think.

“Best part of twenty-five years, I reckon.”

“Long time.”

George nods again, and something about the face reminds me of him as a child, and then I see him dead and frozen in Lublin or some other city neither of us had heard of a month ago and my throat catches a little.

“Well then, I hope that you know I’m not a coward; at least I don’t think that I am.”

My friend sits forward and rests his arms on the table, the letter peaking a little more from his jacket.

“Then why not go?”

“Because, George, I don’t have a nation to fight for,” I reply earnestly. Thankfully, George seems to catch my drift but says nothing. Instead he looks at me, as though waiting for clarification.

Our entire lives young Englishmen like George and myself have been denied a home in which to take pride. We have pined for England, that stolen birthright. Some of us without even realizing it. From the time of our earliest school days we were made to know that she was not ours and that the calloused hands of our ancestors who built her counted for nothing after all (as though they had not done so for us and us alone). Everyone was English, and so nobody was. The land was not special. It was a patch, an economic zone and nothing more. I couldn’t fight for that if I tried; it would be like going to war for Tesco or Amazon. I tell George as much and I’m hoping he understands. Surely he’s seen what’s been in front of his nose all these years.

“I don’t mean to sound defeatist, but that’s how I see it, George,” I say. I’m uncomfortable. For the first time to my recollection, I’ve admitted out loud that I am without a home, a nationalist without a nation.

“Quietly into the night. Is that it?” George scoffs contemptuously. I can understand why, if he thinks I’ve given up. I shake my head.

“No, but I won’t kill to save face, or die because them who’ve robbed me tell me to. If they want nowhere men, if they want consumers, a spineless herd or citizen of the world, well, that's what they'll get. They can't claim the man in me now by waving the Union flag in my face. They've caused this mess; let their sons die fixing it."

"Our great grandfathers went," George says.

"Where was yours?" I ask.

"Normandy."

"One of mine was in Burma. The other one was a sailor. I don't think they'd have gone if they could see what's become of England, George. Do you? I don't imagine they'd be too proud of us either; six days a week in a megacorp, tracked everywhere we go, and more attention paid to Netflix than Rotherham, probably wasn't what they had in mind for us. And don't get me started on London, or the rest."

George doesn't reply. He can't. Patriotic delusions to dead lands can't withstand scrutiny. Perhaps I should have left it there, but I don't.

"Look, if those fuckers are coming over the channel, then I'll fight. Until then, no," I say. I think I'd had him until that point. Something about the image of foreign hordes coming over the water, landing on the isle and without a passport between them, it seems to dilate the jet black pupils of George's eyes. You could almost hear his heart beating "Rule Britannia."

"Well, if that's the way you see it," he nods firmly, "but I'm going," he declares decisively. My brow furrows as though pulled by an invisible thread weighted by my dropping jaw.

"Look!" I snap desperately, "I wasn't saying 'give up,' but there are other ways."

"And you feel free to pursue them, but for me, I'm going to do my duty."

"DUTY!" I cry, swallowing back the insulting string of slurs that try to follow. Exasperated I slump back in my chair and shake my head. *Perhaps there's no hope,* I wonder. *Maybe he's given up and this is suicide without the stigma.*

Rising from the seat I step away from the table but stop to say one final piece.

"Look, you want to go, I can't stop you. But don't pretend that you're following in your great grandfather's footsteps. He had everything we didn't. Know what he had?"

"What?" George asks bitterly.

"Children. If you go out there, George, if you die, it'll be like you never existed; you'll be gone and forgotten like smoke in the wind."

For a moment I watch him, making sure that he's heard what I was saying. He seems to understand and so I say I'm going for a smoke and leave him to think things over at the table.

I promised God that I'd never weaken myself with cigarettes again, and I've been true to that word, but cigars were never discussed. Around the back of the horseshoe bar, by the pool table, there's an exit leading to an alley. I step out, pulling my donkey jacket tight against the cold and lifting the collar. The alley is unlit save for the glow from the pub window. I can see snow beginning to fall in thick flakes now, ready to blanket the dry ground as the air bites at my exposed flesh. Inside I can hear the music and laughter, and on the road the occasional car passes. Otherwise all seems still and calm. I revel in the solitude.

From the pocket of my jacket I remove the silver cigarette case. On the plate, worn but still legible, the letters H.E.D., my great grandfather's initials. Inside are several knobbled cheroots, the tobacco grown and rolled by my own hand. I've heard it said that I'm an old soul. I take that to mean I didn't go mad with the rest, although in truth I did for a while, though I found my way again. Besides the tobacco I grow vegetables. I also keep a few chickens and brew my own beer. There's a son on the way too, so I can't complain.

Removing one of the thin cigars I strike a match and draw the creamy smoke into my mouth. *That's how it's done,* I remind myself. *A strong home and a strong family, that's your nation. Forget those sinister suits in number 10.* Leaning against the wall I look up to the coal black sky and the falling snow. Now the idea of dying for this sorry excuse for a country really does feel stupid, but I understand. George doesn't have a family, and a man needs something to die for, I think.

I take my time to smoke. When I'm finished I step back inside to the warmth and the rumbling chatter, the mourners' eyes on me and the whiff of piss and urinal cakes wafting from the bathroom. The dartboard is free now. Back at the nook I catch George scratching something into the surface of the table with his arrow. He's paid his pint some attention now, drank half while I've been gone, and as I approach he looks up at me, the hostile scowl washed away by a soft gratuitousness.

"You okay?" I ask. George nods.

"She'll not have kids. She says that she wants them eventually but..." George frowns and shakes his head.

"She's a modern girl, George. She's bothered about work and two for one cocktails, how many likes she can get on a selfie, that sort of thing. You're just an accessory to distract her. A cat could take your place in that relationship, and one probably will one day."

"Are you worried about becoming a dad?"

"Not really. I worry for the future, but what generation hasn't? I'm excited," I say, and George and I both smile.

"I want children."

"I know. Can't do it if you're being shot at or dead," I say, sorry to return to the lecture but unable to escape it.

George doesn't speak. Instead he stares through me, nodding slowly. It's enough. We're friends but really it comes closer to brotherhood. Without a word spoken I can tell he's reconsidered, that he'll see sense in time and perhaps find a little hope. I couldn't stop the war, or save the rest, but I can keep my brother's blood from spilling for nothing. It's a small victory in the grander scheme, but one I'll take.

"Come on," I say, "dartboard's free."

George takes his darts case and pint and stands. On the table, scratched into the oak, the declaration that "George was here!"

May he be for many more years.

May England live long upon the breath of his sons.

The Tale of Auroch: A Fable

J. Michael Kearney

Cattle die, kindred die,
Every man is mortal:
But I know one thing that never dies,
The glory of the great dead.
(Havamal 77, Auden)

You know this story. It was in the beginning of all things, when God formed the Sun and Moon and Stars, and beneath them made the world, and in it and on it he placed sea creatures and birds and beasts of the land. There were some that were strong, some that were swift, some smart, and some of great size. To give all these creatures order, God made for them a ruler, and he called the ruler Man. He made Man in his own likeness, because God is the ruler of all things.

But Man loved to rule too much and grew arrogant and defied his own ruler. He was cast out from his realm of Eden, into the wilderness to survive on his own strength and smarts—but the beasts of the land still trusted him and were ruled by him, and he knew their needs and their quarrels, and he helped them.

But Man was not alone: there were great creatures who lived before the Earth was formed, and they saw that Men had daughters, and together they made monsters and giants, creatures called Nephilim, and the sons of Men were so frightened and impressed that they worshipped the Nephilim and called them gods, and the Earth was ruled by these half- breeds.

God looked at this Earth, and He saw that it was not as He had made it to be. He decided to destroy it and begin again. So God found the only man who refused to worship the Nephilim and worshipped only God. He had learned the stories of his ancestors and knew why he did not live in Eden. Noah was everything God had wanted Man to be, and God told him his plans to destroy the world. He told Noah to help him make the world again: all this you already know… and now you will hear about something you do not know.

Now, it is important to know that after he fell, Man pleased God by making sacrifices—and some animals made good sacrifices, like cows and sheep and chickens and doves, and some did not. God told Noah to bring seven of all the animals he could sacrifice, and two of all the animals he could not and to place them all in an Ark.

So Noah gathered animals of all kinds: he gathered the swiftest and the strongest and the largest, and among the strongest and largest of all animals was mighty Auroch the bull, and Noah took him and his wife upon the Ark.

And it rained.

And rained.

And it rained until the whole Earth was covered in water and everything that could not breathe under the water was dead. And then, one day, it stopped.

When the Ark had come to rest on a high mountain, Noah released the animals to go make the world new—but he kept those he could sacrifice to God. The animals knew why he had kept them, and knew it was their purpose, so they were content.

But Auroch was not. He knew he had survived because Noah had seen his size and strength, and he did not wish to be a sacrifice, even to God, because his spirit was wild.

So Auroch went to Noah, as animals used to do in those days, to convince Noah to let him go. "You will kill me and offer me to God," he said. "Because I am so large and so powerful, you think I will make a great sacrifice." Noah congratulated the bull on his intelligence.

"But you have not thought of my people," Auroch continued, "and how they will live in this new world. Will I not do better by siring many children as strong and great as I am, and they will better be able to defend themselves against those who seek to kill them?"

And Noah, like Man had been meant to do, listened to Auroch and considered his argument, and in the end decided that although he knew his motives were not pure, he was nevertheless correct.

"You are right," Noah said. "In this new world, you will be few in number, and your children will need strength."

"But, Auroch," he said, "I see your heart, and I know you have fear and arrogance in it. Fear of death, not fear of God. You are wild, and so you will live in the wild, as my ancestors did when we acted out of arrogance."

So, he sent Auroch and his wife far into the North, where his son Japheth would later go to conquer and settle with his own children. God saw what Noah had done, and he knew Noah had judged rightly, but he also knew Auroch was not the only animal whose heart had become wild while men fell into worshipping the Nephilim and had not ruled the animals as they should have. He therefore separated men from animals and gave Noah and his sons permission to eat the flesh of animals as meat and taught Noah and his sons to hunt and fish.

Then the animals stopped seeking help from men and lived on their own accord, and Auroch and his family, too, ran away from Japheth and his family.

And Auroch had many, many children, and they filled the forests and the wilderness of Europe. Auroch grew old and died, but before he did, he taught all of his children and grandchildren about Noah and the Flood and how men and animals had lived when he was a calf.

After that, the children of Auroch roamed free in the wilderness, but without the help of men, they fell prey to fights and hunting-beasts like the great bears and dire wolves and massive cats of those ancient days. One day, they decided they had enough of this living, and they gathered together in a great meeting of the cattle of the world.

At this meeting, some of the children of Auroch argued that their ancestor Auroch had told them of a time when men were made to rule animals and help them in their disputes and fights. They should therefore go to men and ask for protection from the bears and wolves. But another group of the children of Auroch, who had inherited his wild heart, said they would never be ruled by the children of Noah who had driven their ancestor into the wild.

And a great fight erupted, and bulls locked horns and fought and struggled, until at last the eldest of all the children of Auroch bellowed above the noise.

"There is no way to resolve this fight except by spilling blood! Haven't enough of us died, killed by wolves and bears and cats? Let us all live—let those who wish to go to man go—and see how they fare. Those who wish to live as we have always lived can follow me, return to the wilderness, and survive from strength and smarts, just as man had done when he was cast out by God."

And he disappeared into the woods, and half of the children of Auroch followed him and the others went to men, to the sons of Japheth, and asked for their protection. Men, though, had grown shrewd and wily in the days after Noah and his sons had died and demanded a trade for this protection.

The children of Auroch asked what men needed, and the men said, "We need food to feed ourselves and our children, so we can fulfil God's command to multiply and subdue the Earth."

The children of Auroch thought about this and spoke among themselves, and then at last they said, "Then we will give you milk to drink, and you may make food from it, called cheese, and just as we once were given to God in sacrifice, we will permit you to choose from our number to take as food."

"But," they insisted, "for this you will guarantee our safety from all our enemies, and that we will always have food to eat and water to drink and places to sleep and care for our own children!"

Men accepted, and these children of Auroch became cattle and are now these cows and bulls raised by farmers all over the world. But the wild children of Auroch refused the name of Cattle and called themselves *Aurochs* after their ancestor and menaced man's fields and flocks and homes. Men began to hunt them, and as they hunted them, the Aurochs grew wilder and fled further and further away.

Men chased after them, until at last there was only one. That last Aurochs was hunted and felled in the East of Europe. When he fell, men and cattle alike mourned him, and the cattle lowed a sad song:

We cattle will live on, safe and calm
Under watchful eye and soothing palm
But who will know us when we are gone?

Auroch! Wild your spirit, untamed and bold
Remember, you cattle, your sire of old:
Live forever, great Auroch, mightiest of bulls!

First Words

Ludwig L

Son, it's going to go something like this: you're going to emerge headfirst, your skull still loose tectonic plates and your eyes almost useless. You'll have no hand-to-eye coordination, no motor skills to speak of, and not a balanced bone in your body. Forget trying to find your bearings or do any kind of reconnaissance. You won't have time for that: as soon as you're out, a large man in a white coat will cut you loose and you will be transferred to an adult-sized woman on a bed, the same woman who hosted you, fed you, and kept you warm for nine months consecutive. She's your mother, so be nice. If she weeps on your face, if she briefly cuts the flow of air to your lungs, just take it. It's called love. In time, you'll understand what that means, you'll understand that there is nothing else like it, that it is possibly the only thing that makes sense in this crazy, upside-down world.

So here we go: once you're out, first thing you do is make a fist—go on! It'll be the size of a plum and about that soft, but it doesn't matter, it's symbolic and it'll feel good. Once you've done that, push out a long, sharp cry. With all these giants manhandling you, you'll need to put your foot down one way or the other. Just shriek your lungs out, I promise it'll feel good. Besides, your voice will fill the surrounding void and it will give you a sense of the dimensions and emptiness of this place, your new home. This is when I will call back at you. This is when you will hear me for the first time. I'm your dad. I'm here to guide you and get you on your feet. I'm here to make sure that your first stumbles are not injurious, that your first scrapes do not go south, and I'm here to make sure that, as long I have breath in my lungs, the world's demons do not come anywhere near you.

If you are anything like me, you will feel a strange mixture of joy and consternation in these first moments. You will feel free and liberated, but at the same time, it will all seem a bit menacing and mysterious. That's ok. At thirty-five, it still feels that way to me. Don't worry, I'll be right there.

Now, a note of warning: one of the first things you'll experience—if not *the* first thing—is pain: the sting of light in your eyes or that choking feeling when fluid runs down the wrong tube. Take it in. It's all valid. Any experience—giants fondling your feet; the smell of fetid breath on your face—is valid. A spit bubble is experience, laughter is experience, but so too is chickenpox or a thump to the head. Some experience you'll receive free of charge. Some, alas, will be inflicted on you unsolicited. In all events be patient; it comes slowly. At least, it will seem that way until it all comes too fast. I'm here to make sure it reaches you in a way that you can handle and assimilate. So if I hold you back from time to time, you'll know why. Once you've seen how this place works, and the traps that have been laid out for you, you may even thank me for it.

And now, on to the most important thing: Congratulations! You have started on the road to truth, son! You will start to understand things now; you will acquire knowledge. You will discover that there are appearances—things said, written, or pretended—and there is truth; the two are not always the same. Often they are not. I'm running ahead of myself, I know, and we will talk about this again, many times, but I wanted to mention it right from the start. Before you can apprehend truth, you must observe. That is where you will begin. Thankfully nature has so rigged things that it is also in these early days that your eyes will clear up from the amphibian fog that has been with you for over nine months. These eyes are your most important tool, son. Use them. Look! I will often say this to you. Look! See what lies before you and take it in. This is more important than what you are told and, for the most part, even what you think. Use your eyes. What you see is what you see. Never forget that. Men will try to tell you all manner of bunk, but before anything, look, and then draw your own conclusions.

Well, you don't need to worry too much about "conclusions." That will come later. For now, use your eyes and behold the wonders of the world: cumulus clouds, the human body, the spectrum of colors, the night's constellations. You will be peering through these peepholes an awful lot, only closing them to sleep or shut-out insects and particles incoming. You will be amazed a hundred-fold before you become blasé. You will not comprehend what you have just tapped into. You will feel exalted, if not a bit divine.

These will be your wonder years. Enjoy them because they are few in number. Before you know it, you will commence twelve years of state-mandated training in reading, writing and arithmetic—we will try to avoid that; we will do as much of that at home, I promise—and before the age of ten you will have suffered a few minor indignities. Perhaps you will be bullied. You will certainly be insulted more than a few times. This too is experience. Just get through it. Fight it with everything you've got. I will be right there behind you all the way.

In the following phase you will be, shall we say, exploring; you will start to go off on your own to test everything you think you know. Alone and with others, mostly with others, although perhaps not always with the right people. Some of them you will call your friends, only to discover in time that they are no such thing. Believe it or not, but you will learn a lot from these false friends. Not directly—you will learn nothing from them directly—but they will help you understand what a true friend is, and that is a valuable lesson on its own. Your friends are your fortress. Your friends can breathe life back into you when you're on the ground and, shall we say, on your last breath. If you do not have friends in life, son, you will not make it. Learn that. Learn that quickly.

This is also the time when your voice will start to break and your body will throb with impulses. Your mind will at times be obsessed with one thing or another: girls, certainly, will be one of those. While we are on the subject: if at some stage you find yourself crying for help from the bottom of the shallow ditch called teenage love, forgive me if I don't come to the rescue. That too will be part of your experience.

Then, suddenly, before you know it, you will be a man. I will be much older then, and at this point it is I who will be looking up to you for wisdom, son. By then this world might have slipped out of my grip quite entirely. I will help you up to this point. I will teach you everything I know. I will learn things just to teach you. All of that I will do. But understanding this world and where it is going, well, at some point, I will hand that over to you, and it will be for you to tell me and to tell your own children. You will guide us, as I will guide you now.

You can forget everything I've told if you remember only this: What I said about your mom and love; that is the most important thing we can teach you. Live with love in your heart, son. You do that and that same love will live outside of you and all around you wherever you go. It will bring order and peace in this world, which—you will soon find out—needs so much of it.

I welcome you, my son. We are here for you.

Your Father

Altar Angel

Nathaniel Lucas

The rod of gold has faded out again. It is all I know of night and day in unit 1002, hovering as I have since Anno Domini 1858, when Father O'Riordan called me down with fanfare to Christ's altar in front of a capacity crowd in the Lady Chapel of Saint Chad's, Chisholmwell. The view was great in those early years, majestic, all the apostles gleaming in their windows, and the stream of penitents and daily communicants. For well over a century I patrolled this altar.

Several times I had to scare away some dodgy characters with banging on the window (sorry, St. Bartholomew!). One couple had even undressed in preparation for a desecration that I could not allow. I started the organ playing Bach's toccata, and I don't know what the vicar thought of the red pumps he found the next morning. Other angels look askance at human interaction, but in extremis it is allowed. A full incident report is filed with Archangel Michael. Once I saved the tabernacle from falling in an earthquake.

Despite remaining here for all those years, never venturing beyond the nave and sanctuary, I have my ways of knowing the ways of men. Snippets of chat after Mass, the many vicars' few expressions. Saint Chad's, Chisholmwell fell into decrepitude. The young, it seemed, no longer cared for themselves or Creation or their Lord. And the little children I knew grew up and went above and the place was decommissioned, deconsecrated by an old Archbishop and the parish merged with Saint Cuthbert's down the road.

But they forgot to say the prayers that would have loosed me, and I'm a stickler for the rules. That's how God made me. My altar was sent to unit 1002. Mrs. Fairbanks covered up our Lord's resting place with boxes full of books. The place where once a day, or sometimes twice, since 1858 the Lord of All appears on earth. Forgive her Lord. Amen. They placed the two angel candlesticks, which by the way look nothing like me, on the floor, surrounded by the robes and cassocks and paraphernalia that Saint Cuthbert's had no use for.

I admit it is a bit pointless, staying here. No not just a bit, entirely so. But those are my vows. In the dusk, cluttered with stale elastic, mothy smells, the presence that makes my presence presses in, warmly pressurizes unit 1002 with His charge and the smallest speck of powder and stalest plastic lives, and upward through soiled cassocks to me, the storage complex, Saint Chad's decommissioned steeple-top, and the still-veiled stars He suffuses.

Michael comes to visit once a decade. He says God is working on the problem but can't promise anything at the moment. Men and their ways obstruct His will. I could go rogue and leave, but the work is necessary even here. The demons prowl, infesting unit 1002, thousands upon thousands of neglectful souls, jealous of the good, wary of my flaming sword. And what does an angel have but his word?

When the golden rod is lit, I hear voices outside unit 1002. An auction. It sells for $275 then the voices move on. The next day the door rolls up and the light streams in like a flash of beatific vision. They pile the boxes of books away and I rejoice to see that sacred spot freed once more. They load the altar onto the bed of a truck and me with it. Some demons follow half-heartedly along the road, but they trail away as they despise the light. To think I have not been outside for more than one hundred years! We enter a yard where piled up are heaps of scrap wood, broken chairs and tables. It is not so bad and the men who work here look in need of Our Lord.

Then the crack and the buzz, like what some crazed demons do with their gnashing of teeth. It's a machine at the end of the yard, and the wood gets fed in and ground up. I contemplate giving the men torn ligaments or pulled fingers to stop this madness, this desecration, but while I could, I cannot. A wrong is wrong; I would become a demon. The Lord will tolerate no tormenting for His sake. O Father O'Riordan, this is the end of the assignment God through you gave me. I fix my gaze on that lovely haunting place, then into the pile of particles, into the sparkling blades, and out and up into the heavenly realms again. Have I failed? Lord, forgive them. Amen.

The Barricade

Ndabaningi

He couldn't recall what he'd been drinking at the *braai* all those months ago. It didn't matter, but he focused on trying to remember; it was a way of drawing his own attention away from the uncomfortable thought that, whatever it had been, there'd been too much of it. He looked across at his acquaintance, now talking to one of the others in his always-intense way, and shrugged.

It was colder now. The sun was still enlivening the western sky, projecting color and life over the distant mountains, but as soon as it had dipped below the line of sight, the cold had rushed in. He shifted in the shell of his greatcoat and blew a stream of foggy breath into the evening air.

The lockdowns had changed many things and stood to change a whole lot more. But he felt "over it." The State of… State of… What had the government… the *useless buggers* called it…? "Catastrophe"? "Calamity"? not "Emergency…" At this moment he couldn't remember and couldn't care. He was over it. "Disaster." That was it. Another childlike, simplistic way of seeing things. Typical. The present fun and games would change a whole lot of things too. People, bombarded as ever by the lying press, the massed ranks of opinion makers, the useless bloody ticks clustering on social media, would be guided back into the fold. No, it would be a number of "folds"—one more detrimental than the next. Some would quietly start packing their bags, hopelessly unable to express what they knew to be true, oppressed by the feeling of facing a void, living in an Africa they could no longer even pretend held a future for them. Among them would be the realists who had just looked away for twenty-seven years—kept their heads down, got on with it. Others had deluded themselves and had suddenly, rudely, unpleasantly awoken. And, of course, there would be yet others eagerly guzzling down another helping of Rainbow Nation twaddle. "Unity!", "diversity!", "we all stood together" when faced by this "threat to our Democracy." They would invoke the memory of Madiba, the Great Nelson Mandela, who'd taught us all to live together, who'd overcome our "dark history," etc., etc. The pabulum of platitudes would be stirred and served, a congealed porridge, sour enough for those willing to trust their own taste, wolfed down unthinkingly by all too many more. Frank smiled. He was tired and amused by the tumbling imagery. Tonight, none of that mattered. Tonight was a glorious vindication. And there, standing across the road, at the other end of the barricade, now talking to a young, bearded Indian with an American rifle casually propped up between them, was the short, stocky embodiment of that little victory.

The *braai* had been the same as most he'd attended over the years. Young families from the surrounding farms had come together to celebrate something, a handful of guys from the local village, some from further afield, joining in. Perhaps it had been a public holiday—one of the many strewn across the calendar to celebrate the new order ushered in back in '94. They mostly had vaguely communist origins—Workers' Day, Women's Day, Youth Day—and Whites didn't take them seriously, not even liberal ones. It was an excuse to get together, have a few drinks, and, if you farmed or owned a business, forget how many of your African employees were at that very moment getting properly *dagiwe* on your dollar and working up towards a week of absenteeism or, if you were less fortunate, to crashing your tractor and damaging your equipment irreparably. Had it been a sporting weekend? Were the Sharks playing? The Springboks? That was always a serious matter. In any event, it had been a good day. *Wors* and steak, chops and rashers grilled by the men, helpings of *paptert* and an array of "modern" salads prepared by wives and girlfriends had been the order of things—with plenty of banter and joking around, all washed down with cold beer. Then the brandy came out—*Klippies, Ricky Louw*—and the shooters—*Jaggies, mampoer*. He didn't remember what he'd been drinking exactly, nor how much. But he did remember when the wheels came off. One shallow, foolish, insufferable, accepted truth too many had set him off. He'd been talking to a younger woman about current affairs and the state of the country. She was pretty, but he'd put that sort of thing aside as he became more engrossed with the subject. She had been receptive enough, surprisingly so, given her age and urban background and the fact that she was a student at one of the liberal universities (*were there any that weren't liberal...? Not in South Africa*). They had started discussing the absolute inversion of truth peddled, disseminated, reinforced constantly by the media. "Lies" was a hopelessly mild, almost meaningless understatement to describe the dark, evil miasma rolling from the presses, buzzing across the airwaves, flickering on millions of screens. They had explored a number of recent cases where the vaunted "fourth estate" had contrived to convey the exact opposite of what had happened or, having failed to do so, had marshalled the facts and subsequent opinion to such an extent that it had over time amounted to the same thing.

Inversion. From there they had explored some of the shibboleths that had so insidiously wormed their way into the very fabric of South Africans' thinking and being. Racism, the "troubled past," a "history of discrimination," exclusion.... And so the conversation had ultimately circled back, like a path across the hills of Natal, to the greatest of them all. The Great Idol, the Golden Calf, the Holiest of

Holy Cows. The Saint, the Living Ancestor (now sadly deceased, so sorely missed): Lord Mandela. Madiba and his "Madiba Magic." Frank was old enough and aware enough to remember how it had happened, how an obscure terrorist, whose face no one had seen in two decades, had walked into the limelight and had been transformed, instantly, into a global "icon." Years later he'd watched a documentary. He'd heard (again) an American narrator following the tall, yellow-complexioned man walking from that minimum security prison-in-name-only holding the hand of his murderous wife (so murderous her most ardent leftist adherents had ultimately failed to rehabilitate her). He remembered how, by the end of that choreographed walk, that stilted figure, that terrorist-slash-nobody, had become a "statesman," how that word, "statesman," had been seeded into his consciousness. And he'd witnessed how, over the years, the stature of that man had been raised to godlike heights. He remembered how his own kinsmen, his people, had been conned into voting Yes in a stage-managed referendum and how, ultimately, they had been fooled into loving the man. And this particular man, even after having been so generously released after having only served time for a capital offence, a *hanging* offence, still sang of murdering them, the Whites on live TV—in his vernacular (Xhosa), which the press had, rather remarkably, not translated. And he'd always been suspicious. He had known. He understood Mandela's vernacular. It was close enough to the Zulu he'd heard and spoken since childhood. The absolute bloody chutzpah! Worthy indeed of that golem's master. Astonishingly the girl was nodding along, agreeing.

She'd occasionally interject with an example of her own, an example of some particularly egregious fawning idolatry. And, it was at exactly this moment that Brandon van Heerden, the short, stocky braggart, had interrupted him. It hadn't cramped his style. It hadn't ruined his chances with the girl; that was no longer the point. It was what he'd said. *Mandela saved us from civil war....* Looking back, he wasn't sure exactly why that had set him off, triggered him to the extent that it did. It was, after all, just the usual bog-standard, boilerplate guff one heard every day in South Africa or wherever South Africa was discussed. Perhaps it had been the Covid thing—the lockdowns, the isolation, the barrage of circus-worthy media froth. It had certainly had an effect on everyone's "mental health." The booze had definitely played its part, particularly the *mampoer*. Proper karate juice, that. But, more likely it was maybe the fact that it was coming from a successful farmer, someone who ought to know better.

Someone who actually did know better. Brandon didn't care if people called him a racist; he merely always described what he saw and experienced in his daily life. He was no race-blind ignoramus. He wasn't shy about his "lived experience." He certainly spoke out against all the vaccine nonsense—not a *donder* was he going to have a stupid jab for a mild variant of some disease that posed no threat to someone of his age and relative health. He'd loudly proclaimed that he didn't care what people called him and lifted his sleeve to show childhood vaccine scars; he was hardly a "tinfoil hat anti-vaxxer" but couldn't give a toss if people called him one. In short, he'd always seemed to Frank to be an independent thinker. And yet, there he was mindlessly spouting the received wisdom, repeating the narrative. In any event, it had ended with a lot of shouting and some shoving. Luckily some of the lads had intervened before it could escalate into something more serious, something irreparable with bridges burned and years of bad blood. But it had left a bad taste in his mouth nonetheless. Being called a conspiracy theorist, paranoid for not believing the press, had not really bothered him. Hearing the nonsense for the umpteenth time, "*it's not all about race*," "*they're not all like that*," etc., etc. was just par for the course. What he had found troubling was the thought that van Heerden *did* believe the press, that he *had* in fact internalized the lies. And, if that were true of someone in his position, what hope was there for the rest of the people? What about younger people who had been exposed to the propaganda all their lives? What about people who had limited experience of the real Africa, who only interacted with urbane, White-presenting, fellow citizens? What about townies?

Today all of that had changed. All of that nonsense had dissipated like the fog of breath in the cold air. Reality had intruded as it always, inevitably, did. He smiled to himself, noticed that van Heerden was looking at him and gave him a thumbs up. The shorter man grinned and returned the gesture. On this day, the 9th of July 2021, the province of KwaZulu-Natal had exploded into an orgy of looting and destruction. And, yes, it was all about race. Race and tribe. Zulus, riled up initially to support the ex-president who was facing jail time for contempt of court, had used the impetus to rampage across the province. *Not all Zulus*, of course, but Zulus nonetheless and *only Zulus*. The police, most of whom were Zulus, did nothing. They stood down and allowed the mobs to plunder and destroy unimpeded. And then something else happened, something remarkable. Groups of citizens spontaneously came together to defend life and property. Groups had *collectively* faced the challenge, collectively for the first time in twenty-seven years. And, yes, it was all about race. Race and tribe. Whites and their Indian allies had come together to set up barricades and roadblocks to fend off the mindless, rampaging crowds. Frank and Brandon had arrived almost simultaneously at a shopping center on the outskirts of the nearest town. Behind them smoke rose from downtown; it was too late to do anything about that, but a group was gathering to make sure the tide went no further. What they were going to do about it was the subject of animated discussion. There were twenty of them. They were mostly farmers and people working in the agricultural sector, and they were armed with shotguns and hunting rifles and a smattering of handguns. And then the

Indians arrived. Armed to the teeth. Kalashnikovs and AR-15s and any number of other automatic rifles were brought out. They hadn't forgotten the late 1940s when the Zulus had attacked the Indian community, killing men, women, and children. *Let Whitey forget, let Whitey believe in the Rainbow Nation, let Whitey allow himself to be disarmed.* They knew their own history; they passed things on from generation to generation. They weren't about to be caught out. And while they were still talking, discussing strategy, the horde had arrived. Noisily emerging from the railway bridge tunnel to the north, the looters began loping towards the center in groups that grew in number before their eyes. Frank and the others took up their positions, and as the masses came into range the Whites exchanged glances. *Who would fire first? Who risked being destroyed in the media? Who would have their life ruined as a "violent racist vigilante"?* The Indians looked out over the hastily thrown up barrier of tires and shopping carts and...began to fire. They had not been portrayed as evil perpetrators for decades. They had not been relentlessly psychologically attacked since 1990. They were unconstrained by self-doubts. They saw the threat before them and reacted. And then, just like that, something gave. Some tension suddenly broke. The White men rose to meet the attack. With the first explosion of buckshot a collective sigh of relief seemed to go out from them. They were free to act at last.

That first volley dispersed the rioters, and for the rest of the day the pattern had repeated itself there and, as it turned out, in countless other places. Things appeared to happen very quickly, and yet time paradoxically also seemed to stand still. By mid-afternoon scores of sturdier barricades and better, more strategically placed roadblocks had gone up. Attacks were "discouraged," prevented, and repulsed.

Looters were even ambushed and relieved of their ill-gotten gains; minibus taxis and other vehicles used in the commission of crimes were destroyed. The farmers had set up radio contact, and a steady flow of information helped co-ordinate defense efforts. Whites, Indians, and a handful of Africans, mostly non-Zulus, held the line. Citizens, acting collectively, came to do what the police and military simply could not.

And now, as night came on, Frank found time to reflect on the many vindications this day had brought. Vindications of what he knew, what he believed, what he'd always said, even, perhaps especially, what he'd drunkenly said at that braai all those months ago. Whites had legitimate interests in this country, as they did in others. Only acting collectively could Whites defend their interests. Collectively they could work with other people. Despite the Whites being painted as evil racists for thirty (forty?) years, Indians had instinctively turned to them and lent them their aid. They knew the Whites were their best bet and were more than willing to work with them. They had brought their greater firepower; the Whites had coordinated and led the efforts. The Narrative was bunk. The media were the enforcers of that narrative and would do anything to harm Whites. They were incentivized to do so, even when the individual journalists were unaware of it. Stories of perceived racism carried greater value than those covering real (mostly Black) crime, even crime of the most violent kind. Things had barely kicked off and a British online paper had already ginned up a piece about White "militias" being violent. Militias. A word never used in a South African context but poisoned in the eyes of international readers by the toxic efforts of the media reporting on American matters. He'd shown his comrades that particular article on his phone. They had shaken their heads and muttered angrily. Many biases had been confirmed for Frank on this day. Yes, it had been vindication after vindication. Victories, even. A day of victories.

Shortly before sundown a tall, lanky, White man had arrived. He'd lugged a number of heavy bags from his car and proceeded to set up a tripod. Van Heerden, short stocky Brandon van Heerden, had nonchalantly sauntered over and asked the man what he was doing. The man had smiled enthusiastically and said he was a journalist for a national outlet. Van Heerden had put a pudgy hand on his shoulder, smiled up at him and said: "You are going to pack up all your *kak* and *fôk* off. Right now. And if you pitch up at any of our other roadblocks the boys aren't going to be as friendly as me…"

Glossary

Braai	barbecue (Afrikaans)
Dagiwe	drunk (Zulu)
Wors	boerewors ('farmer's sausage'); traditional sausage, mostly in a coiled shape (Afrik.)
Paptert	side dish of baked porridge prepared from maize meal (Afrik.)
Klippies	Klipdrift brandy (slang)
Ricky Louw	Richelieu brandy (slang)
Jaggies	Jägermeister; imported German herbal liqueur (slang)
Mampoer	home-distilled fruit brandy; traditionally made from peaches (Afrik.)
Donder	thunder (Afrik.)
Kak	shit (Afrik.)
Fôk	… (Afrik.)
Ndabaningi	Nom du plume "(man) of many affairs/interests" (Zulu) Note: many Whites working in rural areas are given African nicknames

A Nice Denny's

Grant Norman

We had been driving for close to four hours when we decided to stop. We needed gas and food. The baby was awake and fussing, so she needed attention as well. Pulling off the highway, we followed a sign that had been visible from the highway, a two-for-one deal on a gas station and a Denny's. It was just a few minutes after two p.m., so our only companions at the gas station were a hatchback in front of the Denny's and a pickup truck. I helped my wife get the baby out of her car seat, and the two of them went inside while I filled up our gas tank.

The gas station wasn't quiet, not with the howl of the wind, the gurgle of my car filling up, and the annoying update on the latest internet trends that was being blared from the screen on the pump, a minute or two out of sync with the one next to the man filling up his pickup truck on the other side of my stall. Still, it felt good to stretch my legs and enjoy the fresh air, even if it was biting at the exposed skin of my face and hands. I wasn't able to enjoy it for too long before the gas stopped pumping and I got back into my car and parked three spots from the hatchback. I locked up and started towards the door, taking a brief look behind me at the flat land before going inside.

My wife was still changing the baby's diaper in the bathroom, so I walked through the glass door to the Denny's to get us a table. I was greeted by a woman in her early-to-mid fifties. She had tired eyes, but the corners of her smile were visible behind her mask as I walked up to her station. "How many will it be?" she asked me.

"Just three, well, two and a baby."

"Oh, a baby!" she said, and in an instant those tired eyes became bright and alert. "You'll be needing a high chair then, and a kid's menu. Let me get you set up, and then I'll grab those for you."

There wasn't anyone else in the Denny's except for a lone man sitting in a booth underneath the television set that he was watching in between bites of his burger. The hostess sat me down at a table kitty-corner to him and promised once more to be back with the chair and menus. My wife was done by then, and I waved her and our little girl over as soon as I saw them enter the restaurant. Holding the little one's hands, my wife led her in a series of wobbling little steps over to the table until they were close enough that I could pick her up. True to her word, the hostess had returned and immediately started cooing over our little family as she put down the chair.

"What a little darling!" she cried. She reached for our daughter, to ruffle her hair or pinch her cheeks, or something, but her hand stopped almost as soon as it had risen, and it fell impotently by her side.

I smiled at her, trying to convey some deeper understanding when I said, "Thank you very much."

Despite the restraints placed on her by the state and social convention, she lingered by our table. "How old is she?"

"Almost a year old," I said.

"And already so big! And with so much beautiful hair!"

Words came easy with this stranger, and I started to tell her about how we were on our way home after visiting family on the other side of the state, and how the relatives had been so happy to see our daughter and spoiled her rotten while we first-time parents got some much-needed rest. I only stopped when my wife asked a question about the food, how big the portions were for one of the items on the children's menu. Both the hostess and I smiled sheepishly, and she dutifully answered and left, with a promise to bring back some water hurled over her shoulder.

As I set up some of the Cheerios we had packed for the baby to eat, I thought about how nice this little interaction with a total stranger was after over a year of hiding behind closed doors and masks, or being cut off from people in the most elemental way. While the baby seized a handful of cereal in her hand and stuffed her overflowing prize into her mouth, I remarked to my wife, "She seems nice."

"She must be a grandma or an aunt," my wife replied without looking up from her menu's selection of soups.

"Yeah, something like that," I agreed and turned my attention to my own order.

We still needed a few minutes after the hostess returned with our waters, but she didn't leave us, not completely. Instead, she leaned up against the booth across from us, on the table of which rested a sheet of paper saying "Stop the Spread! Do Not Use!" She watched our family quietly while we deliberated. I asked her a question about one of the sandwiches I was considering, and she answered brightly. Then, we placed our orders, and she asked sweetly, "And what will the little angel be having today?"

At the sound of her voice, our little girl looked over her shoulder and up at her with big, awe-struck eyes, earning a big laugh from us adults. "She's definitely a people person," I said with a ruffle of her thin hair.

"Take it from me, sweetie, that can be a lot of fun or it can get you into a lot of trouble," the hostess responded with a laugh. Then she collected our menus and headed off to the kitchen with our orders scratched on a small notepad in the pocket of her apron.

After she brought our food, we ate quietly in our booth, savoring the chance to slow down and enjoy ourselves. The volume on the television was low, but I could still read the words ticking by on the bottom of the screen. A lone man had attacked the U.S. Capitol and killed a police officer, the story bracketed on either side by commercials for Applebee's and car insurance. It was very tempting to pull out my phone and to try and find out more, but before I could make that mistake, I looked across the table and saw my wife and child, engrossed in a meal and unaware of what was going on in a faraway city to people and places who had never cared for them. Their ignorance was their bliss, and I turned away from the somber faces and sensational reporting on the television to be present with my family instead.

After a few minutes of this, the hostess returned to take our plates and then to bring us the bill and a small box for what was left of the food we had ordered for the baby. "Take as much time as you need," she said. "You can pay up front whenever you're ready to go."

We still had hours of driving left ahead of us, so I helped my wife with getting the baby unbuckled from her high chair, and with a kiss on the cheek and a promise to be back soon, they went down the hallway to check her diaper in the bathroom once more. I packed up the food and toys that we had brought into the baby's backpack and then picked up the bill and headed to the front of the Denny's. The hostess was standing there, and she watched my approach with a smile. But her smile was not as wide as before, and after I had swiped my credit card, I thanked her for helping us. "It was very nice to meet a friendly face on the road," I added as I scrawled my signature across the small screen on my side of the desk.

"Oh, of course, it was my pleasure," the hostess said. Then she looked past me towards where my wife and daughter had gone. "You have a very adorable little girl; makes me think about my granddaughter."

"How old is she?"

"She's older than yours; turned two a few months ago." She laughed a bitter little laugh. "I didn't get to see her though. I haven't seen her since this all began." She didn't do more than wave her hand vaguely around the air between us, but I knew exactly what she meant. "It's not right," the hostess said, "for a grandma not to see her granddaughter, is it?"

"No, it's not."

She sighed and handed me the customer copy of my receipt. "I'm supposed to be getting my second shot next week though, then I'll be able to go down and visit her. She's so little, my daughter is worried that she could catch it. But it'll be safe to visit her soon, and then I can start making up for all of this lost time, right?"

There were so many things that I could say in response to her plea. I could have launched into an overblown explanation of why all of the restrictions that were making her unhappy were only so much security theater, but I didn't. Instead, I just smiled at her and said, "That's right. Soon, you'll be seeing her all the time."

"Thank you," she said. My wife and daughter were returning, and the hostess looked at them wistfully. "You do have a beautiful family."

"I know. I'm very lucky."

"Never forget that," she said. Then, I walked over and held the door open so my wife could lead our toddling little girl out into the windy air. She only managed to take a few steps before it was too much for her and she started screaming to be picked up. I bent over and obligingly lifted her into my arms and carried her the rest of the way to the car. I helped get her into her car seat while my wife got in the driver's seat and started the car. The baby was wide awake, so after she was buckled in, I climbed in next to her in the backseat.

We pulled out of the Denny's parking lot, past the gas pumps, and back to the highway. From her seat up front my wife said, "That was very nice. That was my first time at a Denny's, and it was much nicer than I thought it would be."

"Yeah, it was very nice," I agreed. As I held a board book in front of my daughter for her to read, my mind wandered back to the restaurant, already nearly vanished in the rearview save for the sign. I thought about the hostess and her granddaughter, I thought about the television, and I thought about the mask that I had forgotten on the table of the Denny's. I still think about that encounter now and then.

Welcome Back

Carl Penda

Caution: the granter of long life? Or, yet another hazard, lurking in the wild world, stalking, waiting to maim and kill? Just as every man had a mother who, in his childhood, safeguarded him against those unexpected dangers that affect only the young, so does he foster his own inner guardian—to more or less of a degree. This was especially true of Mike, an engineer whose presuppositions for danger—warranted or not—had inspired him to build a nuclear fallout shelter in his own backyard. His friend John teased him for it, until finally, after one world-changing newscast, Mike's paranoia (he called it "prescience") was vindicated...

The fuzzy old television cast a dull glow across the interior of the one-room shelter, silhouetting the two men as they listened to the report:

"Ladies and gentlemen," the anchor said, her voice dark and dour, "this is a pre-recorded broadcast, as our news staff has been evacuated. We strongly advise anyone who has not evacuated yet to do so immediately. This will be your last opportunity. The administration has confirmed that China has given the order to launch their missiles. Their countdown was reported to have begun just before this broadcast. This is not a prank; this is not a drill; nuclear missiles will be en route to the United States within a matter of hours. We have not received a guarantee that our country's missile defense can stop the attack, due to the sheer volume of missiles expected. This is why you must make your way with what supplies you can to a safe zone or shelter. If you do not have a fallout shelter of your own, look to someone you know; otherwise we have displayed information on the screen about the available public shelters for you to use. Good luck, and Godspeed."

With one last glimpse of the outside, Mike swung the heavy door shut and secured the giant iron bolt. The fallout sign above the doorway loomed over him.

"Take a good look at it," John said. "It's your new headstone."

Concrete-bound, Mike avoided deliberating over future uncertainties. Rather, he set about with John arranging supplies in different areas of the shelter, double-checking stock and organizing. That was the deal: Mike granted his friend use of his shelter and some supplies, while John would bring more supplies and help keep tidy. Crates of rations they stacked in one corner. Immediate-use items, like first aid, they laid out on shelves, and they made certain that their few perishables were all in the fridge—while triple-checking that the fridge indeed worked. All that done, Mike tacked a calendar to the wall. John watched this last act from a dark corner and sighed, but said nothing.

One single, solitary "X" on that calendar marked their first day in the shelter: two aggressive perpendicular lines denoting the cost of their survival. If any nukes had dropped, these men were too deep in the earth to notice. The Xes were indeed among the biggest changes in that room over time, marking another day—then another, and then another, until the friends lost count despite continuing their marks. Eventually, they even needed to turn the page: a new month in the safety below.

One day—or night—Mike woke in his cot. His watch read 7:00 a. m. He sat up and looked at John. So far his friend had been good about the day's tasks, but today he appeared to be sleeping in.

"John," Mike said.

John remained asleep.

"Hey, John. Come on, man."

"Ugh," John said.

"It's 7:00 a. m!"

"Just how the hell do you know?"

Mike waved his watch around.

"Oh yeah?" John retorted. "And how do you know that thing's not... fast, or slow, or whatever? We'd never be able to tell! Maybe it's actually 3:00 a.m. right now."

"Maybe," Mike said. "But if we stick to it, then we'll at least have a consistent schedule."

"Why does it matter at this point...?" John said.

"We've got nothing else to go by," Mike said. "Am I going to have to carry you through every day or what?"

John capitulated and got up with Mike to commence the day's routine—though not before he faced the giant shelter door and took one long, wistful breath. Mike simply got himself to work.

The two emptied out a few ration crates and looked over their contents. It was not long before John, holding the clipboard, began doodling in the margins of the inventory sheet.

Practically talking to himself, Mike said, "Monday, Tuesday... we can do the dehydrated eggs each day this week... 3 counts of the chicken and broccoli if we want to space it out..." He looked at John to see he wasn't paying attention. "Hello!"

"Alright alright!" John said. "Just remember, the real reason we packed the shotgun was so I can blow my head off when we're out of the chicken and broccoli."

"Always the drama queen," Mike said.

After inventory, they had their daily workout. John presently worked his shoulders. Breathing in deep with each upright row, he closed his eyes, and his mind wandered across images of green trees, a soft breeze, and the sound of birds. His reverie got cut short by another sound: Mike, doing squats with the nerdiest expression on his face.

"Forty-six... forty-seven... forty-eight..."

"I know it's your thing, Mike, but you actually shouldn't count," John said.

"What?"

"You shouldn't count your reps."

"It's how I make sure I do the right amount each day," Mike said.

"You can't progress that way."

"Progress?"

"Yeah, progress," John said. "As in, actually move forward. Move ahead on something, anything, instead of remaining in the same place all the goddamn time. What you should do is hit as many squats as it takes to feel sore and then start counting."

Mike looked cockeyed at John.

"Trust me. It'll make you feel stronger."

"...Okay, I'll give it a shot," Mike said.

"There you go," John replied. "Some things you shouldn't just do by rote."

That night—it felt like it was still night—John woke up and noticed Mike was still asleep.

"Mike..." John said.

Mike groaned.

"Hey, Mike."

Grumbling, Mike looked at his watch. "Dammit John, it's 3:00 a. m.!"

John ignored Mike's tone. "What do you miss the most?" he said.

"Oh, for God's sake..."

"Really. What do you miss the most? A few things stick out to me, but I can't decide on number one."

Mike thought for a moment. "Well, I do miss the National Library. Lots of exciting time spent there, and I could hardly bring enough of my book collection to the shelter. And... I miss my workshop, of course. And I guess the internet. I bet that won't come back in our lifetime, if we even get out of here..."

John looked at Mike sidelong. "That's it? That's what you miss? ...The damn library?"

"Yeah...?" Mike said.

"What about, I don't know, children laughing?" John asked. "Or, women!

You know. Women? Long hair, breasts, dresses, that kind of thing? Or what about hiking through the woods on a sunny day? Or the sun in general?"

"Yeah, I guess..." Mike said.

John rolled back into his pillow. "Man, I don't get you sometimes."

Days continued to go by, according to Mike's trusty watch. Eventually the Xes had nowhere else to go on their calendar, and the men had to start marking the back. With each passing day, Mike never lost sight, nor focus, nor attentiveness, nor ceased adjusting, checking, marking, tallying, and rearranging —with regard to their supplies. At his suggestion that they begin rationing their dental floss, John finally snapped. He dumped the box of floss and began to unravel them, one packet at a time.

"Look at yourself, John! You're losing your mind!" Mike said.

John proceeded to wind the floss around and around his neck, cinching it against the flesh. "I am losing my mind. That's exactly what's going on! I can't do this anymore. I can't just stay here in this... this tomb forever! It's nothing but subsistence-living and routines and drudgery..."

John marched towards the shelter door, but Mike held him back.

"Don't! We have no way of knowing what the situation is out there!" Mike said. "By most calculations, it would take years for nuclear fallout to clear up. I'd have to check my notes on exactly how many years—but it's definitely more than we've been down here!"

"I don't care anymore," John said. "I really don't. We're already as dead as we'll ever be. I need to see for myself."

"No—"

Mike yanked John back from the door. Following his momentum, John shoved Mike, throwing him into a cot. Now free, John ran for the door and fiddled with the bolt.

Seeing he could not fight John, Mike ran for the locker that contained the hazmat suits and raced to don one in time. Just as he had the suit up to his shoulders, a bright light fell across his face. He was too late.

There stood John, silhouetted by the blinding light of the open shelter door. He stepped out into the sunlight. Mike, resigned, joined him, the hazmat suit only halfway secured.

They saw Mike's house, still standing. They saw his back yard. And, down by the street, they saw... a woman walking her dog. The two looked at each other in utter confusion.

Then, John—figment of Mike's imagination that he was—disappeared into thin air, and in his place stood Mike, alone, half-dressed in a hazmat suit.

It was a regular day in town. There were people jogging, going to and from work, children playing, and no evidence whatsoever of any nuclear explosions.

"Contrary to all expectations," said the news anchor, "the US missile defense successfully intercepted every missile that was launched in the attack. Despite the administration sending strong warnings to China, no nuclear retaliation has been planned, and the president is now engaged in talks to deescalate the situation. We'll have more to report on that later. Now, let's listen to what some of the evacuees have to say on their way back home..."

Mike sat in a bustling coffeehouse, watching the back-dated broadcast on his phone. He'd chosen a seat next to a big picture window, overlooking a park that was home to trees and birds, all bathed in the midday sun. Whatever voice John had provided Mike, whatever suppressed drive or subterranean instinct, it had done its work. *You got me out of that hole,* Mike thought. *What else do you have in mind?*

"John" took little time to respond.

The barista, a rather lovely young lady, brought Mike his latte. He looked around, dazed, and said, "It feels like I've been away forever. Never thought I'd see the world again."

She gave him a coy look. "Welcome back."

And then he asked her out.

Though this account does not include whether Mike was successful, what can be said is: it did not kill him.

Small Victories: From Rosa Parks to Robert E. Lee

Mrs. Saxon

Many years ago, our oldest child enthusiastically came home from her expensive private school in our small town in rural America with an A+ on her book report. The book report was on Rosa Parks, and the mind of our daughter was filled with outrage for poor ol' Rosa, who had to sit at the back of the bus. Our oldest is prone to strong emotions and loves her family, her animals, and her morals fiercely. If her grandmother gives her an apple pie, she runs to get her siblings to share with them. She loves fiercely, cares deeply, and learns fast. I asked the teacher about alternative books, and she presented MLK and other black subjects. The Rosa Parks book report, in combination with noticing that our child was not learning much at all in this expensive private school, led us to pull her from school and begin to homeschool our children. While my immediate concern was whether or not I would be able to teach the children well enough, my husband's initial concern was the possible lack of social contacts.

Getting started was not easy. As English speakers, in an English speaking country, there are a lot of homeschool curricula available. I naively imagined it would be easy; a lot of the curricula seemed perfect, only to find out that many recommended books normalizing biracial relationships and encouraging girls to go to college and having a career before settling down. While girls can go to college, it should not be lauded as the only or most respectable option available, while at the same time portraying starting a family early as an unsuccessful option. I discovered that a large portion of the material was not much better than what our nice private school had to offer in terms of quality, accuracy, and encouragement for dreams of the future. It did not take me very long to separate the wheat from the chaff, and once I got to the good materials, we all got more comfortable with homeschooling. The children and I settled into a nice balance of order and chaos, mostly due to the baby and toddler running freely around the house. I figured out everybody's learning styles and what really matters to us. Math was a struggle for our oldest, and after a grueling year of re-learning years of math lessons and unlearning years of spirit crushing Common Core learning, she is now easily keeping up with her math work.

I had the great privilege of teaching my son to read, and to show him a love for reading. We still enjoy many quiet moments after bedtime where he reads to me, and although bigger words are (age appropriately) still a challenge, he enjoys to read. While my husband brings home a much appreciated paycheck, which is undeniably necessary to our lives, I get to educate the children. There are many days where I feel the weight of the value of what I do on my shoulders. I am incredibly privileged to be able to shape the minds of our children, and to instill good values in their minds and souls.

My husband and I enjoy the company of our children, and we do not send our children to a place where they pick up on undesirable behavior such as homosexuality or anti-white sympathies either from the system or their system-damaged peers. Each evening, we have dinner at the dining table and we talk about what occupied our day. The children tidy up the most used areas of the house three times per day, and generally speaking our home is clean, but coated with evidence of our daily lessons and daily living. Some days are such a challenge that a moment of peace represents the peak of luxury. Frequently when either one of our children, or I, have a difficult day, we get the minimal amount of "homework" done, and then we pack a backpack with a healthy lunch and a few books and we all go outside. As homeschoolers, we have the ability to recognize our need for a break, and we can act upon it. Anyone with a multiple-child household can attest that a bad mood can be contagious. Rather than rolling the boulder back up the hill by forcing the children to study despite emotions of frustration and anger, we just go outside. We have an overstuffed closet with weather appropriate clothing: we are ready for rain, snow, hot sun, and mild autumn days. Even the baby has a nice snow suit and can be hauled in a carrier through the woods. We allow ourselves to live. At first, I wondered if we learned "enough" on days where we spent more time outside than we did inside, at the table. Now I know that those outside days are just as important as the inside days, as we learn how to cope with stress, we learn to rejuvenate ourselves, and we appreciate that which is gained from exercise and time spent in nature. Just recently, our oldest came to me with a chicken in her arms and told me that she thought the chicken might have fractured her toe. She had thought of several solutions to heal the chicken and did so all on her own with the use of our chicken books. I will be hard-pressed to find a public schooled fourth grader with such initiative and care. I have created several unit studies on subjects that we value: big heroes like Robert E. Lee, folk heroes like Johnny Appleseed, and gifted artists such as Rembrandt and Audubon. We focus on technique and materials used when we try to copy paintings, or create a painting of a subject of our choosing in the style of the artist. The children have different ages and abilities, so I take time to explain to my son that it is alright if he is not as good at drawing as his sister, because she is older and has had more time to practice.

Before we were dedicated homeschoolers, I would visit with a friend (and her toddler) and thoroughly enjoy those hours of adult conversation occasionally interrupted by our toddlers. When I started homeschooling, my friend would occasionally ask if I was ready to send the children back to school yet, so I would have time for myself (and for her). When I lamented about the children's bad days, she offered the helpful suggestion of sending them back to school, because "school is not so bad." I declined. Years have gone by. My friend's oldest child is being bullied relentlessly by the Current Year's top rung of the school social hierarchy: gays, trannies, and non-Whites. This has become a daily occurrence, because my friend enjoys her free time without children running amok in the household. Our children are all thriving, happy, and run (age appropriately) amok, but are mostly able to clean up their own messes in the hopes of it going unnoticed.

The children and I talked about how we will spend our summer and what projects we will take on. Every school-aged child in our household is going to grow one plant, except for our oldest. She started enough cherry tomatoes so that every one of us can snack on the fruits of her labor. We are getting more animals, and more parts of our yard are being turned into vegetable garden each day. When I stop and look at the children, I see that they are connected to the land and place their family above all else. They know where their ancestors came from and what they did for them. As young children, they are trying to figure out their place in life, and they are basing that on our teachings, not those of a system that hates us.

Fairly recently our oldest children went to a playground where they encountered a blue-haired, school-ground bully and her little gang, who picked a fight with our youngest child there. Our kids immediately stood up for one another and ended the fight rather swiftly. The offending group of children quickly left the playground, while our children were able to play and enjoy themselves. They have learned to stick together like a pack, or as I often call them, "Team Wolf." My husband no longer worries about "how to properly socialize the children." He knows precisely what they will be socialized into becoming.

On a regular basis we celebrate our children's successes. Generally speaking, our children are thriving and are growing up with a healthy mindset and know the truth about history. We celebrate European history and revere in the stories of our ancestors' past, including those of Norse, Greek, and Roman mythologies, The Brothers Grimm's and Hans Christian Anderson's fairy tales and many, many more. Our children enjoy and relish the stories that I read to them, and they happily narrate them back to me. When they do not narrate stories back to me, they take their sketchbooks out and illustrate the stories. We read about other countries' cultures and aim to portray these peoples as they actually are, no noble savage myths, no victimology, and no blank slate depictions of some kind of universal human nature. The children are able to appreciate other cultures in other countries as solitary cultures that need not be merged into others. They have a solid understanding of the Roman Empire and its marvelous beauty, as well as the nobility of those European nations that fought against them. My husband is able to share his love for history with the children at dinner time, and these are moments where I get to sit back and watch an affection for their heritage develop further.

Some days we have grand science projects, and rather than trying to teach early elementary aged children how a dike works, we built a few in a large transparent tote and learned which one worked best and why. When the children are at the beach, with great pleasure they attempt to construct some rather impressive water retention methods. We also have found pleasure in our everyday learning, and I gladly share my kitchen with the children as they learn to cook simple dishes. When they are young adults, they will be ready to cook a healthy meal and at least grow a few vegetables and herbs to season their food.

When the children struggle with a subject, I am able to take the time they need to get things explained and straightened out. Sometimes that takes an extra thirty minutes, but sometimes it means that we spend a week studying fractions, reducing and increasing recipe quantities, and cutting up various circular shaped dishes, or serving the toddler his sandwiches in eights or sixths. We are on our own schedule, and we live independent from a school schedule. I have fully embraced that the children are in such-and-such "grade-ish," because one child might be in the age appropriate grade level for math, but work at a higher grade level for reading. We enjoy a flexible and understanding educational system where the children excel without extra homework when they just need more time to learn and process things.

I wanted to write a piece on small victories, and I suppose if you look at our family from the outside, bringing the children home to be educated is a small victory. The average outsider would assess our children and conclude that they are learning and appear to be able to hold a conversation with adults. This would lead them to conclude that *in this specific instance*, homeschooling them has not failed the children and they are still learning. That would be a small victory.

However, when I look at our family from my perspective, I would not describe our homeschooling journey as a small victory. After all, our oldest is now on top of her math, and the children are not influenced by the anti-White agenda in modern schools. To the contrary, within our children we are cultivating a deep reverence for their ancestors, a love of their race, a passion to reclaim their birthright so that they may pass it onto their own children one day. On grand scale, one individual family opting out of the anti-White system would seem a small victory, but our enemies fear it nonetheless. Thousands of our likeminded kinsfolk raising their own children to stand proudly upon the shoulders of their ancestors spells the undoing of our enemies and the ultimate victory of our people. We teach our children that the future of their race lies within them alone. We only succeed by means of our own work and our own determination. We teach our children that no one can secure the future of our people but themselves. Hail victory, be it great or small.

Shoot

Seax

Interrupted reveries. The man felt the dust blowing off the shelves of his mind. Little Akashic records with their books all overturned. He found himself again, sitting, slumped ever so slightly, cradling a revolver in his hands. Old, now. Funny—he'd always assumed that the tools he bought would age much better than he would. Instead he saw hairline scratches, a beginning of a pit here or there from those months he had forgotten he'd even owned a piece. And yet there he sat, older really on the inside than out. Tired, from the grind.

"Dad," the man's son's voice rang. Dad looked up; for a time he almost thought he could see his boy's voice echoing through the falling leaves of the trees. "Dad, what're you doing?"

"Thinking, Kiddo."

"You do that a *lot.*"

"Yeah I do..."

"Are we gonna shoot now?"

"Ayuh."

Kiddo looked on passively. Dad wasn't sure if he was excited or not. Evidently when they said your kid will ape your every movement, they were right. Kiddo had a great poker face, a shame Dad never learned poker for to teach it to him.

"I suppose," Dad began, caught by an errant thought before catching himself from sinking back into the reveried sea, "that we ought to start at the beginning. Gun safcty."

Kiddo nodded.

"This is a revolver. Ain't got no safety. Well, nothing to write home about anyway. Look here," Dad lowered his shooting hand and thumbed a small notched switch, "red is dead. Understand?"

Kiddo nodded. "Why red?"

"I like to think it's ironic humor, but it's probably because the manufacturer thinks it's easier to see."

"I don't think it is," Kiddo said.

"Well, red's faded over time. Y'alright. Flip the switch up, the hammer don't fire all the way. Don't ever dry fire these. Ain't never tried and find out what happens, they say it bends the firing pin." Dad murmured. "This little guy here," he added as he pointed to the pin behind the hammerhead.

"This is really boring, Dad."

"That's what we call tough titties, Kiddo. Guns ain't all bang-bang Injun wars. There's precautions." The man nodded his head side to side. "Some of which I've forgotten. Used to know a guy that memorized some damn list of rules or other. Verbatim. Allow me to paraphrase. Unless you want to kill it, don't be pointing your gun at anything. None of this funny business with the pointing and the laughing. Men have died for less." Dad took a breath. "Keep your piece aimed down when you reload. And, clean your gun often enough that she don't rust. Here we go."

"Can we shoot yet?"

"Nope."

Dad took a breath. "Loading," he said. "This fires 22lr shells. That's long rifle. Read somewhere that these are among the first kinds of bullets the Pioneers developed for to replace the powder horn. Or something like that."

"Powder horn?"

"Black magic, Kid, don't worry about it. Couldn't tell ya if I wanted to." Dad chuckled, "22lr bullets..."

"Who're the Pioneers?" Kiddo asked.

Dad grinned, his poker face effectively dissolved. "Glad you asked." He tilted his head side to side as he checked his memory banks. "Long time ago things started getting crowded in New England and Virginia and all the other uh-states, so folks started moving out west. Further west anyway."

Dad smiled. "They carried guns that looked a little bit like this," he said as he rotated his wrist, causing the revolver to slowly spin in his grip. "They crawled up out of our forests and fields and streams and drug themselves all across the map in covered wagons. That's the first mobile homes, by the way...waaay cooler than the trailer park where that dumbshit from the co-op lives." Dad chuckled. "The men had their sidearms and their longarms, and they used them to tame the Wild West."

"How'd they tame it?" Kiddo asked.

"They had to fight off Injun Braves, animals..." Dad shrugged. "Real enemy was probably the elements. Hot as hell the further south ya go." Dad paused. "Look here," he said, pointing to a small, spring-loaded button, "when your safety's on you push this tab and pull the loading pin—that's what holds your cylinder in place." Dad proceeded to do what he had said, and with the pin removed he tilted the gun so that the cylinder fell into his waiting palm. "Six shooters," he smiled, "always wanted to be a cowboy growing up."

Dad reached into his belt pouch and counted out six shells with his fingertips;

he held a bullet between his fingertips and gingerly loaded it into the chamber. "Roaming the land, no laws, no government. No goddamn taxes. No peaceful protests. No alien and remission acts." Another bullet. "None of it." Another bullet. "A man could live by his wits. And if he didn't like his neighbor..." Another bullet.

"He'd kill 'em?"

"What? No! Well, maybe sometimes. But murder is wrong." Dad loaded another bullet. "The thing that makes a man not an animal is he can control his aggression." And another bullet. "It takes discipline to be a good man. A man with a hammer looks for nails to pound, I know that's true. But you can't always take the easy way out."

Dad counted out the bullets: 1, 2, 3, 4, 5, and... 6. "That makes us no better than the ones that make it easy to want to be a cowboy."

"What d'ya mean?"

"You give into every impulse, you're an animal, t'ain't no coincidence we live in a big friggin' zoo."

"I don't understand," Kiddo said.

"That's why we're here," Dad said. "Someday you might have to use this. Someday I might have to. What you don't want is to get to where you look forward to it. Then you've lost."

"Lost what?"

"Yourself." Dad shook his head. "Oh now look at what you did, you gone and made me get philosophical."

Dad chuckled. "See here how I've cocked the hammer?" He thumbed the hammer. "Listen, there'll be clicks." Slowly Dad pulled his thumb. Kiddo cracked a smile as he heard them. "Pull the hammer back all the way, you hear the four clicks. You're ready to fire."

"Now," Dad said, "lining up your sights. Your uncle Rob taught me this; he was in the army. You see this little u-shaped looking thing? You want the tippy top of the little nub at the end of the barrel to fill that spot. Kapeesh?"

Kiddo nodded. Dad extended his shooting arm, closed an eye and took a breath. "Plug y'ears, Kid." And he fired. He lowered his revolver and leaned forward, squinting; he had hit about four inches from the bull's-eye.

"If I was a Cowboy, that would've been a very wounded brave. *Provided* he didn't club me with a tomahawk first."

"I don't get it, Dad," Kiddo said. "You're telling me you'd wanna go across the country in a wagon, but not shoot the gun?"

"The Pioneer didn't want to have to shoot Chief Runamok," Dad said. "He did what he had to. It's a hallmark of a sick society where we make up motives that don't fit the bill... The White Man did what he had to, always did up until around the time I was born. Now here we are, maybe wondering if someday we're going to have to do things we don't want to."

"Like fighting Injun Braves?"

"They won't be brave, and they probably won't be Injuns."

"Who?"

"Can't say, find out if it ever happens."

Dad took another shot. Two inches. Inside the center line, close to the heart of the target. "It never changes. Our ancestors weren't cowboys and they didn't have revolvers. But they'd a known about powder horns. New England was settled with flintlocks and blunderbusses I think. Real pirate stuff." Dad shot another round, this one landed some six inches up from the bull's-eye. "That might've been a throat," he mused. "Hard to steal stereos when you can't breathe." He sighed. "But once you settle your homestead, you're in a nest; in the natural world you'd have to defend it. A man had to be ready in a moment's notice. It's why we had minutemen later."

"They fought the British, right?"

"Right-o," Dad said. "Now there's a difference between defense and offense." Another shot. "In the natural world." He took a breath. "But we live in a world governed by lawyers." The last shot. "Nothing is natural."

Dad pulled the pin and ejected the chamber. "Don't touch that until I say," he said as he walked over to the target. Six shots, clustered around the bull's-eye, all within six inches of the core, with three close to center.

"Home is all that's ever mattered," he said as he returned to the firing line, "and that's why this is important; home doesn't matter to everyone in the same way. There's all kinds of people who want to take what you have. Just like the Puritans had to fight the French and Injuns and the Pioneers had to fight Injuns and a different kind of nature. And Mexicans, I guess. Don't know as much border history as I ought to."

"I thought we don't have borders anymore," Kiddo said.

"Not officially," Dad answered, "but I don't think the Pilgrims or Pioneers worried about borders. The people they fought didn't. Open borders are for lawyers. You know where your home is, where it begins and ends. All this yah-yah with lawyers and legalese is claptrap. It's pissing in the wind; they tell you it's raining but your shoes are still cold. And wet. And smell bad." Dad shook his head. "Whatever," he grumbled and waved to the gun. "Load it."

Kiddo looked to the revolver, Dad could see his gears turning. Thoughts of adventure and duty playing against each other in his little noggin. Slowly, with hesitation Kiddo picked up the revolver chamber and quietly extended his free palm. Dad dropped six shells in that palm and smiled quietly as Kiddo gingerly slid the first into the slot.

Et Cetera

Mark Time

John Fuller trimmed the sail on *Et Cetera* as he cleared the Love Lighthouse at Cape Hatteras. Checking the GPS, he still had thousands of miles of hostile Atlantic water before he reached Spain. In days of yore, Europeans embarked on desperate westward voyages to reach the warm sands of America. That day, one of their progeny set his compass eastward to escape this world. Behind him laid miles of white shores, the stars and stripes, and a stack of papers. These papers ruled his life from stem to stern.

Chief of these tyrants were the divorce papers. A close second was the yellow slip bearing a diagnosis of terminal illness and its pricey medications. Various bills, diplomas, and certificates formed the foundation of John's paper life. He lost the house in the divorce and lived out of a storage unit as he awaited his impending death. The doctors told him he had a year to live at the most. Astride this mountain of paperwork sat a final page, greater than all before or since: a bill of sale for a thirty-five foot sailboat named *Et Cetera*.

In his younger days, he sailed competitively for the Maine Maritime Academy. As his marriage sank into the depths, he found solace in renting little five footer boats on the lake at the local state park. Gliding effortlessly across the surface, John could forget the churning waters of turmoil around him. By month three of his final year, his life continued to be covered by paperwork like autumn leaves. Under the bill of sale sat the receipt for a loan he never intended to pay back—the price of *Et Cetera*. Taking her out on practice sorties by the shores of North Carolina, the final stages of his plan fell into place.

The night before getting underway, he carefully checked the weather report. John Fuller gripped the rigging with a prolonged sigh. *Et Cetera* bobbed peacefully as it rested next to the pier. Looking over its sleek, white hull, John ran his hand along the chrome railing. The stillness of midnight entwined the pair on the eve of their fateful journey.

First the Caribbean, then Tenerife, then mainland Spain. John couldn't believe he was really doing it. As soon as the last mooring line laid cast off on the pier, he would finally be untethered to his Kafkaesque existence on shore.

As *Et Cetera* plowed out into the open ocean the following morning, John ducked his head under the yardarm as he made his southerly tack towards the emerald waters of the Caribbean. To his right, the continent menaced a death by a thousand paper cuts. To his left, a thin band of islands reached toward John to keep him pinned against the land. In front, the bow jumped and cut through the briny waves towards the end of his life. Unlike the meaningless slow burn of perishing in a hospital, John Fuller would go out like an enterprising sea captain.

The wind and the sea spray invigorated life within him that sat dormant for decades. At last he was free. John's soul peaked out from its shell like a hatching chick, full of the promises of new life. Checking the GPS again, he found he was making good speed and maintaining a steady track. All the man-made barriers to his freedom evaporated with the morning dew as the sun rose higher.

John's face was wet with spray, which concealed a growing flow of tears. Moisture from the ocean and his eyes watered the shriveled root of his soul. Suddenly, another source of water landed on his countenance. A solitary droplet from above heralded the arrival of a torrential downpour. John shielded his eyes to look towards heaven. The Atlantic marshaled her forces for a surprise attack to oppose the fateful sailor. He gripped the helm with white knuckles, struggling to grapple with the fast setting reality of weathering the storm. He was certain the forecast reported clear skies. This freak storm threatened to upend both *Et Cetera* and John's ambitions of transiting the frigid waters to the east.

Tacking back and forth as the winds whipped up sheets of spray, he struggled gallantly to keep her steady. At last, lightning struck the mainmast, frying the rigging and setting a small fire. He sat dumbfounded and blind as he fumbled around the deck of *Et Cetera*. When he regained his senses, he saw the growing inferno towards the stem.

Springing into action, John cast his coat on the flames and hauled down the mainsail. Miraculously, both he and the sail survived the strike. However, *Et Cetera* foundered dangerously in the strong winds.

Clambering to the stern, John pulled furiously at the cord to start the diesel engine. After a few harried yanks, he attained ignition and propulsion. Buffeted by titanic gusts, he noticed he was in present danger of being dashed on the shoal. In the adrenaline soaked moment of decision, John Fuller curtailed his ambitions from a trans-Atlantic voyage to simply keeping *Et Cetera* off the rocks. He took the rudder in hand and drove directly into the wind. The diesel engine groaned tremendously while fighting back the forces dragging John back to his fate. He twisted and wrung the throttle like a soaked rag in a desperate attempt to make headway. Looking at the billowing, dark sea, John's heart sank with the realization that he was making exactly zero knots. Neither advancing nor retreating, *Et Cetera* remained locked into an equal struggle between the engine and the wind.

John continued to clutch the throttle like a lifeline as the seconds and minutes drifted under the keel. He checked his surviving equipment and found that the only electronic device still functioning was his VHF radio. Sitting at the lower corner of the plastic sat a small red button marked "M" for mayday. Pressing it would alert the vessels in the area that he was in need of immediate rescue. John put this thought out of his mind as he battled the elements.

As the wind whipped and chafed around him, he at last saw a small amount of progress. First one knot, then three, *Et Cetera* heaved forward. John let out a raucous cheer as the land behind him edged away. In tandem with this cheer, the last drops of diesel poured out of the fuel line. The engine lurched, sputtered, then unceremoniously died. John gave way to a despairing scream. Drifting quickly towards the breakers, he coped with his situation. He figured he could still return to land, avoid his creditors, repair his ship, and get back out onto the water before his terminal year was through. He reluctantly accepted this backup plan and dialed the distress signal.

After a short while of listless drifting, a navy salvage vessel hoved in view. John waved his arms in depressed surrender to the forces pulling him back to land. At least he could try again after the repairs. Welcomed onboard to the navy vessel, John watched impassively as they lashed *Et Cetera* down with the towing line. He noticed a worried look from the captain. After some hush conversation, he informed John that the towing lines were intended for large container ships and were too heavy for the sailboat. The rescuing vessel had no other lines aboard.

Ignoring their warnings of the dangers it posed to his boat, John demanded that they make an attempt to bring *Et Cetera* back. Otherwise she would suffer the ignominious fate of being dashed on the rocks. Shrugging his shoulders, the captain assented to John's wishes. The navy vessel heaved about and set its course back to land. Without a sufficient catenary bend, the heavy towing line shook and tore at *Et Cetera's* pristine hull until the fiberglass showed significant fissures. First the front towing cleat snapped. Next, the sailboat turned sideways and buffeted against the choppy seas.

The captain informed John that *Et Cetera* would not make the journey intact. The defeated sailor demanded that they continue on. The sailboat was more like a lifeboat off the sinking ship of his life. Concerned for the safety of navigation and crew, the captain overrode John. Sending out a message to the surrounding vessels, he declared *Et Cetera* a hazard to navigation. In ten minutes, he would commence sinking the vessel. John cried out in terror as he heard the words pass over the captain's lips. Rushing to the forecastle, he saw several sailors loading up a fifty caliber machine gun.

The captain stood on the bridgewing overlooking the scene with grim understanding. The sailors bristled at John's advance, but the captain motioned for them to stand down. At the end of his tirade, John took in the mournful scene of *Et Cetera*. It was heeled over nearly to the point of capsizing as it dragged along under the heavy steel cable. The formerly proud and beautiful hull limped onwards like a mangled dog after its owner. The navy vessel made proper arrangements to decouple the ship from its tow and circled *Et Cetera* like a shark. Their haggard passenger made grave threats and entreaties to save his boat to no avail.

At last, the captain descended to the forecastle as the sailors trained the dual barrels of the machine gun on John's most prized possession. The gunnery officer asked the captain for permission to fire. Hesitating for a moment, he closed his eyes and clenched his jaw. Motioning to John, the captain instructed him to stand on the firing platform. The sailors gave each other concerned looks but acquiesced to the officer's demands to step away from the gun. A glimmer of hope turned to black despair as John realized what the captain wanted him to do.

He gripped the weapon's controls with trembling fingers as his thumbs drifted to the trigger. John saw his escape from the mountain of paperwork writhing in agony through the sights. *Et Cetera* fought to stay afloat like a wounded animal but floated helplessly towards the rocks. John turned a tearful eye towards the captain. Pursing his lips, the officer nodded with assurance and empathy. Between giving *Et Cetera* a hero's death or letting her be eaten by the land, the choice was clear.

John increased the pressure on the trigger until a thunderous burst tore across the stormy seas. Only one of the six bullets found their mark. The rest caused large geysers of water to shoot up next to *Et Cetera*. John took a brief pause to pay respects to his sinking dream then let out a prolonged hail of fire. As the hot lead slung downrange, each shot carried his troubles away. With a blank mind, he kept his thumbs planted on the trigger until the belt ran dry. When the smoke cleared, *Et Cetera* was nowhere to be found. The sailors hooted and hollered at the carnage, but the captain chastised them to keep quiet. Standing up straight, the officer demanded they engage in a moment of silence.

In the cool, stark silence of the sea, John looked with blissful detachment at the billowing cauldron where *Et Cetera* once was. Some wreckage floated on the top like a transient grave marker of his escape. The navy vessel would bear him back to his captors and the tyrannical stack of papers. This thought failed to trouble John. He had striven valiantly against the tide, out from under the thumb of his nightmare. For a brief few hours, John was utterly and totally free. In that ephemeral, ecstatic state, he lived more than all of his years of paper existence.

When they pulled into port, John Fuller stepped ashore to face the consequences of his breakout attempt. The creditors, lawyers, doctors, and bureaucrats awaited to receive their pound of flesh. The faceless monstrosity that ruled his whole life on a throne of paperwork seemed less frightening to John now. He lifted his eyes to heaven as he strode confidently down the gangway. They would take his money, possessions, even his life—but they would never gain his soul, his spirit, those precious hours of freedom—et cetera.

Spark, Compression, Timing, Fuel

Mark Time

Spark, Compression, Timing, Fuel. If you have those four things, generally you can get an engine to run. What did Jim have? Nothing about his life had any sort of spark. Working long hours at a retail store and living with several roommates, the drudgery dampened any sort of passion. What about compression then? Of course there was pressure. This element dominated his life. Under cycle after cycle of debt, spending, dead end jobs, dead end relationships, and the crushing futility of post-modernity, it was remarkable Jim could withstand the compression. Many couldn't. His three other roommates all gave way to drugs, porn, and any other release they could find. The timing was all off for Jim. He was born into the lost generation of young men who had no mountains to climb nor stars to explore. Everything was either on a map or already classified into a series of soulless formulas.

On a smaller level, opportunities would come and go without any success for Jim because he never prepared beforehand. He would always write off putting in any sort of meaningful effort. After all, it's all meaningless, right? Well, he had no spark or timing. Surely there must be fuel? In reality, Jim chugged along on fumes. The great reservoirs of religion, family, and community had all been thoroughly drilled out and exported to other causes. The only things keeping him alive were the inevitable chemical processes taking place in his body set in motion by the regrettable episode of his conception. In order to get Jim running again, a good bit of work needed to be done. A full teardown to be sure and most likely a replacement of all the internals. Most would just relegate him as totaled beyond repair to the heaping flesh junkyard of twenty-first-century America. After all, why go through all the effort of resurrecting the soul of this gutted man?

He saw it on the side of the road. It had a sign that said, "For sale, just junk, make offer." Jim was on the way to work and was already running late. The motorcycle was devoid of any body paneling. Corrosion had already set about its work of returning the machine to dust. Jim slammed on his brakes to take a closer look. He left his phone in the car as he ran with a magnetic draw towards the derelict motorcycle. A slovenly looking lump sat in a folding chair in the shade of a tree several yards away. Jim had no technical knowledge nor had he ever ridden a motorcycle. Yet somehow, he felt compelled to give the machine a deeper look. Running his fingers on the rusty metal of the frame, he straddled it and put his hands on the bars. Instantly his mind gave way to visions of cruising down a winding forest road. Jim got an electric sensation of a far-off freedom.

"You just gonna look? Or ya gonna buy?" The lump crushed Jim's ecstatic trance.

"How much?" he replied.

"It's got plenty of compression. I tested it. Gotta be worth at least $500." The greasy man shifted in his folding chair.

Jim dismounted the bike. "How did it get like this?"

"I rode it for a while and then just got tired of it. Parted it out some and got tired of messing with it."

The neglect of this formerly beautiful machine stirred anger in Jim. The years of abuse wore long. He shared a sense of camaraderie with the motorcycle.

Unaccustomed to the practices of bartering, Jim simply paid full price. Missing his shift to retrieve the money from his apartment, he engaged in the first spontaneous act of rebellion in his life. That $500 was just about all he had. With no way of getting the bike home on a trailer, he simply rolled it home. Jim sat shocked in the parking lot of the apartment building after retrieving his car.

"What did I just do? I can't afford this! It's just a piece of junk. I don't know anything about how to fix this." He sat on the curb across from the machine.

His upstairs neighbor, Billy, walked out on the balcony to smoke a cigarette. "What'd you get?" he bellowed.

"A piece of junk." Jim put his head in his hands.

"Does it have compression though?"

He thought for a moment. "Yeah the guy said he tested it."

Billy, an older man with a large paunch, sauntered down the stairs to take a look. "Spark, Compression, Timing, and Fuel. It's as simple as that," he grunted after approaching the man and his machine.

Jim crossed his arms. "It's got to be more complicated than that. How do mechanics charge so much?"

The older man put a hand on the throttle grip. "Nope, that's it. It's simple." he pushed down on the suspension. "I didn't say it was easy though."

"Can you help me?" Jim asked expectantly.

"I suppose I could." Billy stroked his stubble. "But it's just a piece of junk, right?"

The young man shifted, "Well, it's got compression though?"

"Unless you see some value in it, it's just some scrap metal," Billy waxed contemplative.

Jim looked over to the motorcycle again. As a sculptor views a block of marble, he grasped the titanic task ahead of him. Hesitantly he repeated, "It's got compression."

"You gonna commit?" Billy crossed his arms.

"I mean—"

"Yes or no?" his neighbor pursed his lips.

With a sigh, Jim ran through all the times he dared to start something and let it pass him by instead. He could just try to sell it and get his money back. Or he could plunge into the unknown.

"Yes!" the word appeared like a lightning rod from his mouth.

Billy smiled. "Look at that, we've got some spark!"

His neighbor's declaration rippled in his mind. Jim had never committed to anything that didn't involve instant gratification.

After receiving a dressing down from his boss at the retail store the next day, he slaved through a nine hour shift. Rushing home, he saw Billy sitting next to the bike with a toolbox.

"Bout time." He sniffed the evening air. "C'mon, let's get to work. I hooked up a battery and it cranks right over. Put this spark plug in."

Jim took the small metal implement in his hand. Following instructions, he guided the plug into the ignition boot.

"Now place it on the cylinder head and take a look." His neighbor pointed to the top of the engine.

In truth, he could've pointed to the rear tire and Jim would be none the wiser. Billy took a deep breath and pressed the starter button. As the engine cycled over, Jim watched in eager anticipation at the little rods of electricity jumping across the electrode.

"It's working!" he cried.

Billy nodded. "I know. You almost wrote this thing off. This thing's still got plenty of life." He patted the front tire. "Just needs a little TLC."

"What's next? We have compression and spark. I suppose we should do the timing?" Jim repeated what his neighbor told him last night.

"Hold your horses. Before we go about ripping apart the engine, let's just shoot some fuel in there." Billy grabbed a spray can labeled "starter fluid" from the pavement.

The young man shook his head. "But there's not even a fuel tank."

"Sometimes you can get away with just a quick hit of this. If everything else is good, we should hear some ignition. It won't run for long, just a few seconds." His neighbor gave the can a couple shakes.

Jim thought about his own life. He remembered the dozens of times he resorted to a quick dopamine hit over working towards genuine satisfaction. Just like the engine, this would only keep him going for a few seconds until his mind would go dormant in a meaningless malaise.

After a few spritzes of the fluid, Billy gave the starter a few cranks. The engine tumbled over and over but to no avail.

"What's wrong?" Jim concealed his immense heartbreak.

His neighbor remained silent as he set about removing the generator cover. "Oh geez." Billy shook his head.

"What?"

"Oh man." His neighbor pursed his lips.

"What's wrong?" Jim's heart sank.

Billy stood up and wiped his hands. "Well, the timing is totally out of whack. Frankly I'm surprised there's spark at all. The cam chain might not even be there otherwise we'd hear it rattling around. The spark is probably governed by the computer but it's telling it to fire at the wrong times." He paused to grip the throttle. "We've gotta tear it apart unfortunately."

The prospect of a long, drawn out effort depressed him immensely. "Maybe I should just sell it."

Billy furrowed his brow. "Up to you, man. It's got life in it. I know it."

Jim's disposition sagged into gloomy despair. Just like everything else in his life, this would fizzle too. He didn't even notice when Billy packed up his toolbox and left. After stewing for what seemed like hours, Jim sighed and got up off the curb. The sun was already well beneath the horizon as darkness swept into the parking lot. After walking a few steps, he tripped on something. Jim managed to gather his balance and see what was in his path.

"Billy must've left this here on accident," he remarked to himself as he picked up a large screwdriver.

Jim took it in his hand and walked toward Billy's apartment dreading the next day of work. When he reached the second floor, he heard a great deal of commotion coming from the room a few doors down from Billy's. The door suddenly opened, sending a sliver of light out into the night. A woman fled and ran towards Jim. A beer bottle flew out, along with a tirade of curses, and shattered on the balcony.

The woman yelled towards Jim, "Please help me! He's gonna kill me!"

Taken aback, he had no time to react before a surly man came barreling out after her. As she approached, he could see that she was exceptionally beautiful.

"Oh, who's this? Huh?" the man growled.

Confusion overtook Jim as he struggled to react. All he could manage was a steely silence.

"I'll mess you up, man!" The figure approached him rapidly.

Jim held up the screwdriver. "Get back!"

The man hesitated for a moment when he saw the sharp end of the tool pointed at his throat. Jim was far from physically imposing, but the screwdriver made the man think twice about a fight.

"Oh you wanna fight like a pussy? Ok maybe I'll bring my weapon next time." He gave a death glare to both of them and turned around. After a few steps he paused. "I'm going to kill both of you. Bank on it." Then he kicked the shattered glass on the balcony.

As the man walked away, Billy came out.

"What was that all about?" he asked Jim.

He explained what happened and turned towards the woman only to see that she had already retreated inside her apartment.

"Geez, she didn't even thank me." Jim shook his head.

"Well you were there at the right place at the right time. She's probably just shook up. I know her; she's a nice gal. Her name's Vivian." Billy paused for a moment. "See what I mean about timing?"

The young man handed over the screwdriver and chuckled. "I'm not sure how much I really did."

His neighbor patted him on the back before heading in for the night. "You did good, kid."

Jim again stood dumbfounded in the stark blackness of the night. As the adrenaline subsided, he was reminded of his lengthy shift at the store tomorrow. Heading off to his apartment, Jim didn't sleep a wink.

After struggling through his shift, he came back to the parking lot to see Billy working on the bike.

"I've got some good news for ya!" he called out. "You know what I said about timing? The cam chain just skipped a tooth. The tensioners were notoriously bad on these things. By some miracle, the junkyard had one laying around. Even better, I found a gas tank! It's from the previous generation, but it'll do." Billy patted the frame. "Just a few more bolts and I bet it runs!"

Jim could not believe the stroke of immense luck. "Why are you doing all this work for me?"

His neighbor chuckled, "You're a lot like this bike. Somebody just needs to stop and invest a little bit of time."

The young man fidgeted uncomfortably. The feeling of not being alone in the callous system of modernity was utterly foreign to him. After putting his belongings in his apartment, he returned to the parking lot.

Billy took the starter fluid and gave the intake a quick spray. After a crank, the engine screamed to life for just a few seconds. Nevertheless, those transient seconds resonated in Jim's soul like some heavenly symphony. They both let out a triumphant yell.

Billy took the fuel tank and connected up the lines. "I already made sure it would kick into gear." He swatted Jim's back. "You ready to learn how to ride?"

The prospect terrified him. The last time he even rode a bicycle was years ago. After fitting the tank, Billy turned the motorcycle on and fiddled with the idle. Jim almost hoped it would break down again so he wouldn't have to face the hair-raising prospect of riding the motorcycle through the barriers of his comfort zone. He had no such luck. The bike gradually settled into a smooth idle as it warmed up.

His neighbor took it on a quick loop of the parking lot and then put down the kickstand.

"Ok, get on," Billy commanded.

With trembling fingers, Jim ran through the motions of pulling in the clutch and feeling for the brakes. He got into first gear with a hesitant, jerky motion of his left foot.

"Let it out slowly and give it a little bit of gas," his neighbor nodded reassuringly.

Raising the RPMs, Jim let the clutch engage. With a jolt and a shudder, he was underway on the vessel he had seen in his vision. It was exactly as he had seen it when he first put his hands on the handlebars. With his knees in the breeze, he took a deep breath. The warm summer wind rushed by him and cycled through his nostrils and the bike's intake alike.

Both were drinking deeply of fuel. Jim circled the parking lot with a few close calls next to some parked cars and stalled it next to Billy.

"C'mon, get that clutch in when you stop!" his neighbor chastised.

Jim shook his head and restarted the engine. After a few more laps of the parking lot, he even felt confident enough to shift up to second gear.

"Look at you go! We oughta get you your license," his neighbor joked.

Putting the bike in neutral, Jim nodded with a smile. Just as he was about to set out on another lap, he saw a dark figure looming on the second floor of the apartment building. His heart instantly knew what was happening.

"Billy, look!" He pointed to the balcony.

His neighbor whipped around just in time to see Vivian sprinting from her apartment towards the stairs. In a heartbeat, Billy leapt up to render aid.

"Wait, Billy! What should I do?" he called out after his neighbor.

Turning his head as he ran, he called out, "You just get her out of here! I'll stall the guy!"

Vivian came tumbling down the stairs and bumped into Billy. He directed her towards the quivering young man on the motorcycle. Not far behind, the aggressor pursued with murderous intent. The woman ran towards Jim. His mind accelerated beyond the redline.

I can't take her for a ride on this! he thought as time slowed in the heat of the moment. He looked briefly over to his car. As the man started attacking Billy, he knew there was no time to make a quick swap. Jim's keys were back in his apartment.

Before he could finish his train of thought, Vivian was already on the backseat of the motorcycle.

"Let's get out of here!" she yelped.

Jim sat frozen for a moment. As Billy attempted to fight off the attacker, he looked back briefly at the pair. With a grim smile he gave an imperceptible nod as his opponent drew a knife. Jim let out the clutch and gave the bike a healthy helping of throttle. The front wheel kicked off the ground for a brief second as they peeled away. Winding their way down a forest road, the riding came more naturally to Jim. His vision came to its final fruition. She laid her head on his back and held tightly to his body. The warm fires of affection began to well up in tandem with the rapidly cycling engine.

A few years after their wedding, Vivian gave birth to a boy. They named him Billy. As they forged their new lives together, they drank deeply of spark, timing, and fuel—never mind the compression.

Goodbyes and Clear Skies

Turn_Coat

Eliza's face was streaked with sweat and rain as she opened the door to her apartment. The streets of Seattle were dirty with soot and human waste beneath a cloudy, thunderous sky. Eliza felt nauseous, having covered barely a third of a mile before tiring and at-pace returning home. The rain descended in a dreary haze glowing with the city buildings and traffic alighting steep streets.

As Eliza pitched open the cheap, plastic door to her apartment, water fell from her back onto an even cheaper carpet. "Alright," said Eliza breathlessly, "I'm back."

Eliza's roommate made a show of ignoring the return while playing with her phone in an old armchair. The girl was a properly rotund woman named Capricorn. She had actually legally changed her name to Capricorn. Eliza had no idea why, and at this point was a little scared to ask.

"When's your boyfriend going to be getting home?" asked Eliza.

"Five or six," answered Capricorn grumpily. "Depends on the bus."

Eliza glanced at the clock. Capricorn's boyfriend was the third roommate in the apartment and worked fast food. He'd come home greasy and tired and plop his lanky ass on the couch right next to his adipose addled partner.

"I'm going to take a shower before he gets back."

Capricorn harrumphed in response, but didn't say anything intelligible.

It had been about two weeks since Eliza had come to the realization that her life had been stagnant, and that her friends wanted it that way. You can throw crabs in a bucket because any one that tries to climb the rim will be pulled back down by one of his comrades. Maybe that's what life was like now: sit in the office, work a meaningless job for miserable pay, and do that forever.

Water splashed down the shower drain. Eliza checked herself in the mirror. She wanted to look good, not just exist or do the bare minimum. Sure, life sucked, but there was more to it than this—there had to be. Just work until you die? As much as her friends had given her hell the one time she'd mentioned it, she wanted to have kids and a family one day, not… this.

Eliza exited the shower swathed in an old, teal towel.

"You should really take care of yourself better," said Capricorn.

"I'm good," said Eliza, casually traversing their shared living room.

“No seriously,” said Capricorn. “You should love your body more, instead of trying to change it. I’ve seen you with your salads and with your jogging. You’re placing undue stress on yourself; you’re going get hurt. I’m just *worried* about your wellbeing y’know.”

“I’m sure you are,” said Eliza, hoping for a swift end to the conversation.

“We should go out tomorrow,” said Capricorn, “maybe grab some ice cream or something.”

“I’ll see if I have time after work,” said Eliza.

“It’s just that—” Capricorn was cut off by the front door rushing open and Jonathan returning from work. His hair was thin and matted while his shirt was stained from a day in the grease pit, as he sometimes called it.

“Oh hey, you’re back!” Capricorn stood, leaving a decidedly pear-shaped indentation in the chair where she’d rested for the day, and waddled across the floor to hug him. “It’s great to see you. How was work? I was just thinking about making some food.”

Eliza laid down on her bed. Crabs in a bucket. Maybe they liked living in this shit-stained, dreary city where it took three roommates to afford a minuscule studio.

* * *

It took several weeks of tacit maneuvering. Capricorn continued to make focusing on exercise or diet difficult. Still, once Eliza had grown accustomed to infrequent concerns for her health, it stopped bothering her so much. After a particularly long run, closing in on a mile now, Eliza was resting on their communal couch when Capricorn sat down on her chair in the corner and spoke.

“You should get a boyfriend,” said Capricorn. “I’m happier now that I’ve allowed Jonathan into my life.”

“I don’t know, maybe I just haven’t found the right guy yet,” said Eliza.

“Oh, it’s easy, just scroll on your phone and take your pick,” said Capricorn, showing off her phone for emphasis.

“I’m not interested in just a one-night stand,” said Eliza.

“It’s fun! I’ve been out with dozens of guys. It’s like ice cream: you can’t settle for just one flavor for the rest of your life. Jonathan accepts that about me. That’s why he’s okay with my occasional fling or date. I can’t be held hostage like a bird in a cage,” said Capricorn. She brushed a lock of brightly-hued hair out of her face and looked at Eliza encouragingly.

Eliza removed the keys from a hook near the door. “I have to get to work.”

What Capricorn had said stuck in Eliza’s mind for the remainder of the day. Maybe the big girl was right, one-night stands were a hell of a lot easier than some messy relationship. Eliza’s last boyfriend hadn’t turned out too well anyway.

Evidently it worked for Capricorn, though Eliza worried a little what *type* of guys were interested in a one-night stand with that behemoth of a woman. Call center work was mind numbing; it was half paperwork and half talking to angry people. Her coworkers all seemed miserable as she was, mashed into ill-fitting cubicles like chickens in an industrial pen.

Where did you even meet people anymore? Social media was trash; only people over sixty or seventy even attended churches or social gatherings. People didn't even meet in bars; you arranged a date on some app before you got there, and if you showed up alone, you'd probably be leaving alone too. Everything had to be impersonal. Pick him up and then ghost him like trash if he didn't match your taste. It was easy.

Eliza's afternoon jog was dreary again. The sun did deign to make a brief appearance on the corner of Tenth and Alder as she was passing by a series of tents. The bright colors of the vagrant encampment contrasted the dull concrete of the sidewalk.

When Eliza returned home, she cooked dinner and shared a dish with Capricorn before sitting in the shared living room. She tried scrolling through the digital profiles of various men in the area. "I don't know," said Eliza, turning to look at Capricorn still ensconced in her carpeted armchair like it was a throne. "What do you look for in a guy?"

"Whether or not he's any good in bed," said Capricorn with a rolling laugh.

"No seriously," said Eliza.

"I wouldn't worry about it; guys will sleep with you no matter what. Just pick out a guy you think might look alright without his clothes on."

"It isn't exactly appealing to get fucked by some guy who will just sleep with anything. It's supposed to be about more than that," said Eliza.

Capricorn shrugged. "Like what?"

Eliza shrugged. "Maybe a husband, or kids?"

"Kids?" said Capricorn derisively. "Who would want a little cum goblin running around and under foot all the time? We should be happy as who we are. Why commit to something when there's no reason to? Just enjoy your life."

Eliza wondered if Capricorn enjoyed her life. "What about when we're older? Don't you want kids someday?"

Capricorn shook her head. "Hell no, I don't want that kind of responsibility. When we're old we'll go on vacations, travel, see things and go to new places. It'll be an adventure! Kids won't be anything like that; it's just a bunch of whining and screaming. Damn kid in my house would get beat to death. That's why I made Jonathan get a vasectomy. Birth control really should be the man's responsibility anyway."

Eliza shook her head. "When did that happen?"

"I dunno, six weeks before you joined the lease on my apartment."

* * *

Isn't it human nature to raise the next generation and have someone remember you once you've grown old and died? Lineage mattered; it mattered to Eliza's mom and dad before she'd gone off to college here in Seattle—at least she thought it mattered. Eliza had trouble getting to sleep that night and only succeeded after resolving to call her mother for advice. Change was an important part of life, and it seemed like the world just wanted stagnancy. Corporate overlords demanding drudgery while she slowly wasted away until she was as gray and featureless as the city's concrete copse and dim skies. She remembered being outside once upon a time when she was a kid. Where did those days hiking trails in the Cascades with her father go?

In the morning, she once again woke around the same time as Jonathan. He smiled at her as she prepared for the day, but he looked exhausted. She watched him out of the corner of her eye as she applied a minimal amount of makeup. "You alright?" she asked.

He shrugged. "Capricorn just kept me up late last night, talking about what Mel Jackson did yesterday."

"Who?"

"Just some internet celebrity," said Jonathan, looking blearily out their apartment window at the rising sun. "Guess it's important to her. So I guess it's important to me. Apparently the guy said something about keeping his daughter at home, and Capricorn was incensed. Whole bunch of people online calling for the guy's head."

"Eh," grunted Eliza in acknowledgement.

"I dunno, it's just hard," said Jonathan.

"I mean, we made last month's rent OK," said Eliza.

Jonathan spoke hesitantly. "Sort of… I had to get a payday loan last month to be honest."

Eliza took a deep breath. No, she wasn't going to offer to help cover. She really wanted to; she could see how tired Jonathan was. He'd been working day in and day out for the last two weeks, and now she knew why. He had to cover the payday loan *and* this month's rent on behalf of himself and Capricorn. She even knew that look in his eye: he was hoping that Eliza would offer to help, but she wasn't going to do it. She knew better. "Well, I might be able to help with the payday loan… *if* we can cover this month's rent." Dammit. Dammit dammit dammit. Eliza shook her head. Why did she say that? Well, obviously Jonathan needed the help, but that wasn't her job. It wasn't like Capricorn and Jonathon were *her* kids. Just roommates.

Jonathan relaxed a little, “I mean… I don’t mean to get in the way, but it *would* really help us stay afloat.”

* * *

“Hey, Mom,” said Eliza when the other end of the phone line picked up. It had been a long working day and she’d considered not calling, but stuck to the previous evening’s plan anyway.

“How’s it going, big city girl? I haven’t heard from you in ages,” said her mother, who’d never really *wanted* her daughter to leave the house.

“It’s going OK. I know, I should call you more. I’ve just been thinking, it’s like I’m spinning my wheels out here y’know?”

“Well, that’s how it is sometimes,” said her mother. “I’m sure someone will recognize how talented you are. You’ve got a degree after all. It should be pretty easy to find something; just show them what a great worker you are. When I was your age, I worked plenty of different jobs and had to apply to five or six different jobs before I found something that I enjoyed doing.”

Eliza silently rolled her eyes and remembered why it was she so rarely spoke to her mother. Somewhere in the last thirty years life had completely changed, and her mother simply didn’t seem to have noticed. She imagined how nice it would be to get a call-back after only five or six job applications. Try fifty or sixty, assuming you passed an automated credit check. You’d be lucky to get a rejection letter in your email six months after the fact. “I’m working on it, Mom,” Eliza said.

“Maybe you should think about buying a house. It’s a great investment,” said her mother. “Your father and I bought ours for around seventy-five thousand dollars when we were young, and now it’s worth ten times that! Your dad always said that a house was the greatest investment a family could make.”

“You remember that guy I dated in high school?”

“You mean that little, black-haired boy? I think his name was Lawrence. He moved to California to try and become a musician. I never heard what he’s up to now,” said Eliza’s mother.

“No, the guy I dated my senior year, the blond guy. Caleb.”

“Oh yeah! Him. I think he got an engineering degree and moved to Iowa or something to work for John Deere. That’s what his mom said anyway. Don’t know why someone would move out there; there’s nothing to do. Takes all sorts I guess.”

* * *

“Dude, I’m telling you, the weirdest thing happened.”

“Fucking hell, Caleb. You finally get around to hooking up with that Lithuanian girl you were talking about at work?” said Scott over a crackling phone line.

“No man, I… I dunno. I don’t know how to get to the next step with her. I’m not even sure she’s interested.”

“Alright, hang on. Just a second.” There was a muffled commotion on the far side of the microphone before Scott spoke again. “Then what happened?”

“So I dated a girl in high school,” said Caleb.

“OK, and?”

Caleb fiddled with a refrigerator magnet. “Apparently she got ahold of my mom and asked for my phone number.”

There was silence on the far end of the phone line for a moment. “Did she give the girl your number?”

“I told her she could. That was a few days ago,” said Caleb.

“Uh-huh… well, that’s kinda weird. What was is it about?” said Scott.

Caleb pawed through his clanky, old refrigerator looking for something to cook. “That’s what I asked when she called me.”

“She actually called you? For real?”

“Yeah, weirdest thing. She said she’d just been thinking about things and had got to wondering what I was up to these days. We talked for like three hours, man. Do you think she was hitting on me?”

“If you thought she might be hitting on you, she was *definitely* hitting on you. Can’t take a damn hint to save your life. Wait, so your ex from fucking high school was hitting on you over the phone? Is she hot?” asked Scott.

“Eh… not like a ten out of ten. She was heavy in high school, but she says she’s been working out and shit. I’m just not sure what to do; my plans are all fucked up now. Do I try to get back together with this ex or…?”

Scott considered on the distant far side of the phone line. “Dude, your life is fucking weird some days.”

“I know, right?! I’m not sure what to do.”

“Pfffft… I don’t know. Get on a video call with your high school friend to see how she’s doing now, and ask your coworker to go to the gun range with you. There you go. Next logical step for both.”

“You sure that’s a good idea?” asked Caleb.

“No. But it’s the best I got. If your coworker isn’t cool to go shoot with you, then she’s not worth wasting any time on anyway. Get a video chat with telephone girl and see what you think,” said Scott.

“I… I suppose that’s true,” said Caleb. “Next logical step, see what happens.”

“I mean, what else would you do? Sit on your ass and wait? What’s the point of raking in a hundred thousand dollars a year if you've got no one at home worth spending it on? Go for it! A hell of a lot better than you'll find scrawling through profiles."

* * *

A ruckus round of laughter shook the table, and Eliza's attention returned to her immediate friends. To Eliza's left was Kelsie, a girl that Eliza had met a few years ago as a coworker. Kelsie was in her late twenties and enjoyed the bar scene, always getting slovenly drunk when the opportunity presented itself and using that as an excuse to sleep with whoever was handy. Seated to Eliza's right were Aaron and Ramona engaged in a loud conversation complaining about their corporate landlords raising rent again.

"I don't know," said Ramona, "at least in our parents' day you could just let the landlord smash in exchange for cheap rent once a month, but that guy looked like he couldn't smash an Easter egg."

This elicited more laughter from Aaron. "Did you see how hard it was for him to get up the stairs for the inspection? Fuckin' property management firm. My window *still* has a leak."

Eliza sipped a mixed drink and tried to enjoy herself. "Come on guys, let's go dance."

"Ah, no, I'm good," said Aaron.

Kelsie, whose dress already bordered on salacious, was up for the dance floor though, and soon the two of them were trying to outdo each other. Eliza allowed her mind to wander as she danced. Within ten minutes Kelsie had taken a break and gone back to the bar for a pre-processed pizza, a luxury that Eliza had stopped allowing herself over two months ago. Actually, Eliza thought, she didn't really feel tired from dancing either, not like she used to anyway. The hard work she'd been putting in had been paying off.

Kelsie and Ramona were talking about their most recent boyfriends. Ramona tended to go through a relationship every month or two, with Aaron being a perpetual fallback fuck-buddy. Kelsie didn't even bother doing anything serious.

"He was good in bed, I don't know, just didn't feel the chemistry y'know?" said Ramona. "I feel like it'd be, y'know, effort to stick with him."

Kelsie spoke, slightly slurring her speech. "You always get the best guys and just throw them away! He was going to get a doctorate or something, right?"

Ramona shrugged. "Just not my type. Besides, you're one to talk."

Kelsie shook her hair and smiled. "I do who I want, when I want. I should have brought a date out here; got a guy on the hooks right now. He's *obsessed* with me, chasing me around and texting me."

Ramona grinned. "Is he hot?"

Kelsie smiled back. "Yeah he is, told me he owns a nightclub."

"What about you?" asked Kelsie to Eliza. "I could hook you up with a guy. You aren't online enough to meet anyone."

"I'm OK," said Eliza.

Ramona looked at Eliza for a long minute. Maybe she was acting out of character for this quiet celebration of drinks and music, sufficiently so for Ramona to catch on at least. "Wait, are you seeing a guy?"

"I'm thinking about it," responded Eliza.

* * *

"You ever get Lithuanian girl to hit the range with you?" asked Scott over voice chat, the sound of some video game barely discernible in the background.

Caleb paused before continuing. "Nah, actually she kinda surprised me."

"How?"

"When I asked she was all like '*I heard you were from the Seattle area, that you also didn't like it out here in the country.*'"

"Bruh," said Scott simply.

"Yeah, so I guess that isn't ever going to happen," said Caleb.

"Yeah man, fuck that. What about the other girl you were talking about?"

Caleb fidgeted a little. "We've been talking every few days about life, books, about politics… Watching a few old shows together."

"Politics?" There was a pause as Scott was clearly thinking on the far side of the voice chat. "Like real politics?"

"A little," replied Caleb.

"Huh," said Scott, "didn't think anyone in that city would have it in 'em."

"I've been impressed," said Caleb. "Once I started talking about some of the dissident ideas, the ones you're not allowed to have on social media, she said everything kinda started making sense. The focus on family and qualifying the spiritual good of our people over materialism, it appeals to her."

"Well," said Scott, "good for you two; guess you'll have to start dating."

* * *

Two weeks ago Eliza would have just been doing this out of stubborn determination, but now she had *someone* that she wanted to actually look good for. It was a new experience. After decades of "ever size is beautiful" bullshit, Eliza had finally decided to stop pretending aesthetics were arbitrary. There was beauty, and there was ugly, and they weren't in the eye of the beholder.

Eliza and Caleb had made their boyfriend/girlfriend status official a week ago, and it had served only as more motivation. Maybe she'd be able to have a family anyway; all she had to give up were those big city delusions she'd developed years ago at the age of eighteen. This wasn't a place of wonder and opportunity; it was one of used needles, homelessness, broken glass, and concrete. *I'm going to go work in the big city and get a degree and have a career.*

Long distance, Eliza and Caleb watched stupid, childish cartoons together and managed a few conversations on politically sensitive subjects. The conversations with her long-distance boyfriend were novel, thought Eliza, to talk to someone who didn't share all those urban taboos. She'd spent so long tiptoeing around social eggshells that she hadn't even realized what the world could be like without doing so. It was nice.

* * *

"She lives with a roommate and the boyfriend."

"She lives with her boyfriend?" asked Scott.

"Her roommate's boyfriend. Says he's been wage slaving for years. They're pretty progressive as far as partisanship goes," said Caleb.

"That makes sense. I couldn't imagine living in a house like that. When the hell are you two getting together anyway?"

"Well, I flew out last weekend to meet her in person." Caleb glanced out the window of his small home as he continued talking. "It went well. We watched some movies together; she showed me around the city and took me to a dance club. We stayed in a hotel. She said that her roommates would have lost their minds if I'd stayed with them."

"Yeah, I bet they would've; it's good to hear you two met up. How was she?"

"It was great! We had a great time. I remembered why we'd dated in high school for that year before I took off to get my degree."

There was silence on the line for a few seconds.

"Shortages are getting worse," said Scott. "How are they where you are?"

"Nothing too bad yet," said Caleb.

"You've got to get her the fuck out of that city."

"I know.

* * *

Today was moving day and Capricorn was furious.

"If you leave like this, we sure as hell won't give you back your deposit!" said Capricorn angrily from where she stood on the compressed living room carpet.

Eliza shrugged. She wasn't going to get her deposit back no matter the conditions that she'd decided to exit their arrangement under. "I know. Maybe it will help you two cover rent while you look for someone to take my place."

Capricorn glared at her. "You're just being selfish; give us at least a month."

"I didn't know I was going to be leaving in advance," lied Eliza. Eliza had been accustomed to telling the little white lie before now, but this was different. She'd lied for weeks about planning to leave, and now she lied to Capricorn's face about what her ultimate plans had been. Why? Eliza wondered what had changed.

For nearly a full two days, Capricorn had tried to raise hell as Eliza had packed her pitifully small distribution of belongings into a few dozen cardboard boxes. Capricorn was even less happy when Caleb had finally pulled up in front of the apartment in a beat-up, red pickup truck with plates from a state deep within the American heartland.

"I'm here," texted Caleb when he finally parked outside the high density apartment block. His truck barely fit onto the shoulder of the narrow asphalt road; he had to jump two tires up onto the curb.

Eliza opened the door of her shared apartment and walked outside beneath the heavy coastal clouds to wave at him. "You made it!"

Caleb nodded. "Took me an hour to get the U-Haul trailer though. Credit check database went down or something. Let's get your boxes."

Capricorn finally arrived on the front stoop and glared daggers at Caleb. He wore a pair of rough work boots and Carhartt jeans and obviously didn't belong anywhere in a city like this, and judging by his swagger, obviously didn't care. "These your roommates?"

"Yeah," said Eliza softly.

"Howdy," he said to Capricorn. "How's Seattle these days?"

Capricorn scoffed at him. "I can't believe that she'd just abandon us like this." Eliza watched as Jonathan emerged from the apartment to stand next to Capricorn.

Eliza and Caleb began removing boxes from the cramped apartment, one after the next. Eliza had a hard time meeting Jonathan's eyes. She knew that leaving on short notice might wreck him financially. Of course she also knew that if she'd provided a month of warning she'd be lucky if Capricorn hadn't tried to destroy either the travel plans or her property. Who knew what that girl could do… Eliza had seen Capricorn end friendships and commit property theft over feelings of abandonment.

"We should never have let you into the apartment. You're never going to be welcome here again! Good luck finding somewhere to live," said Capricorn angrily. "Jon, she's not allowed in the apartment anymore!"

At one point Jonathan attempted to intervene directly, at Capricorn's behest, but a cold look of indifference from Caleb had ended that, the sort of look between men that constituted an acknowledgement, a threat, and a willingness to act in ways that coastal elite culture believed they were too civilized to partake in. After that, the loading got easier, though Capricorn at no point stopped the attempted delays.

Eventually the U-Haul was loaded and the pickup stuffed. Caleb was in the cab starting the engine when Jonathan came over to Eliza and simply stated, "I don't know how we're going to pay rent next month."

Eliza wanted to apologize and offer him financial help, and defend her actions. She could see a tired pain in Jonathan's eyes. He had hopes and aspirations and dreams too, just like she still had. Eliza bit her lip and tried to speak, angry with herself for leaving like this and angry at Capricorn and Jonathan for making it the only palatable option.

Caleb spoke from inside the old truck as the engine rumbled to life, loud and confident, "Well, I'm sure the two of you will figure something out. Best of luck!"

Was it smug and self-assured? Sure it was. Coastal elite types like Capricorn and Jonathan had been shitting on Caleb for a long time, especially since he'd moved to Middle America. At the same time Eliza respected him for not intentionally rubbing salt in the wound she was leaving in the household. She didn't say anything, simply got in the passenger's seat and the two of them left.

Eliza watched as the city highway turned to cold and bony mountains, then opened into wide plains and distant, green fields. The concrete and rebar of Seattle were behind her. The stony grasp of those tendrils were still trying to heave her back into their embrace, but weaker now, the connection or addiction severed.

While she sat in the passenger's seat of Caleb's truck, she realized what had changed, why she'd felt so comfortable lying to Capricorn for weeks before exiting their living arrangement: it was about who Capricorn was, what she now represented. Eliza glanced over at Caleb who was fiddling with the radio. The few cars in front stretched away until it was only the two of them on the road between swelling oceans of green, growing grains. Capricorn and Eliza were of different peoples, a people different from herself and Caleb. Eliza wondered when her sense of moral universalism had unobtrusively evaporated. Instead it had become centered about a new family, a new people, new ideas.

* * *

Eliza looked out from her front porch across the open prairie. *Her* front porch. She hadn't even realized places like this existed. In an intellectual sense she knew they did, but it never really struck her that these were places one could physically travel to. Her phone rang, an irritating little buzzing emerging from her purse like an angry hornet. She picked it up.

"Hello?"

"Hey, Lizzie, we haven't heard from you in ages. Wondered if you wanted to run out and get some drinks or something. You don't call us anymore. Ramona is all up in arms about what the police did the other day. All cops are bastards. Where've you been anyway?"

"Oh, I've been out for a bit. I moved actually," said Eliza.

"Oh really? Where to? You're still in the neighborhood right? We're going to hit up that new club I told you about in downtown. You want to come with us?"

Eliza watched the dimming sun closing the day on a clear sky. "No… I won't be going out downtown tonight."

The times ahead might be hard. War, betrayal, famines, and more lay past that beautiful horizon of aquamarine darkening to a deep pastel purple. Still, she thought, she'd definitely rather be here with her new fiancé among the farmers and fields. Better than remaining trapped in halls of asphalt and glass fighting with some kitschy, urban bureaucrat over the last can of beans in a Walmart parking lot.

An Excerpt from a Story about Possession

Memento Vivere

In the stretch of time since returning home, the color of spring had waned into dullness. The once comfortable warm days with their cool breezes reached an unbearable crescendo of sweltering heat.

He was sitting on the porch step, which creaked loudly under his shifting weight. The worn-down paint chipped off in broad, peeling flakes. He was certain it had not been retouched since the last time he sat there; that was years before.

He could hear a neighbor speaking loudly, complaining of work, the displeasure of a meeting and having more numbers than a human being should rightly be tasked to process. The vague shape of a head could be placed in an open living room window from which the neighbor's voice projected. He wondered if the man in the window knew he was speaking for an audience or if he simply didn't care.

Looking through other windows, one could catch clues of living room occupation: the glimpse of a silhouetted hand passing by mid gesticulation. Families idled together within on a summer's day which they found too hot for work or play and especially too hot for rest.

It was altogether a stifling day, made tolerable only by the assumption of a breeze and that sweet tea brewed out of his mother's kettle and served readily with ice. He could hear the occasional muffled word of Paul, only able to understand in part: "...rich enough for computer games and too poor for air conditioning..." He imagined his mother absently nodding her head, a glossy expression indicating she was generously paying half-attention. Her hand clutching a frosty glass from which she took short, delicate sips. Something about what Paul was saying bothered him, though it was hardly the kind of thing he could articulate and expect to be understood. That maybe the discomfort was the point, that without it days like these would never be memorable, but would instead fade into a similarly temperate haze of recollection. And besides, if we all had air conditioning they'd expect us to work all the time regardless of climate.

"Aren't you hot out there, Bill?" came a call from behind him. He was a little surprised as he thought no one was aware of him resting on the step. "Well, I'm sure hot in here." Whatever could be said of his brother's abrasiveness, he had a keen perception. Bill took in all the sleepy goings-on outside before standing, sighing in unison with the step beneath his feet. The screen door opened to him a portal of darkness before slowly his eyes became acquainted with the dim lamplight-illuminated living room. As it all came into view, he laughed to himself to see that the scene was almost precisely as he imagined it a moment ago.

He threw himself lazily down on the couch beside his mother. She was scratching off lottery tickets while Paul rocked gently in dad's chair. The TV box chattered quietly, innocent white noise in the background filling up air-space. He adjusted himself, already uncomfortable at the contact of cushion and accumulated perspiration. "How'd you guess where I was?" he asked to Paul.

Paul drained what ice water had accumulated in his glass and set it down on the table. "Where else would you be?"

Silence fell on the idle three, none of them feeling the urgency to break it. None of them had anywhere at all to be, and for the moment, nothing at all to worry about on the horizon. Bill realized he couldn't recall the last time he felt that way. Childhood? Probably. His time in the city had been so wracked with senseless anxiety, when the darkness lingered beyond every street corner, within every alley, behind every door, and in every face, that he'd forgotten actually what it felt like to just be all right. This was not a feeling that could be experienced with a sedative cocktail. A doctor couldn't give it to you. A flash of fear came over him as though he'd forgotten he was due someplace important; his eyes briefly darted across the room. It was a fear that was quickly displaced, and it faded into irrelevance.

He stepped out into the kitchen and poured some tea over a few cubes of ice, which crackled as they drowned. "So then," he began, returning to his place, "where's Joey?"

"Upstairs," said Paul, shaking his head. "Computer games."

For a man like Paul, complaint was such a well-acquired skill that it appeared natural. Though it only showed through in little ways, cracks in the veneer; he was at this moment, Bill could intuit, merely happy at being alive.

Paul tilted his head to look outside, his legs stretching with each rocking motion of dad's chair. "It's good to be home."

Bill couldn't help but agree.

Honorable Mention in Short Stories

The Door

Casey McDonough

For our wrestling is not against flesh and blood; but against principalities and powers, against the rulers of the world of this darkness, against the spirits of wickedness in the high places.

Ephesians 6:12

For the weapons of our warfare are not carnal, but mighty to God unto the pulling down of fortifications, destroying counsels.

2 Corinthians 10:4

The day the Boy was born, a door was opened. Nothing entered through it for quite some time. For most of the Boy's earlier years it simply hung on its hinges. Not more than an occasional breeze might cause the door to swing idly and drift nearly shut, but never close.

Gradually, the Boy grew up and began to form a mind of his own. He was soon running and playing jovially with the other boys his age, often spending his days outside from dawn till dusk as every boy should. It was during this formative time when a tick first crawled its way through the door. It latched on to the Boy's chest and tried to burrow itself into his heart. This same day, the Boy cursed his own brother, for he had made him terribly upset, but the Tick's grasp was not strong enough to overpower the child's innate admiration for his older brother. Before the Boy went to bed, he made sure his brother knew he was sorry, and the Tick lost its grip. The insect fell to the floor, and defeatedly crawled back through the door from which it came, but still the door remained open.

Every now and again over the next few years, a tick, a fly, and sometimes a worm would wriggle its way through the door, one at a time, and attempt to make a home for itself inside the Boy. Flies found that the Boy's instincts were too quick to make a landing for more than a passing moment, and the ticks' strongholds were never quite strong enough to hold for more than a day or two.

The Boy was attending a friend's birthday party the day a worm first ate its way into his young heart. His friend was given a shiny new toy, something the Boy had instantly wished was gifted to him instead. As the Worm gnawed at him from the inside, the Boy convinced his friend to give up his new toy in exchange for one the Boy could trade him from his own collection, knowing that the toy he would trade him was probably going to break soon. By the time the Boy's mother drove him home with his shiny new toy, the friend's trade-in was busted and the gluttonous Worm had stuffed itself completely. Satisfied, the Worm decomposed into the Boy's blood stream and was soon flowing through his veins. The Boy played with his shiny new toy completely unaware of the presence of any worm, or the door through which it came.

For years the door stood open, a hidden portal providing undetected passage to a legion of worms, ticks, and even an occasional weaving spider. One night, something truly terrible approached the door, looking for the Boy. It waited for a moment, knowing it could not make its presence too known, too fast. The Creature, a foul imp with long, outstretched arms dripping thick, black oil, reached through the door and lightly tapped on the Boy's heart. The touch of this beast immediately left a stain on the Boy's heart that quickly spread to his brain and suffocated his final breath of innocence. The Boy sat alone in his bedroom, blind to the hideous nature of his dark company, because to him it looked like a thing of beauty, and stimulation. His youthful eyes sat hypnotized by images of pleasure laying naked in front of him. Not once did he consider, nor once was he warned, that what was looking back at him were the eyes of a roaming lion patiently waiting to devour his very soul.

No matter the brighter or darker days of the Boy's life, the Creature never left the boy's side. Taking the form of a leech, it had sunk its teeth deep into the Boy's neck, sucking the life force out of the young child and hanging on to him wherever he went. At the first glance of a carnal thought in the Adolescent's mind, the Leech would fill the Boy's heart with cursory vignettes of the pleasure and love he longed for, providing momentary comfort but soon enough leaving his soul feeling emptier and emptier with every dose. Sometimes the Boy would ponder where this empty feeling was coming from, and hastily this great Pest would send for more leeches to pile on to the Boy's back. For more than ten years, an uninterrupted flow of these filthy bloodsuckers marched through the door and affixed themselves to his shoulders, suffocating him more with every reinforcement. All the while the Boy went on, a slave to the Leech without one attempt to defy his new master. He was blind and could not see the Leech for what it was, and the door remained wide open.

By the time the Boy had reached adulthood the swarm on his shoulders had grown large enough to blanket his entire back and wrapped around his heart like a noose. Among other things, this torment greatly hindered his pursuit of finding a wife, though marriage was something he deeply desired. Many women sensed the infestation inside of him. Some even felt the draft coming from the open door, and as a casualty many budding relationships would suffer a pathetic death. Often there were women who were not alarmed at all, for their souls bore an infection of their own and left them numb to the Boy's.

As grace would have it, the Boy eventually fell in love with a girl who was not so numb, and she loved him in return. For a moment the Swarm's grasp seemed to slip off of the Boy, and this disturbed the King Leech. Through the open door it summoned another wave of reinforcements, and the mass grew large enough for the Girl to see it for herself. Out of love for the Boy and pain she felt at the sight of the leeches, she fought with the Boy, and the two fought, and fought and fought. At first the Boy was careless and confused, which turned to outright denial of the throng of parasites that had taken hold of him. Denial soon led the Boy to justification. "Well, it's no big deal," the Boy would say to the Girl. "Everyone is like this." The Legion delighted in the words uttered from the Boy's mouth.

The army of leeches prepared for total victory over the Boy as he wept alone on his bathroom floor over the love he knew he was moments from losing. As tears dripped off his nose and his head hung low, his soul cried out for help and was quickly answered by a Spirit. All at once, the Boy finally felt the crushing weight of the parasites on his back. He reached behind and plucked one from off his shoulders, but another quickly filled in to take its place. He tried to pick another, and another, but like the heads of a hydra they seemed to appear faster than he could rip them off. Viciously he began tearing fistfuls of leeches and casting them off of his body, digging them out of his heart one by one. The leeches snarled and hissed in retaliation and continued to siphon their way deep into his chest. He stood up and discovered the trail of bugs as they crawled their way onto his back. In anguished fury he began following the trail, stomping out every single leech, tick, and worm he could find that had set course for his heart. The column of insects led him to the threshold of the open door.

Without hesitation the Boy began to shut the door, but before he could the King Leech stood up off the floor and transformed before the Boy's eyes into an attractive woman. As she got closer she put her hand on the door, begging him not to close it. Her lurid voice lingered for a moment in the Boy's ears, paralyzing him. As she laid her hand gently on the Boy's he looked into her eyes and saw nothing but unending darkness. What he had seen for years as a window to pleasure and sensuous gratification was now a window to absolute emptiness and despair. The Boy shut his eyes tight and slammed the door as hard as he could, but something kept it from shutting completely. Once more the Succubus regressed, this time to its true form, a hunched mass under a thick black cloak. With a face gaunt like a leper and an echoing moan, it fiercely pushed back against the door and managed to wedge its fingers inside the door jamb. "You will never keep us out," the Mass spoke to the Boy in a voice pitched deeper than the bottomless pit. "You cannot shut this door." When he heard the voice the Boy opened his eyes and at last witnessed the Creature for what it always had been, not an insect sent to torment him, not a woman to love him, but a hook-nosed merchant who had come to sell him only death.

In desperation the Boy again cried out to the Spirit. The same reinforcing Spirit that moments ago had given him the strength to fight back against the beast. "You have everything you need, for I am with you," the Spirit spoke to the Boy.

“Do it.” The voice on the other side of the door snarled and hissed, cursing the Boy, but the Boy ignored the Black Mass’ cries and snapped its fingers off under crushing strength. For the first time in his life he had finally closed the door.

For the rest of his days, any time the Boy would ease up his restraint against the door for even a moment he risked its reopening and the return of the Beast, welcoming his own destruction. Forevermore he would wage a holy war to kill this Beast, lest he be killed himself. Fed with conviction flowing from the guardian Spirit, he forged an iron will with the sole purpose of keeping this door shut. Though he did not have the power to permanently lock the door himself, for this required strength beyond his capabilities, he quickly realized that his life had been given back to him with the weight of the Horde lifted off his shoulders and kept behind the door. So long as he could keep it closed, he would have a chance to find love and live at peace until the day the familiar Spirit of a Carpenter would come to tear the door down Himself.

Honorable Mention in Short Stories

Marble Redeemer

Rune Stenbock

The market stall bristled with the grotesque glory from every corner of the empire. Macarius Quintus smoothed back the jet-black curls on his head with one delicate hand, held his heavy purse firmly with the other. His grey eyes wandered between the uncanny artifacts on the shelves—conically shaped craniums, strange beasts, alleged cadavers of sirens, fauns, *monocoli*, the race of one-footed men from far *Indus* who would use their one large foot as protection from both rain and sun.

"Are you looking for anything in particular, sir?" asked the shopkeeper.

He cut an unwholesome figure, the shopkeeper. Clad in filthy vestments and afflicted with severe rotting of the teeth, he constantly rubbed his flabby fingers together, as if this tic would somehow bring increased commerce.

"I heard a rumor about a two-headed dog by the gates," said Macarius.

"Purchased, I'm afraid, sir. But sirens seem to be especially popular these days."

"I'm looking for something that lives."

"This one used to live not that long ago, sir, a real-life harpy from the islands of *Strofades*," said the shopkeeper and displayed what was supposed to constitute a harpy.

"That is not a harpy."

"Ah, a true *cognoscenti*," said the shopkeeper and put the alleged harpy away. Let me show you something I display only to customers with the most… refined of tastes.

The shopkeeper opened a door at the back of the stall, motioned for Macarius to enter. Increasing the firmness of his grip on the purse, Macarius entered.

* * *

Returning to his wagon, Macarius looked around, unwrapped the cloth that protected his purchase, marveled at the eerie apparition.

The shriveled husk of a human was crouched in a final position of prayer to its theriomorphic gods. Dry skin stretched over angular bones, the cracked mouth twisted in a desiccated smile. For many years he had heard tales about the mummified priests of *Aegyptus*, and now, finally, he had found one. Reveling in the joy of acquisition, the sensation was quickly dispelled when he became aware of his lighter purse.

Once again, the grip of his hand had been all too lax. He had spent more of his master's coin on the mummy than he had intended. He had gone against his master's instructions. The mummy wasn't alive, nor would it ever be. And living things was the sole matter of his master's interest. Yet for all this, he hadn't been able to stop himself from making the buy.

Macarius wrapped the mummy in its cloth, locked the wagon, and made his way to the slave market with the purse in an even firmer grip. He prayed to the gods that he would find what he was looking for at the slave market, prayed that his funds would suffice.

* * *

The slaves were aligned on a wooden ramp, chained by hands and feet against the backdrop of masts, ships, and the sea. The air smelled of salt, rang with the cries of gulls.

Macarius moved through the throng of people inspecting the slaves. He paced the ramp, all the time followed by a man in a red toga who tried to act as if his eyes weren't on Macarius. Coming to the end of the ramp, Macarius saw a miserable-looking creature sat on the ground.

She had brown skin, slanted eyes, and an enormous growth that wrinkled red and rotten from her neck to her waist. The tumor must've weighed about as much as an eight-year-old child. Macarius called the attention of the slaver.

"Her price?" asked Macarius.

"Her price?" blurted the slaver. "My good sir, if you want slaves, I have others of much better stock. Yes, Numidians who work all day in the sunlight. Gauls who can—"

"Her price?"

"One thousand *denarii*, good sir."

"For a deformed slave?"

"Ah, but that's what makes her valuable, no?"

"If there's any value to her, why has no one purchased her?"

"Because she's deformed!" exclaimed the slaver and had a long, throaty laugh.

"Is Julius Balbus still slaving at these docks?" asked Macarius, looking around. "I hear he takes fair prices for his slaves, and his customers seriously."

"To hell with Julius and his inbred peons!" shouted the slaver. "Stay with Argrider, and he will make sure you leave satisfied. The deformed one is yours for six hundred *denarii*."

"One hundred *denarii*."

"Anyone can see she's worth at least five hundred!"

"Anyone without eyes. One hundred and twenty *denarii*."

The haggling continued. Argrider the slaver paced, spat, gestured, cursed the gods in one breath, praised them in the next. Macarius stood still save for the occasional smoothening of his hair. He kept his temper even and his right hand on his purse, where three hundred *denarii* remained after the purchase of the mummy. The man in the red toga stood back, watched with piqued interest.

The haggling ended. They arrived at the sum of two hundred seventy-five *denarii* for the deformed slave. That is when the man in the red toga intervened.

"You have softened, Argrider," said the man in the red toga. "Selling the cursed one for under three hundred *denarii*."

"May we conclude or business?" asked Macarius.

"Allow me—Five hundred *denarii*.

"Sold for five hundred *denarii*!" shouted the slaver.

"I thought we had an agreement?" asked Macarius.

"We did, good sir," replied the slaver. "But now, Argrider has a new one."

Argrider led the man in the red toga away to conclude the transaction. Macarius glanced longingly at the neoplastic splendor of the deformed slave. Then he left the docks, cursing the gods. They had not answered his prayers.

Anxious about having to revisit the shopkeeper, Macarius made his way through the throng, gripping his purse until his knuckles whitened. It would not do to return to his master empty-handed.

* * *

The landscape around the *Via Appia* vibrated with the life of early spring. Creeks gurgled with fresh water as the last snows of winter melted, trees stretched their branches towards the sun, and farmers wept sweat from their brows as they worked the soil.

Macarius sat atop his wagon, gazing at the wanderers, riders, carts that traveled the road. Up ahead limped a bent old man hobbling forward with the aid of a withered staff. As Macarius' rode up beside him, the old man addressed Macarius.

"You look like you have a seat to spare for an old man."

"Depends on where he is headed," replied Macarius.

"Rome."

Macarius climbed down, offered the old man his arm. Leading him to the wagon, he inspected the old man.

Furrows creased the weatherworn face, his hair hung thin and white, his vestments were poor and dusty, yet despite his unimpressive figure, there was something about the old man's appearance that elevated him above the dirt that clung to his person. Perhaps it was his azure eyes—youthful, alert, brimming with wisdom.

Arriving at the wagon, the old man stopped when he saw what was stowed in the back. He inspected the grinning mummy and the other monstrosity that lay beside it. Lifting it, the old man saw wings, talons, hair, human skin. When he looked even closer, he recoiled.

"What is this supposed to be?" trembled the old man.

"A harpy," replied Macarius.

"If that's a harpy, then I'm Theseus."

"It is a harpy to the one who purchases it."

Macarius grabbed the man by the arm, led him around to the steps, and helped the old man onto the wagon.

"Why do you travel to Rome?" asked Macarius as the old man took his seat.

"I go there to tell the tales of the heroes of old," replied the old man.

"You're a poet."

"I am but an instrument of the muses. And you? What could make a man travel with such ghastly companions as you have stowed away in the back?"

"I am a *teratologus*. I travel throughout the empire in search of these 'ghastly companions,' which I bring to my master in Rome, where he sells them at the *teraton agora*, the Market of Monsters."

"So people do indeed purchase these things?"

"They do."

"Why?"

"They collect them."

"Surely, one must be disturbed to collect such monstrosities."

"Surely," said Macarius and sat the horses in motion.

* * *

By midday, they came upon the Pontian Marshes. The sun hid behind gray clouds, as if the gloomy swamp wasn't worthy of the rays of Sol. Twisted willows dipped towards the murky waters, their tentacular roots crawling over the boggy ground. From the reeds came the melancholy calls of invisible birds, and the rancid air buzzed with mosquitoes.

Macarius prepared to set the horses to trot when he heard song coming from the marshes. The voice was frail but beautiful. So beautiful that Macarius held in the horses, forgot about the mosquitoes, listened. When the song ended, he jumped down from the wagon, moved closer to find the source of the song.

It was a child. She was pale, thin, miserable looking, yet she possessed a quality that set her apart from other children, a salient feature that no true *teratologus* could miss noticing.

It was her head. It was many times too large for such a scrawny child, so large in fact, that the child seemed unable to stand up, propped up against a willow tree as she was. The head was misshapen, knobby, tautened, a dark fuzz lay plastered to her scalp, and the eyes seemed small and alien embedded in that vast cranium.

"You sing well, child, but can you speak?" asked Macarius.

“I can,” spoke the child with a fair voice.

“Where might your mother be?”

The child pointed towards a spot behind Macarius. He turned around, saw an emaciated woman standing half-hidden in the reeds.

“I mean no harm,” said Macarius and held up his hands in peace.

Slowly, the woman approached, her arms looking like sinews about to snap under the weight of the water pails she carried. Macarius took the pails from her, carried them towards the willow tree where he put them down. The woman bent down to water her deformed child.

“Now,” said Macarius, producing his purse, “how much do you want for your child?”

* * *

The sun saw it fit to appear again when the marshes gave way to a hilly landscape where cattle bleated and smoke from farms drifted lazily towards the cobalt sky. If the pleasant weather affected the poet, he gave no sign. From under his bushy eyebrows, he glowered between the deformed child in the back and Macarius.

“How much will your master profit from the child?” asked the poet.

“Live monstrosities bring in much coin,” replied Macarius.

“And you deem the profit worth the separation of mother from child?”

“Next time the harvest comes up short, who do you think will go without food? The child who can labor, or the child who can’t? I did both mother and child a favor.”

“For being a *teratologus* you sound very much like a simple slaver.”

“And for being a poet, you whine like an old housemaid.”

They rode on in silence.

* * *

The road snaked upwards through the hills, circumnavigating vertical drops that not even Roman engineering could master. On the steep inclines grazed cattle, overlooked by their herders who sat basking in the spring sun.

“How about a tale to make our journey more enjoyable?” asked Macarius.

“My tales would be lost on you,” muttered the poet.

“Just because I deal in the grotesque doesn’t mean I can’t appreciate its opposite.”

“What would a *teratologus* know about beauty?

“I wasn’t always a *teratologus*. Once upon a time, I did other work.”

"Doing what?"

"Sculptures. I used to make my living sculpting."

"Sculpting is a fine way to make a living."

"It's a fine way to starve."

"Were your sculptures that bad?"

"They were beautiful. But in Rome, beauty went out of fashion a long time ago."

They rode on in silence.

* * *

They came to a bridge that spanned over a deep ravine. There, they had to wait until the caravan of wagons coming from the other side had passed. Macarius produced a goatskin, took a swig of wine, offered the goatskin to the poet, who drank deeply.

"Ah!" exclaimed the poet. "Therein dwell the muses!"

"Why not take advantage of them while they course through your veins and tell a story?"

"You're not one to give up lightly, are you?"

"Might pass the time of waiting."

The poet turned to Macarius with a shrewd glint in his azure eyes.

"Have you ever heard the tale of Hercules' twelve labors?" asked the poet.

"Only fragments, as a boy."

"Pass me the wine."

Waiting for the caravan to pass the bridge, the poet told Macarius the tale of Hercules' twelve labors. Macarius listened with rapt fascination, forgetting everything but the heroic deeds the poet described. Neither he nor the poet noticed the deformed child in the back pricking her ears, soaking up every one of the poet's words.

* * *

The dark dome of night stretched above the walls of Rome. Inside the walls towered stupendous buildings, rang the calls of guards, and glowed the fire of a hundred thousand torches. Macarius steered his wagon through the Gate of Capena and entered the city proper.

The streets were crowded, filthy, stinking. Clusters of two and three-storied apartment buildings rose from the ground. Among the buildings moved merchants, soldiers, drunkards, hagglers, hustlers, half-naked whores.

"Welcome to Rome," said Macarius.

"Crown of the empire indeed," sneered the poet.

"Where would you like to be let off?"

"Here is as good as anywhere," said the poet.

Macarius held in the horses, helped the poet off the wagon. He pierced Macarius' eyes with his azure gaze.

"Did you listen closely to the tale of Hercules?"

"When the muses speak, one listens."

"Then you understand what morals the tale wishes to impart?"

Macarius stood silent. So swept away had he been by the tale and the talent by which it had been told that the presence of mind required to divine any morals or larger meaning from it had been lacking.

"To Hercules and the ancients who composed his tale, monsters were not something to be bought and sold," said a fair voice. "Monsters were meant to be slain in combat as a way for heroes to better the world, to put their strength and virtues to the test, and a way to prove themselves in the eyes of the gods."

Macarius wondered at the strange, child-like quality the poet's voice had assumed. But when the poet turned to the wagon, he understood it wasn't the poet that had uttered the words.

"There's more to this head than its deformity," said the poet and nodded at the deformed child.

"Not to Rome," said Macarius.

"Perhaps not to all of its citizens," said the poet with a shrewd glance in his eyes. "Take heed of the tale of Hercules, Macarius. Those who deal in monsters end up as monsters."

And with that, the poet hobbled down the dark city street, disappearing into the shadows.

Macarius covered the child beneath a leather tarpaulin. Then, he picked up the mummy, produced a rope, and tied the mummy to the underside of the wagon. When he was done, he rose, and caught sight of the alleged harpy.

The sight sent shudders over his entire body. He knew that it wasn't a harpy. He knew all too well what it really was. And in that gloomy street, he did not like the way the thing looked at him.

He shook the shudders away, resumed his place on the wagon, and sat the horses in motion. Making his way to the *teraton agora*, Macarius prayed that the bindings of the mummy would hold.

* * *

Macarius entered a covered courtyard illuminated by torches. It was dominated by a circle of large cages. Behind the iron bars sat midgets, humpbacks, giants, hermaphrodites, men with gigantic cocks. At day, they would be displayed to the *curiosi*, patricians and plebeians come to gawk at the misshapen and malformed. At night, they sat in their cramped cells, drinking, drowsing, enviously staring at those who moved about freely. As Macarius held in the horses, a familiar voice reached him from the shadows.

"Ah! At last he arrives!"

A man with fine clothes, ringed fingers, and the smile of a hyena strode towards Macarius.

"Master Lucilius," greeted Macarius, "may your business ever prosper."

"They will indeed with this latest shipment. What strange new wonders do you bring your master this time?

Without waiting for a reply, Lucilius jumped up on the wagon to inspect the wares stowed within. Macarius glanced at the mummy bound underneath as his master rocked the wagon in anticipation. The bindings cracked ominously.

Lucilius rummaged through the back, lift the harpy, inspected it. His smile turned from that of a hyena, to the snarl of a wolf.

"Good Macarius better explain what this is supposed to mean, spun Lucilius."

"A harpy, Master," said Macarius trying not to glance at the mummy.

"If this is a harpy, then Lucilius is a cyclops."

"The market in Capua was all but empty, sir.

"Is that so? Then perhaps good Macarius could explain why Nerva Porcius' *teratologus* just returned with a slave with an absolutely exquisite growth on her neck?"

"He must have purchased it before I had the chance, Master."

"Did I send Macarius, most trusted *teratologus*, to Capua to find excuses? Did I send him to return with useless trinkets and a vulture with the head of a whore sown on?" asked Lucilius and displayed the theriomorphic abomination passing for a harpy.

"I have no doubt you will be able to sell it, Master."

"Lucilius can sell shit to flies; that is not the issue. Do you know what the issue is, Macarius?"

"You sent me to find living things, Master. Which is why I also purchased this."

Macarius removed the leather tarpaulin from the deformed child. Her deep-set eyes blinked in the sudden torchlight that baptized the oversized head in flickering reds and oranges.

"One of the *hydrocephalii*!" exclaimed Lucilius, rocking the wagon in excitement. "They are rare indeed! From whence does she come? From the barbaric woods of Germania Magna? Or far-off Hibernia perhaps?"

"I'm afraid not, Sir," said Macarius and watched Lucilius' excitement fade. "The child stems from the desolate steppes of *Sarmatia*, where it was revered as an oracle to their heathen gods."

"Extraordinary!" exclaimed Lucilius, his excitement returning. "You know how to surprise your master. Now, just hand Lucilius the remaining funds, and he will—"

"I'm afraid I return with an empty purse, Master."

"Then I am afraid Macarius will go with an empty stomach for a while." Lucilius hopped off the wagon. A loud thud was heard.

Macarius looked at the ground, where the mummy lay, its bindings come undone. Just when Lucilius turned to find the source of the thud, a voice rang out through the *teraton agora.*

Both Lucilius and Macarius turned to the deformed child, who sang with a voice clear and beautiful.

"It sings?" asked Lucilius.

"As she was trained to do by the Sarmatian priests."

"It better keep silent at the market tomorrow," sneered Lucilius. "That voice detracts from its delicious deformation."

Lucilius snapped his fingers. A slave picked up the child, carried her away. Macarius stared after the child, who waved to him. Before Macarius could return the wave, she was gone.

* * *

Basilisk's teeth, manticore wings, a cyclops' heads, conjoined twins floating in a glass jar—Macarius took in the altar of the grotesque and the familiar feeling of fulfilment it always brought. For years Macarius had traveled and bought and collected, each item carefully selected with consideration to the abominable harmony that permeated his collection, each artifact carrying with it its own history and memory…

The purchase of the enormous teeth from a destitute *praetorian* in *Syracusae*, the bidding war against a wealthy patrician in *Carthago Nova* that left him the owner of the leathery wings, the acquisition of the one-eyed head in the forbidden market in *Alexandria.* And now, thanks to the child, he had the mummy. With reverence, Macarius placed it among its morbid peers.

The altar dominated the main chamber of his *insulae* where he would eat, sleep, and sometimes entertain guests who would come to marvel at his collection. And when it was complete, there would be no end to the guests' praise. Only a few more items now… Macarius took a step back, beheld the altar.

Out of the teeth grew a basilisk—scaly, slimy, endowed with glowing eyes that turned men to stone; between the wings formed a manticore—human head, feline body, scorpion's tale; the one-eyed head grew a body, grew in stature, towered over the altar; the mummy rattled its teeth in hoarse prayers, flexed the taut sinews under its parched skin. Macarius rejoiced as his collection came alive. It was without a doubt worth a week's empty stomach. Then, a barbaric howl sliced through the *insulae.*

Out on the altar came a man clad in nothing but a lion skin, wielding a gnarled club. His body was all muscles, in his eyes burned with mad fury. He attacked the basilisk, dashed the giant lizard's brains out before it could petrify its attacker. Next, he grappled with the manticore. Taking it by its venomous tale, the man impaled the manticore with its own stinger, delivering poisonous death. The cyclops flew into a berserker's rage, and for a moment, it looked like it would overtake its antagonist. Yet so fierce was the fury of the man clad in lion skin, that eventually, the cyclops fell—cranium cracked, the sole eye hanging out from the sole socket by a thread. Seeing who the man's next target was, Macarius sprang forth, snatched the mummy from the altar. He fell to the floor, mummy cradled in his arms like a small child.

Moments later, he rose slowly, fearing his collection to be in pieces, but even though his prized artifacts were in the same perfectly grotesque condition as before, relief didn't come. He put the mummy back on the altar and left his *insulae* to search for the poet. Maybe he could explain his vision of Hercules. Maybe he could explain why the collection had suddenly lost its appeal and fascination.

* * *

Macarius roamed the night in search of the poet, *tabernae* after *tabernae*, but even though he searched all night, he did not find him. And when the first light of dawn climbed the Roman walls, he found himself, as if by chance, at the *teraton agora.* There, he heard the beautiful voice of the child, telling the tale of Hercules' twelve labors.

The monsters sat inside their cages, gripping the bars, listening with rapt attention to the child. Such a glint was in their eyes that no monstrous retina ever bore. Such a glint, it made the caged creatures appear to Macarius for what they perhaps really were—humans. Yet when he entered the circle of cages, the human gazes turned monstrous, all their hate and scorn directed upon Macarius. Nonetheless, he made his way to the cage of the child.

"How come you know the tale of Hercules, child?"

"I memorized it when the poet told it," said the child.

Macarius looked around, sat down within the circle of freaks, and rested his head in his hands.

"Start from the beginning. Please."

And so, she did. She told the story almost as good as the poet. When he closed his eyes, he could see what she described—the slaying of the Nemedian lion, the capture of the Erymanthian boar, the theft of the Hesperidian apples. Within the dark of his shut eyelids, Hercules slaughtered other things as well—basilisks, manticores, cyclops, a shriveled slave from far Aegyptus. When the tale was over, Macarius opened his eyes. It was already morning.

* * *

Macarius made his way to the part of the market where the stonecutters resided. There, he bought a slab of marble on credit.

When he came home, he opened an old coffin, picked up his sculpture's tools, and dusted them off. They felt strange and foreign in his hands after years of inertia, but they would do for what he had in mind. He sat in the stillness of his *insulae*, visualizing what his work would look like until the marble was delivered. And when the marble was delivered, he went to work.

Macarius labored for the rest of the day and all through the night, taking neither food nor drink. When night turned to dawn, the clang of metal upon marble could still be heard coming from his *insulae*.

* * *

The *teraton agora* was crowded with the *curiosi* who shamelessly stared and pointed at the miserable wretches inside their cages. The air was filled with the voices of vendors who announced the macabre surplus of the empire, and the sun beat down, cooking the covered courtyard. Macarius made his way through the throng carrying an item wrapped in cloth under his arm, sweat pouring down his entire body. Finally, he made it to his master's stall.

"Where is the child," gasped Macarius?

"Ah! Good Macarius, come to inspect business!" exclaimed Lucilius. "Worry not, trusted *teratologus*, they are going phenomenally. I even managed to sell the harpy."

"That wasn't a harpy, Master."

"I know. And so did the purchaser," said Lucilius with a meaning smile.

"The child, Master. The deformed one. Where is she?"

"Sold for the stunning sum of two thousand *denarii*! I though it a hard sell at first when the child refused to stop singing. But of course, there was someone who simply had to have a fair-spoken monster in her collection."

"Who purchased it?"

"I offer not only the finest *terata* in Rome, Macarius, but also discretion."

"I know, Master, but—"

"Never mind my customers. Your services are required early tomorrow.

Rumors abound regarding a woman in *Mediolanum* who is as hairy as a goat. They say even her face is entirely covered. I need my most trusted *teratologus* to investigate if there's any truth to the rumor, and if there is, to track the woman down and purchase her."

"Very well, Master, however—"

"See you at first light tomorrow then."

With that dismissal, Lucilius turned to a customer, a patrician woman who browsed the wares of the stall with a fetishistic twinkle in her eyes. Macarius shook off her gaze and shuffled homewards.

* * *

When Macarius came home to his *insulae*, there was nothing there to greet him but silence and the altar of the grotesque. He sat down, unwrapped the bundle, and placed its contents in front of him.

The sculpture had been intended as a gift to the child. He wondered if she would have liked it. It was rough around the edges, but what could one expect after such a long hiatus from the craft? Still, the work had been inspired. Inspiration… It had been missing a long time. Thanks to the child, it was back. And with inspiration regained, he would make many more. His craft would improve with time. When he was done, the muscles would be anatomically correct, the lion skin wouldn't be undersized, the club not oversized. When he was done, he would be able to do Hercules justice.

Macarius exited the *insulae* and returned inside carrying a heavy plank. He felt the weight of the plank, took a few practice swings, and turned to the altar.

He envisioned himself naked, dressed only in a lion skin, armed with a club. He swung the club, crushed the basilisk's teeth, smashed the manticore wings, beat the cyclops' head to a pulp, disintegrated the glass jar and battered the conjoined twins, and pounded the mummy to dust.

When the desecration of the altar was complete, Macarius threw the monstrous remains away, cleaned the *insulae*, and cleaned the altar. Next, he washed himself thoroughly, lit candles, and burned incense. He placed the sculpture of Hercules on the altar, poured libations, and prayed:

Lord Janus, I pray for a start of prosperity through this act
That I may please you and the divinities
I seek your vision and protection at this initial juncture

Oh, Great Hercules
God of strength and fury

Slayer of monsters
I welcome you to my home
I ask you to look down with favor upon me
I ask you for your blessing
I ask for your strength to be imparted upon me so that I may resist:
The temptations of decadence
The madness of collectors
The allure of morbid gratification
I ask for your strength to be imparted upon me so that I may gain:
The inspiration to create
The fortitude to withstand failure
The strength to withstand starvation
In return, I offer wine and the gift of prayer
I offer the quitting of my profession as *teratologus*, now and forever
I offer this and my subsequent sculptures, now and forever

Oh, revered Vesta, hear my words:
I ask you not to warm my home
Not to warm my heart with your flame
Not to keep me in your hearth's fire
Not look over me
But to look over the deformed child
As though she was your own

So, it is done.

Second Place Winner in Short Stories

As the Spirit Moves

Joe Morris

The sun's light glinted off the stone walls of the Abbey of St. Martin as Brother Francois set his sandaled feet to the dusty path leading through his beloved gardens and out among the fields and forests of the Touraine region. In the worn leather knapsack slung over his shoulder were two rolls of bread from the abbey's wood fired kitchen (one for him and one to be broken up and distributed to the birds he would meet on his daily walk), a few almonds sweetened with honey (for the children who often followed him through the fields to the edge of the forest), and the tools of his trade as a translator and scribe of written works deemed fit for preservation by his brothers and his abbot.

In his pocket was a small cloth bundle that contained his most precious possessions in all the world: the Holy Cross that had been carved especially for him by his woodworker friend Brother Jacques, a small bronze medallion imprinted with the image of St. Michel the Battle Angel, and a small piece of oak carved in the shape of a hammer.

The last item had been pressed into his hand by his peasant mother as she waited with him for the wagon that would take him to his new life as a monk, during his eleventh winter of life. Unable to feed all seven of their children, his mother and father had decided that their quiet and bookish youngest son would be given to the Poor Brothers in service of Christ to live out his days as a monk. Any guilt they may have felt for such a decision would surely be assuaged by the knowledge that their son's lot would be a life of piety, contemplation, and holy service to the Divine. Nevertheless, the young Francois had sensed a pensive sadness in his mother on that cold day long ago. She had pressed the wooden hammer into his hand, telling him in a quiet voice that before the Son of Man came in the person of Jesus Christ, the people of this land, the ancestors of the Franks, had prayed to the Battle Angel in his stead and that the hammer was their sign of devotion to him.

"The Lord Jesus Christ will not hold it against you if you keep it close, my son, and seek the protection of the Battle Angel when at times you feel the need," she had whispered to him, her voice sounding on the verge of tears.

And so he had done at times over the years, feeling in his heart that there was no heresy in doing so, for his elder brothers taught him of the hierarchies among the legion of angels who served the Most High, and surely he as the most humble of Christ's servants could look up to all of them and do them honor. Furthermore, as he worked at translating the many Greek texts his abbot had designated for preservation, he discovered among them the concept of the personal daemon, the spirit of genius or inspiration that philosophers spoke of as guiding action here in this material world. "Always follow your personal daemon" seemed to Brother Francois a most holy and excellent piece of advice, and one not at all in contradiction with commands to "walk in the Spirit" or to do "as the Spirit moves you." He knew from his dedicated and studious translation work that in John 3:8 the Greek word *pneuma* or "spirit" was used interchangeably with "wind," and so Brother Francois heard the whispering of the Battle Angel's gathering storm in the admonition: "The wind blows where it pleases, and you hear its sound, but you don't know where it comes from or where it is going. So it is with everyone born of the Spirit."

It seemed to Brother Francois that this was the way to live his life, blown by the wind of the Spirit, having faith that the small daily actions he was compelled to take would be woven inexorably into the grand plan of the Most High, becoming part of a beautiful tapestry too great for him to imagine. And so he began each day in deep prayer and meditation, seeking that center of silence from whence his every action would become a living sacrifice to the will that was higher than his own. In this way, each and every small act became a victory within a victory.

Each row of his hoe in the humble abbey garden became an act of inspired creation that would one day fill his brothers' bellies after a hard day's work, fueling them for greater achievements the next day. Each child he gave a gift to on his daily walk might keep forever a memory of the encounter that would inspire kindness and charity to their own children, on and on through innumerable generations. When he planted trees on the edge of the green and gold fields of the Touraine, he imagined a tired farmer one day resting in the blessed shade of their outstretched branches, mouthing prayers of thanksgiving to God for the blessing. The good brother couldn't imagine a better way to live life than as a tool in the hands of God, and his fondest hope for the day of his death was to finally be allowed to see the great victories his Maker would weave out of his countless, daily small ones.

On special and very blessed occasions Brother Francois would feel the Spirit whisper to him in a personal and special manner, revealing to him just how a translation should be altered in this or that way, ever so slightly, to ensure the Creator's Will would be passed on just as He wanted.

Brother Francois leaned on his stout oaken walking staff as he ascended a slight incline in the path that rose up and out of the little bowl-shaped valley in which the Abbey of St. Martin sat. He turned to enjoy the view of the city of Tours above and behind the Abbey, its walls and spires rising above the glistening Loire River. He smiled, imagining the bustle of life that swirled within, hundreds of his Frankish countrymen engaged in the daily rites and rituals of life, serving the Creator whether they knew it or not. He swiveled his gaze to the right and the left, taking in the hamlets and farmsteads that were the abbey's neighbors on this side of the Loire. Above one village, closest to the forest that bordered the farmers' fields, a cloud of smoke rose announcing the making of breakfast or perhaps the clearance of wild brush in preparation for the farmer's plow.

He unslung his knapsack and pulled out one of the pieces of bread, breaking it apart in anticipation of the arrival of the sparrows who visited him here, like clockwork, among the lilacs and lavender that grew beside this section of the path. He turned to feed them, a slight smile on his lips, only to be greeted instead by a single black eye that chilled the blood in his veins and clenched his gut in knots.

The raven stared fearlessly into Brother Francois' eyes for what seemed like an eternity before taking flight, saying its farewell with a single hoarse croak. The frightened brother stood rooted to the spot for several moments after the creature's departure, contemplating the message it carried, unmistakably from the Spirit that moved him.

Over the past two months he'd been plagued by a dream, which always began with the sighting of that penetrating black-eyed gaze. He turned to look again at the smoke over the sleepy hamlet. Black smoke… darker than the cooking fires… black as the smoke that had consumed the homes in the bloody nightmare he now feared he was about to live. The sound that he'd taken to be the clanging of a blacksmith's tools in the early dawn light now revealed itself to him as the clashing of weapons in the distance.

This could only be a Moorish raiding party, far north of their usual haunts. The lust of the invaders' caliphs and captains for white-skinned slave girls drove their war parties farther afield, and ever deeper into Christian lands, so the table-gossip of the abbey brothers would have it. Brother Francois nearly wept as he remembered the fate so many of the familiar village children had met in that terrible repeating dream he now knew to be an omen from his God.

But he could not tarry long… that nightmare had also given him a mission. A small victory that, though seemingly nonsensical upon waking, he now knew must be immeasurably important to the battle plans of the Redeemer God he believed, even now, planned to save his beloved country from the pillaging and rapine of the invaders.

Brother Francois clutched his walking stick and slung his knapsack back onto his shoulder, quickening his pace as he followed the familiar steps from his prophetic dream, down through the dry streambed, cutting westward through the unplanted field, then south into the deep green of the tangled beech and oak trees that comprised the nearby forest. His breath came in ragged gasps as he pushed through the tangled underbrush, thorns tearing at his robes, slashing open bleeding gashes on the tops of his exposed feet. From somewhere outside the forest a scream of terror rent the still air, sending a flock of birds into flight. Still, Brother Francois pressed on, his small task taking on world-changing importance in his mind's eye. To combat the fear threatening to flood his veins and freeze his limbs, he began to recite the Lord's Prayer, repeating it in breathless tones again and again to keep his unsteady feet moving through the dark forest.

"Pater Noster, qui es in caelis,sanctificetur nomen tuum. Adveniat regnum tuum. Fiat voluntas tua, sicut in caelo et in terra. Panem nostrum quotidianum da nobis hodie, et dimitte nobis debita nostra sicut et nos dimittimus debitoribus nostris. Et ne nos inducas in tentationem, sed libera nos a malo. Amen."

A flash of tawny-colored flank caught his eye, off to his right, as a well-muscled deer sprang into motion and fled his advance. That fateful feeling of déjà vu gripped his heart, and he remembered how that same sign had guided his dream-self on the path toward the accomplishment of his divine mission. He stumbled and fumbled his way over to where he'd spied the deer and picked up the trammeled and meandering path of its passage. He hustled along in the deer's wake, his movement quickened by the helpful creature's fortuitous trailblazing.

Nearly spent, he arrived at last in a small clearing where the light of the morning sun broke through, filtered into a comforting green-gold by the interlocked leaves of the forest canopy. The halo of light illuminated the root-broken ground at the base of a mighty oak tree, and with that flash of familiar insight he remembered this place as the site where his dream-self had accomplished his goal.

Falling to his knees, he pulled patches of loamy earth away from the largest of the roots, digging like a furious mole into the fertile soil of Francia. He pulled the cloth pouch containing his personal holy items out of his pocket and opened it to examine them fondly one last time. The Holy Cross, the image of the Battle Angel, and the Angel's blessed hammer. Here they would lie concealed, waiting for the purpose for which the Most High had them placed here. Brother Francois retied the cloth bag carefully, and with shaking hands placed it reverently into the cavity he had created next to the root. Carefully he recovered the pouch with soil, tamping it tightly, first with his fists and then with the butt end of his walking stick. Once the objects were securely buried, Brother Francois rose to his feet, making the Sign of the Cross in front of himself three times.

A sense of relief filled his heart, and he nearly laughed with joy. The unmistakable certainty of the signs, matching without fail the events of his terrible dream, assured him beyond doubt that he had fulfilled the Will of the Lord on this fateful day. Whatever plan the Great Redeemer might have for his Holy objects, Brother Francois knew with certainty that it would lead to the liberation of his land and his people from the invaders that plagued it.

This blessed reassurance made his feet light as he turned back towards the rising din from the village, the noise and the scent of smoke guiding him toward the certain and terrible conclusion to this day, which he already knew from the dream would be his doom.

"Yea, though I walk through the valley of the shadow of death..." he murmured under his breath as he marched inexorably toward the massacre taking place in the familiar village at the edge of the forest. He began again to recite the Lord's Prayer, drawing strength from the recitation, preparing his soul to rise from his body to meet his Redeemer.

"Pater Noster, qui es in caelis,sanctificetur nomen tuum. Adveniat regnum tuum. Fiat voluntas tua, sicut in caelo et in terra. Panem nostrum quotidianum da nobis hodie, et dimitte nobis debita nostra sicut et nos dimittimus debitoribus nostris. Et ne nos inducas in tentationem, sed libera nos a malo. Amen."

Brother Francois tramped onward, guided by the rising remembrance that there was one final mission his dream-self had completed. A flash among the trees was the final sign in the dream, that same tawny color as the deer that had guided him to the hiding place of the holy relics. He knew the details would become clear when they were meant to and that the Father would guide his steps. The brave brother could now make out the outlines of burning homes as he neared the edge of the forest, and the screams of the wounded and dying villagers were clear as a bell.

He paused one last time in the undergrowth and prayed for the Lord to make his mission clear. Just as he finished his invocation, he spied a young woman breaking free from the deathtrap of the village, sprinting towards the tree line where he was hiding.

Yes… hair the color of the deer. The sign was clear. His last mission was to help this woman escape, and to… to deliver her child. Brother Francois smiled as the silent Voice of his personal daemon finished the sentence for him. Surely the hour of death was upon him if the reasons for this small victory he was to win were being made so blessedly clear to him. He thanked the Lord for his benevolence and for seeing fit to use him as a tool to save the mother and the child. Upon finishing his prayer of thanksgiving, he gripped his wooden staff tightly in grim readiness.

Behind the young woman two Moorish soldiers vaulted the village fence in hot pursuit. Their snarling visages were savage to behold. In the years since they had arrived on European soil, word of the invaders' taste for native flesh had spread among the terrified common folk. Both girl and boy had disappeared, again and again, into the vast harems the slothful sultans kept for themselves. Whatever the noble reason they gave to the Jewish merchants and turncoat mercenaries who aided their invasion of the mother continent, the only purpose the Moors now knew was slaking their vile lust with the bodies of Brother Francois' people, and he felt a righteous boiling wrath rise in his breast at the thought of this young woman falling victim to such an end.

As the fleeing village woman reached the edge of the tree line, one of her pursuers managed to grab her by the hair, pulling her backwards.

"God save me!" she cried out in country-accented Frankish.

At this, Brother Francois sprang from his hiding place, swinging his staff with all his might. He struck the unprepared soldier hard across the face, driving him back and forcing him to release his grip on the young woman. Wasting not a single instant, the woman escaped into the trees.

With relief and joy Brother Francois faced the enraged and bleeding invader. Even as the man unsheathed his sword with a curse, the Christian monk felt no fear, only joy at having completed his divinely inspired mission. Blinded by blood and pain, the invader's first swing was clumsy, and Brother Francois blocked it with ease, the sword binding up in the tough wood of the staff. With a mighty heave, the monk pulled the soldier forward and down onto one knee.

At that moment the second Moor caught up to his companion and thrust his blade cruelly into Brother Francois' side. With a cry the monk fell, and both invaders set upon him with fury. The monk rolled to his back as the cold steel sent lightning-bolt stabs of pain through him, his eyes seeking and finding the golden disk of the sun. The pain faded as the light filled his eyes, flooding him with golden brilliance to the core. The material world and all its troubles faded to nothing in that light of that perfect illuminating fire…

* * *

Years later that same light filled the eyes of Sir Alaric de Fontaine as he rode at the head of a column of marching infantrymen two dozen strong through the deserted hamlets and barren fields of the countryside between the cities of Tours and Poitiers. The increasing frequency of Moorish raids striking north from Andalusia had caused most of the peasants, farmers, and other rural folk to feel for the safety of the walls of one of the two nearby cities. And now, so the scouts reported, the Moorish general Abd al-Rahman al-Ghafiqi himself was on his way to sack the cities for slaves and plunder.

Two nights before, the young knight had sat beside his patron and adoptive father Sir Guillaume as the duke and prince of the Franks himself, Charles, had briefed them and his other knights and nobles on his plans for the defense of Tours and Poitiers. The prognosis for victory seemed grim indeed. Light on cavalry, chevaliers of skill being scarce in Frankish lands at the time, Charles planned to rely on a phalanx of his experienced heavy infantry against the great numbers of mounted warriors the Moors could bring to bear.

It had been a moment charged with the electric tingle of fate when Charles fixed his stoic, piercing gaze, on Alaric and charged him with taking a raiding party of men to the rear of the Moorish column, where their slaves and loot would be kept under light guard. He was told to free as many slaves as possible and raise a great clamorous din at the rear of the Moorish column.

"Abd al-Rahman and his men have long since abandoned the service of their prophet, and their lust for our Frankish women has turned them to the service of Mammon. When word spreads of a threat to their pleasure slaves and ill-gotten wealth, they will abandon the charge and leave their throats exposed to our holy vengeance," Charles had stated, icy calm despite the import of his words to his young and loyal knight.

Though skeptical of success, Sir Alaric had accepted his mission with a humble bow. He had selected a few skilled men from among his adoptive father's forces, leaving the rest for Sir Guillaume to lead at Charles' side. Though Sir Alaric was a practical man who valued hard facts over spiritual matters like fate, this mission seemed to him a fitting one to die on should that be the result. His mother had grown up in this land and had nearly been taken as a slave herself in a Moorish raid while he was growing in her womb. She had often told him how an apparition of the Battle Angel, St. Michel, had stayed the foeman's hand and enabled her to escape, where she was eventually found and taken in by a young Sir Guillaume when he rode in with a party of chevaliers to drive back the Moorish raiding force.

As the midday heat set in, Sir Alaric led his men into a nearby grove of trees for shade and rest. They would wait until the din of battle raged in the distance to strike at the nearby Moorish column, and the trees would provide cover from the enemy scouts until that time came. The central column of the little grove was a stately old oak that had clearly been struck by lightning. Its trunk was hollowed out and blackened by the fire that often burned at the core of trees after such a strike, though its roots and high branches remained green and living. His men settled in a ring at the center of the clearing, perimeter sentries posted in all directions, ensuring the unsteady tree was given a wide berth.

Dismounting, Sir Alaric tied a feedbag to his steed's face and hobbled his legs. If his men would not have the advantage of horseback in the coming fight, nor would he. His instincts for leadership and skill for inspiring the spirits of his men had won Sir Alaric numerous victories against Moorish raiding parties, and he considered the esprit de corps of his men a weapon more valuable than any fine steel longsword or yew-wood spear. As he patted the flanks of his beloved horse, murmuring soft and comforting words, a great cracking sound nearly deafened him.

Sir Alaric and all his men turned to watch as the old oak tree, unbalanced by the trunk mass that had been consumed by fire, toppled over. The weight and force of its fall was enough to uproot it, and the tangled mess of roots loomed over the party of men as it flung damp Frankish soil high into the air.

A peculiar sight greeted the men who gazed openmouthed at the fallen forest giant. A strand of cloth fibers hanging from the highest root connected three objects dangling from its length. The topmost was a wooden cross, next below it a brass image of St Michel, and the closest to the earth was a wooden hammer.

The shock of the moment had frozen his men to the spot. Though educated in knightly schools to be unmoved by superstitions, unwavering and practical in all crises, Sir Guillaume had made sure to teach young Alaric to honor the superstitious and emotional nature of many of his lowborn troops, and even to use it when necessary to encourage and inspire them. Thus, moved by the strange synchronicity of the objects revealed by the tree's fall, Sir Alaric seized the cord and ripped it down, showing it and the relics around to his men in his open palms.

"The Battle Angel himself, as a herald of God, presents us a sign of impending victory! In the battle to come, we will be the Hammer of God! No longer will the Most High tolerate the yoke of slavery being placed around the neck of Frankish women and children by the hands of foreign invaders! Their prayers, rising from the harems and dungeons of the foe where they have been so unjustly violated, have been heard by our God, and in thunderous answer he has sent US, that through our right arms he may SMITE the guilty! For every Hail Mary whispered over rosary beads clutched in the shaking hands of a Frankish girl, our God has blessed a Frankish longsword! For every faithful recitation of the Our Father prayerfully sent heavenward by the lips of a Frankish orphan, our God has blessed a Frankish shield! For every drop of Frankish blood spilled by Moorish hands, the Lord of Hosts will spill, with our weapons, a river of enemy blood in recompense! In the name of our Father, victory will be ours! God wills it!"

"God wills it!" rose the answer from the two dozen Frankish warriors assembled in the clearing, eyes shining, fears banished by the fateful sign.

Whether it was coincidence or providence, Sir Alaric was satisfied with the result of his words: the surging strength he felt coursing through the spirit of his assembled warband. He tucked the holy relics into his tunic, near to his heart, and motioned for his men to follow him from the clearing to their positions at the edge of the forest.

From their hiding spots they could see the Frankish slaves bound together by strong ropes, and the leering Moors who guarded them. There were easily twice as many Moorish soldiers on this stretch of the enemy supply train as there were Frankish fighters assembled under Sir Alaric, but that did not deter him. They needn't win, or even survive, to turn the tide for Charles, duke and prince of the Franks. Seizing the attention of the enemy host for but a few moments would be enough, and the lust and greed that possessed the Moors of Andalusia meant that there was no better way to distract them than by threatening their slave hoard.

Sir Alaric looked left and right, meeting the eyes of his men, ensuring he had their full attention. He placed a clenched fist over his heart, where all had seen him place the holy relics, and reminded them: "Hammer of God." As he saw them nod, eyes gleaming with battle fervor, he relished the fate-laden moment for an instant before loudly proclaiming: "God wills it!"

With a roar the Franks sprang from the trees, falling among the surprised Moors, flashing steel cutting the invaders down like wheat before the scythe. The swords of Europe's defenders fell again and again, first hacking enemy limbs and heads, then the slavers' ropes. With shouts of joy and praises to God the freed captives rose up, helping to finish off wounded Moors before fleeing for the safety of the forests.

The Moorish guards closest to the front of the column fled toward the main battle, screaming about the loss of slaves and plunder. Abd al-Rahman's captains, fighting more to grow their harems than to spread the word of their prophet, turned to reinforce the slaver caravan. In showing their back to the man who would become Charles Martel, Charles the Hammer, they sealed doom for themselves and for Abd al-Rahman, who fell in battle on the fields of Tours that day.

Sir Alaric also died in battle that day, on the same patch of ground where Brother Francois bled his last. The prayerful or meditative soul, sitting still in a French forest on a starlit night, can still hear the wisdom of these two noble spirits spoken in the rustling of trees and the gusting of the wind. They teach that the small daily victories of good men are seeds that, when faithfully sown, will one day produce a harvest of the greatest divine victories. They teach also that the good God of the Franks will still move heaven and earth to send a savior to His threatened people and a fearsome destroyer against their enemies, if they but say the words, then follow faithfully as the Spirit moves them.

First Place Winner in Short Stories

The Castle

T.R. Hudson

There used to be a cantankerous, old beaver who lived near the stream by our house. He was well known in the neighborhood and harassed the ducks who tried to break his dam. One day a little girl came too close, and the beaver bit her. The girl's father shot the old beaver, and the ducks broke the dam for good. The father left the body on the side of the river, his fine pelt being picked at by some birds and other scavenging animals. A few months passed, and it was as if the old beaver had never been there at all. I've been thinking about this more and more lately.

The dog woke us up. An unceasing combination of barking and howling, whose only slight reprieve was the occasional fit of growling. This woke the baby, whose crying matched the dog, though we could not blame her, even if sleep was a rare luxury these days. Alice went to her, and I was to find out what had Max so bothered. He usually slept through the night, and the baby was learning to as well. A setback, but it was easy to wave it off. I checked in on them before heading downstairs, and Alice had calmed her down, nursing our child on her breast. Looking in on them, I almost forgot about Max.

I got to the pup and did my best to grab his attention. Commands did not dissuade him, and I felt a bit of shame and embarrassment. He really ought to listen better. I looked out the window to see what he was so fixed on; I figured it was a rabbit. I was wrong.

It was dark, but I saw two people camped out on our sidewalk. They had backpacks, and a few garbage bags, and I saw sleeping backs unfurled, though all careful not to touch a blade of grass on my lawn.

My shame and embarrassment turned to pride. "Good Boy, Max," I said and patted his head. His barking subsided, but he kept a steely gaze on the interlopers.

"What's going on?" Alice asked from upstairs, the baby still on her bosom.

"There are people sleeping on our sidewalk."

She said nothing, but the look of concern on her face and the beauty of those two just up the stairs was all the motivation I needed.

"It's okay, I'll take care of it."

I thought about the sprinklers, but it was still technically winter and I wasn't going to crack the pipes just to shoo away a couple of bums. I could go out there, wear the 9 mil on my hip and tell them to shove off. But what if something happened? What if they were on drugs? If they got the gun? No, charging into a siege when you have a perfectly good Castle is a fool's tactic. Alice and our child were my first and only concern.

I called the police. I paid taxes after all. They'd take a while, but I had time. Max had all the time in the world. The house was quiet again, though not peaceful.

I got off the phone with dispatch, and as the motion-sensing floodlights popped on, I saw the two bodies turn into four and wished I hadn't called at all. They weren't just some vagrants, but a family with two small children. The boy had a toy truck and a SpongeBob SquarePants sleeping bag. The little girl, a stuffed unicorn, and some sort of pony sleeping bag. The mother, worn and haggard, was brushing her daughter's long, black hair. The father was making shadow puppets on the ground for his children. He was short and fat and Hispanic. Probably Mexican, though that mattered less than their being on my street at all.

I looked for alcohol and saw none. I looked for needles, but there was nothing, though it was dark and those things could be there, just hidden for now until the children were sleeping. It would be much easier if these were degenerates. I could even cope and say I was being helpful, but that is a lie and weak. Deep down, passed the weakness, I wanted this man and woman to be good.

I wanted to see a man who I might even befriend. I could just go out there, shake his hand, and we'd find common ground between my limited Spanish and his broken English. He'd leave, and no one would need to go to jail or be harassed by the police.

But that was improbable. If I were out there and my child was cold and I was desperate and some stranger approached us to shake my hand and tell me to shove off, I might clock him so hard and go inside his house, if only for a night. I would kill for my daughter. For my wife. No, I'd stay put. And he'd stay out there, outside the walls that I've marked as mine.

I could hear my sister in my ear. She has that Master's Degree confidence conferred to affluent liberal women who live in big, dangerous cities, yet somehow believe they're invincible. She ignores the depravity around her and focuses on avocado toast and rooftop lounges overlooking polluted waters. Family is complicated, but I still love her.

What would Jesus do, I wonder? Help the poor, feed the hungry. Love thy neighbor. But Christ was never a father. And God sacrificed his only child, and I'm not strong enough to do that. No, I'm doing the right thing. I know this, but it's difficult.

What if it were us out there and them in here? I wouldn't want the cops called. I wouldn't want to be sleeping outside some guy's house, putting on a brave face for my wife and kids. This couldn't have been the plan. No, something happened to that man, and something could happen to me, too. How many paychecks can I go without before I'm him? More than one maybe, but not many more. I can't hate him; I am him. If I hate anyone, it's the politicians who welcomed him with open arms and told me to suck it up. If I let him stay, he might tell someone else and then I'm walking Max, trying to avoid human shit, used needles, and piss-soaked cardboard. No. Not today, not ever.

I can see the angel and the devil on my shoulders, but I wave the thought away. That too is a cope. A holdover from my liberal upbringing. It's not evil to have responsibilities. Those two children are not my responsibility. The one up those stairs is.

The patrol car comes around, and they pack up without incident. No one is arrested; instead, they load up in a car that swings by ten minutes later or so. I see the father's face, and he sees mine through the window as the police lights shine through. He nods at me, and I nod back. He understands. He would do the same. If such men ruled the world, it would be better.

But that isn't how it is. Maybe never was like that. Agamemnon always leads the Achaeans. Hector and Ajax are always opposed, and though they trade gifts, they are not friends. They can never be friends, but it would be nice if they could.

The show ends, and I go to bed. Alice grabs my arm and requests that I spoon her. I hold tight like someone is trying to take her from me. A few hours pass, and I can't sleep. I sit in the nursery and watch my little girl. The savagery I'd perform for her, though it disturbs me, finds me unflinching in my resolve.

I walk Max in the early morning, just after sunrise, and inspect their campsite. They left it cleaner than I thought they would. A candy wrapper that might have blown in from the wind and a plastic bag with something inside. Drugs, I bet. I hope for it. But it's not. It's a ziplock baggy of red playdoh. My eyes well up a bit. Guilt? Shame? Maybe, but that's fine. I can be guilty. I can be shameful. But my home is unmolested. My wife is safe and sound. My daughter was protected from the world another day. Sorry, Amigo. The reason you want in is the same reason I need to keep you out.

www.ingramcontent.com/pod-product-compliance
Lightning Source LLC
Chambersburg PA
CBHW051257210726
48287CB00002B/543

* 9 7 8 1 9 5 6 8 8 7 6 2 4 *